Launching RTI Comprehension Instruction with Shared Reading

40 Model Lessons for Intermediate Readers

By Nancy N. Boyles

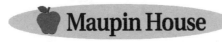
Maupin House

Launching RTI Comprehension Instruction with Shared Reading:
40 Model Lessons for Intermediate Readers

By Nancy N. Boyles

Cover design: Studio Montage
Book design: Mickey Cuthbertson

Library of Congress Cataloging-in-Publication Data

Boyles, Nancy N., 1948-
  Launching RTI comprehension instruction with shared reading : 40 model lessons for intermediate readers / by Nancy Boyles.
     p. cm.
  Includes bibliographical references.
  ISBN-13: 978-1-934338-67-4 (pbk.)
  ISBN-10: 1-934338-67-2 (pbk.)
  1. Reading (Elementary)--United States. 2. Reading comprehension--Study and teaching (Elementary)--United States. I. Title. II. Title: Launching response-to-intervention comprehension instruction with shared reading.
  LB1573.B6915 2009
  372.47--dc22
                    2009032464

Also by Nancy Boyles
Teaching Written Response to Text: Constructing Quality Answers to Open-Ended
        Comprehension Questions
Constructing Meaning through Kid-Friendly Comprehension Strategy Instruction
Hands-On Literacy Coaching
That's a GREAT Answer! Teaching Literature Response to K-3, ELL, and Struggling Readers

Maupin House publishes professional resources for K-12 educators. Contact us for tailored, in-school training or to schedule an author for a workshop or conference.
Visit www.maupinhouse.com for free lesson plan downloads.

Maupin House Publishing, Inc.
2416 NW 71 Place
Gainesville, FL 32653
www.maupinhouse.com
800-524-0634
352-373-5588
352-373-5546 (fax)
info@maupinhouse.com

10 9 8 7 6 5 4 3 2

Dedication

One dreary day last winter my daughter Caitlin decided I absolutely had to join the rest of the world and acquire a Facebook account. I hardly saw the need for this. But to avoid further reinforcement of my reputation as a "techno-dinosaur" I let her set this up—as long as she *promised* not to include any deep family secrets in my profile. As winter eased into spring, I reconnected with several old friends, and that was fun. But my absolute best Facebook moment occurred a couple of months ago when my e-mail inbox announced, "Luciano has sent you a message."

"is this by chance nancy neuman boyles? my elementary teacher"

Never mind that my maiden name was spelled wrong (Naumann). "Yes," I answered, as quickly as my fingers could type. "What have you been doing for the past thirty years?"

And Luciano replied:

"Wow its so great to hear from you, I always talk about you with all my friends and tell them how you made my first school experience here in America the best anyone could ever ask for, and I want to thank you for that, My best friend is a Teacher and he told me to try and contact you and I didnt think I would be able to find you. You are truly a very special person and I never did forget the article you wrote about me. . . . "

A few points of clarification: Luciano showed up at my third-grade classroom door midway through one of my earliest years of teaching. I had no idea how to teach a little boy who had just arrived from Italy and spoke not a single word of English. Back in the day there were no ESL teachers or programs for English learners. But I regarded this as a great adventure and, before the year ended, wrote an article for *Learning* Magazine which I titled, "We Got a New Kid and He Don't Speak No English." In return, Luciano's family gave me a tiny Italian glass slipper which, even now, a whole career later, sits in my dining room china cabinet—a happy memory of that long-ago experience.

So, Luciano, this one's for you. . . you made my day.

And Caitlin, this one's for you, too. You show the promise of a great teacher (even beyond your computer wizardry). As you join "the family business," remember that you just never know whose lives you will touch and the potential you have to make a difference in ways you may not even imagine.

August 2009

Table Of Contents

CHAPTER THREE
Supporting Readers before Reading

CHAPTER FOUR
Supporting Readers during Reading

CHAPTER FIVE
Supporting Readers after Reading

CHAPTER SIX
Getting Students to Independence with Comprehension Objectives in an RTI Classroom

CHAPTER SEVEN
Assessing Students' Response to Instruction 65

PART II
Shared Reading Lessons 77

PART II INTRODUCTION 78

CHAPTER EIGHT
Strand A Lessons: Forming a General Understanding 83

CHAPTER NINE
Strand B Lessons: Developing an Interpretation............................ 167

CHAPTER TEN
Strand C Lessons: Making Reader/Text Connections 213

CHAPTER ELEVEN
Strand D Lessons: Examining Content and Structure 257

Files on the CD

INTRODUCTION
Planner for Shared Reading

CHAPTER TWO
Comprehension Objectives
Pacing Template

CHAPTER THREE
Blank Target

CHAPTER SEVEN
How Am I Doing On Written Response?
Rubric For Assessing Students' Oral And Written Response to
   Comprehension Questions
Anchor Responses
Comprehension Checksheet: Intermediate Grades
Comprehension Objectives
Sample Comprehension Checksheet: Intermediate Level

CHAPTERS EIGHT, NINE, TEN, AND ELEVEN
Targets, *Vocabulary Connections*, and Supplemental Materials
   for All Lessons

Introduction

WHY I WROTE THIS BOOK

I wrote this book because so many of you—classroom teachers and literacy coaches—asked me to write it. Actually, *asked* is too gentle a word. *Begged...bribed...threatened.* Those words more aptly describe the way this book came about. Some of you have approached me after workshops I've given on shared reading and pleaded with me to hand over the lessons I helped write and edit for a district where I've done lots of curriculum work. "Well, no," I have had to tell you, "that district paid me to work on those lessons; those lessons now belong to that district." Some of you—in the Graduate Reading Program at Southern—have offered to come back after receiving your degree, when you no longer even need course credits, if I would just teach a course in designing model literacy lessons. Those of you who know what truly motivates me have offered up large quantities of chocolate in exchange for shared reading lessons. Maybe it was the promise of chocolate that finally inspired me— along with the recognition that a book on planning and implementing model literacy lessons really would be useful to teachers, and ultimately, helpful to students. There's also now the added challenge of sorting out all of the implications of RTI: What does RTI mean to our comprehension instruction? How do we meet the demands of RTI in the classroom?

As a teacher of teachers whose day-to-day work revolves around reading the research and then applying it as I visit classrooms, planning and implementing literacy lessons, even with RTI considerations, seems like not such a big deal. But then, I have access to dozens of journals and professional books, several conferences annually, and did I mention that I've been doing all of this for about a hundred years?!

Literacy instruction has become so complex in the past decade, amid a swirl of federal mandates, state regulations, and district initiatives, that it is a challenge simply to know *what* to do, let alone *why* we're doing it: "Fidelity to the core program!" they charge; we do our best to march in step. "Practice for the test," they tell us; we practice...and practice... and practice. "That lesson needs to be longer (or shorter);" we scramble to make the suggested changes.

But what goes into a good literacy lesson—in particular, a good *comprehension* lesson that meets the criteria for RTI Tier 1 instruction? If we were more confident about that, we'd know what to emphasize in our core program. We'd know what kind of practice makes the most sense for students. We'd know when a lesson was too long or when it was missing some vital component.

This book will answer the key question: What goes into a shared reading comprehension lesson that meets the specifications of RTI Tier 1 instruction? It will also give you those whole-class, shared reading lessons you've been pleading for as models for creating your own lessons. And it will offer some initial guidelines for helping you differentiate your small-group instruction following your shared lesson for RTI Tier 2 and Tier 3 interventions. The logic here is that, with greater knowledge of best practices and the elements of a rich and powerful comprehension lesson, there will be a greater impact on student learning. And fewer students will need RTI interventions at the Tier 2 and Tier 3 levels.

WHAT THIS BOOK IS—AND IS NOT

First, this book is not intended to teach you *about* RTI. RTI is a very comprehensive initiative that encompasses many components. (There are numerous resources you can access that can help you learn *about* RTI.) However, this book *will* help you implement RTI—in particular, Tier 1 comprehension instruction, which by RTI standards must be *high-quality, scientifically-based, explicit, systematic instruction for all students in the regular classroom.*

The forty lessons in this book do meet the precise, rigorous instructional requirements based on the definition above. Remember, however, that *precise* doesn't mean *prescriptive*. It is true that every element of each lesson within this book is explained thoroughly, but that is to give you a vision of what you need to accomplish as you move through the lesson. You will know that you have a good grasp of the lesson's intent when you can put aside the planning template and put your own personal spin on the lesson—without missing any of the significant pieces.

Only one lesson is provided for each objective. Students will almost never achieve mastery of any goal based on a single lesson, even if the lesson is spectacular! You need to teach a *sequence* of good lessons matched to the objective in both shared reading and through your small-group instruction in order for students to attain independence. The lessons here merely *start* the process; it is your job to finish it by creating and teaching your own good lessons.

Next, note that the literacy lessons provided in this book are intended for *shared* reading. The lessons are based on picture books, most of them with a multicultural dimension, that you may already have in your classroom or that you could find in a school or public library, in a book store, or from a source online. They are all presently in print. (I tried to select paperback books to cut costs for teachers purchasing the books themselves. But there were some books available only in hardcover that I loved too much and that were just *too* perfect not to use.)

As the teacher does most of the actual reading during shared reading, it is relatively easy to identify a text and plan a lesson around that text. The lesson needs to be matched to the identified objective as well as students' interests and cultural and linguistic backgrounds—not to their *reading* level.

This book provides a few guidelines for effective small-group instruction (see **Chapter Six**), but small-group instruction is not the main focus here. This book definitely does not include small-group lessons. Small-group instruction requires close attention to students' developmental needs and the resources you have available to meet those needs. I do not know the developmental needs of the students you teach. I don't know which leveled texts are in your book room. I don't know what your data says about which kids need additional support on which objectives. I don't know what you did yesterday with your small groups or how successfully your students met the challenge of the lesson's objective. I don't know any of these things, but you do. That is why *you,* not *I,* need to move your literacy instruction forward by planning your own small-group lessons.

WHO WILL BENEFIT FROM THIS BOOK

This book is intended, in particular, for educators who work with students in the intermediate elementary grades, especially grades three through five, although students as low as second grade and as high as seventh and eighth grades could benefit from the lessons with just a few modifications on your part. This book can be used by classroom teachers complying with RTI standards as they work with *all* students in the regular-classroom literacy block on comprehension instruction—as long as the instruction is based on students' needs as determined by some legitimate form of universal screening. (This might include measures such as DIBELS, DRA, or your state literacy assessment.) The same instructional principles can also be used by ELL teachers, special educators, and reading specialists as they work with struggling readers in RTI Tier 2 comprehension interventions based on students' response to their Tier 1 instruction. This book can furthermore serve the needs of literacy coaches as they design and model comprehension lessons that demonstrate best practices for the classroom teachers in their building.

I hope administrators will look closely at this book as well for the thinking it provides about what RTI Tier 1 reading instruction should look like when they visit classrooms. In fact, the lessons in this book put a "face" on the instructional model described in my book *Hands-on Literacy Coaching* (Maupin House, 2007): what to look for when you're looking for explicit literacy instruction. Note especially that these instructional components go beyond any particular core program or approach to literacy. These are the instructional components that should be present in any "core curriculum," regardless of the program or materials we use or the teaching strategies we employ, so children will learn to comprehend.

DEFINING CRITICAL ELEMENTS OF RTI

RTI includes these components:
- High-quality, scientifically-based, explicit, systematic instruction for all students in the regular classroom
- Ongoing student assessment that includes universal screening and progress monitoring to determine which students need more intense intervention, as well as the appropriateness of the curriculum in meeting students' needs
- Multi-tier differentiated instruction that provides more intense instructional interventions for students who need them
- Parent involvement that keeps parents apprised of the instruction their children are receiving and the progress they are making

Although at first glance RTI appears to be mostly about interventions for students who struggle, that is a myth. RTI at the Tier 1 level is about good first teaching for *all* children. If districts embraced this notion and put a core curriculum in place that met the criteria for "scientifically-based, explicit, systematic instruction," they could prevent reading problems from developing for most students. In fact, they could expect that 80 percent of students would require no further interventions at all!

Note that "core curriculum" does not mean an off-the-shelf core program! A comprehensive, core curriculum could incorporate a "program." But a good curriculum is always more than just a program. A comprehensive core curriculum embeds not only all elements of literacy (phonemic awareness, phonics, fluency, vocabulary, and comprehension), it also includes all essential instructional formats: shared, guided, and independent reading. See the next page for the model I've devised for systematic, explicit reading instruction that I believe meets RTI Tier 1 criteria.

DEFINING OUR MODEL OF EXPLICIT, SYSTEMATIC READING INSTRUCTION

What are these components of Tier 1 reading instruction that are so powerful? Figure 1 on page xv depicts my vision of "doing reading" in the classroom. Note first of all that the focus here is on reading specifically and does not include other aspects of literacy such as writing and oral language; those will require additional time. The preferred length of the *reading* block, then, is **ninety minutes**. This is often the first "wake-up call" to districts. "We only have an hour for reading," many elementary teachers lament. It's sometimes even more grim at the middle-school level: "Our class periods are forty-five minutes long," some tell me. This is a tough call: if you don't have the necessary time on task, you can hardly be surprised when the outcomes are disappointing. Disappointment in this case comes in the form of low student achievement.

To be fair, however, revamping school schedules is easier said than done. My advice to administrators and teachers who respond to my suggestion to increase the length of time devoted to teaching reading each day with pained cries of reduced staff and competing mandates is to help them recognize that this is a *goal*. You don't have to have a ninety-minute reading block in place right now in order to begin to put this plan into practice, but this should be a priority. You should be taking steps to make more minutes available to the teaching of reading.

The next element of the model that needs attention is the column in the middle with the three instructional components: setting the stage for learning, building knowledge, and reinforcing knowledge. These components are described in detail in my book *Hands-on Literacy Coaching*, and therefore, will not be re-explained here. It is important to acknowledge, however, that these are the components of good reading instruction whether you subscribe to a core program, a workshop model, or a district-designed curriculum. These are the components that must somehow find their way into a lesson plan if we want our instruction to truly embody best practices.

Next to the instructional components, in the column on the left, are the essential instructional formats: shared reading, guided reading, and independent reading. The approximate number of minutes devoted to each format within an *ideal* reading block to maximize the impact of Tier 1 instruction is specified in the column on the extreme right. If we know which instructional components need to be incorporated into a Tier 1 shared reading lesson, along with the intended length of that lesson, we can develop an effective, efficient lesson plan that addresses these features. Similarly, if we recognize the role of Tier 1 guided and independent reading as a follow-up to shared reading, we can plan more effectively for those instructional components.

EXPLICIT READING INSTRUCTION

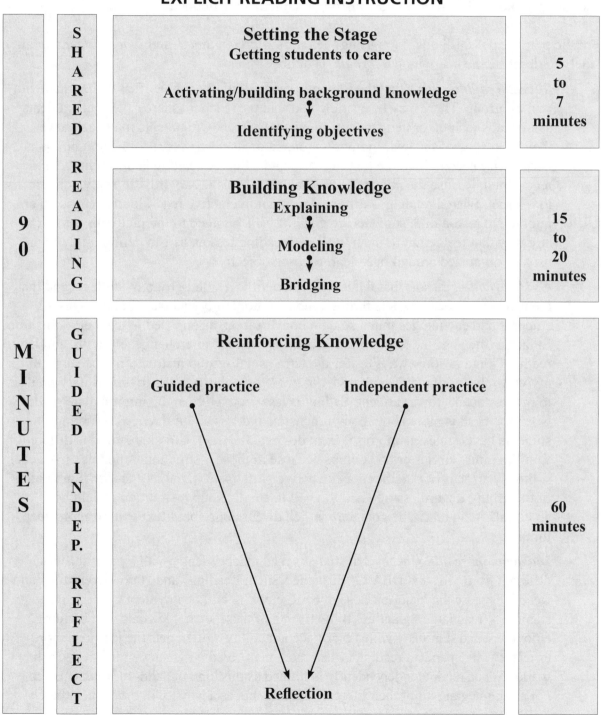

DEFINING SHARED, GUIDED, AND INDEPENDENT READING

I've lost some sleep over what to call the instructional components that I ultimately identify in this book as *shared, guided,* and *independent* reading. Regardless of the label selected, problems follow because different terms conger up different images to different people: "That's not shared reading," some people might assert who see in their mind a class of primary-grade students sitting around a Big Book repeating simple sentences with their teacher. "For guided reading you need a picture walk," other teachers might claim. Who should have the final word as to how instructional terms are defined?

For the purposes of this book, I am using the terms *shared, guided,* and *independent* reading solely to describe the instructional *format.* That is:

- **Shared reading** means that the lesson is shared with the whole class rather than with a small group. There may be a single text that the teacher "shares" with all students as he reads it aloud or that students view on a screen. Or students may each have their own copy of the text. In my opinion, students need *access* to the text but do not necessarily need to hold the text in their hands. Shared reading is different from a read-aloud because the intent of a read-aloud is typically to provide enjoyment, not to instruct. Shared reading is different from an interactive read-aloud because, in an interactive read-aloud, students are generally encouraged to interact with the text in any way that feels right to them; a shared reading lesson, as I'm defining it here, is usually organized around one clear, focused objective.

- **Guided reading** means that the lesson is taught to a small group of students and that the teacher "guides" readers through the text, hopefully in a way that engages all students and encourages much student conversation, as opposed to teacher inquisition. In fact, I often use the term "small-group instruction" interchangeably with "guided reading" (and in some ways prefer the term "small-group instruction") because, in my view, the more traditional model of guided reading applied in the primary grades to move students toward fluent reading is less productive in the intermediate grades when the need is more about comprehension and less about fluency (assuming students have achieved appropriate grade-level fluency). Guided reading is different from literature circles or book clubs because in those instructional models the teacher is mostly an "advisor" rather than an active participant in the day-to-day functioning of the group. Regardless of what you call it, small-group instruction should be about talk—kid talk! The goal here is rich discussions about text that promote deep thinking.

- **Independent reading** means that students read independently with a purpose. This is different from SSR and DEAR ("Sustained Silent Reading" and "Drop Everything and Read") because the major purpose of SSR, etc. is to build enjoyment of reading and stamina to read larger quantities of text. Both of these are noble goals. But building enjoyment and stamina—with a bit of accountability—often gets the job done more efficiently. Independent reading is also more than "reading when you finish your other work." When reading independently is framed as this kind of "add-on," students see it not as an integral part of their literacy learning, but as a way to fill time when there's nothing left to do. Instead, independent reading, as it is defined in this book, means that students apply their understanding of a literacy objective to a text that is easy for them to read in order to practice finding evidence for that objective unaided by a teacher. This independent reading does **not** require pencil-paper follow-up and especially does not suggest that students should answer lots of written questions.

HOW THIS BOOK IS ORGANIZED

Part I: Planning for RTI Tier 1 Shared Reading Instruction—One Step at a Time explains the *where,* the *what,* and the *how* of RTI Tier 1 shared reading: *where* shared reading fits into the literacy block in your classroom, *what* to include in a focused shared reading lesson, and *how* to make sure that you incorporate each instructional component so it has the maximum impact on student learning—helping to eliminate the need for Tier 2 and Tier 3 comprehension interventions. It will also answer those important *why* questions because, once you understand the reasoning behind each part of a lesson, you will be better able to plan and implement more effective lessons of your own. **Part I** addresses the context of shared reading as well as each element of the *Planner for Shared Reading.* This template may be found on page xix at the end of this introduction and also on the CD. Note that all of the lessons in **Part II** are designed using this instructional format. **Part I** includes the following chapters:

- **Chapter One—Finding Your Starting Point: Shared Reading in Context** encourages you to think about the length of your reading block, how your Tier 1 shared lesson will fold into other instructional reading components (guided and independent reading), and how your lesson might look different based on your timeframe—while you simultaneously advocate for a reading block that gives your students enough time on task.

- **Chapter Two—Deciding *What* to Teach (and What to Teach *With*)** provides you with critical insights into the planning that must precede the lesson plan: selecting your objective and your text.

- **Chapter Three—Supporting Readers Before Reading** examines what teachers need to do to set the stage for learning—even before reading the first word on the first page of the text.

- **Chapter Four—Supporting Readers During Reading** defines what it means to truly read *strategically* to find evidence and make meaning from text.

- **Chapter Five—Supporting Readers After Reading** looks at how to help students respond to text, both orally and in writing, and how to help them apply what they have learned through shared reading to other components of literacy, such as fluency, vocabulary, and writing.

- **Chapter Six—Getting Students to Independence with Comprehension Objectives in an RTI Classroom** clarifies how to move from the first Tier 1 lesson used to introduce an objective to follow-up RTI Tier 1, Tier 2, and Tier 3 instruction aimed at helping students meet the comprehension objective independently.

- **Chapter Seven—Assessing Students' Response to Instruction** addresses issues of question validity and scoring validity. It also provides a rubric and checklist aligned with the anchor responses for each lesson (found in the introduction that precedes each lesson).

Part II: Shared Reading Lessons offers those coveted lessons for forty different objectives along with support materials that will add depth to your teaching. The lessons are divided into four chapters organized into the same four thinking strands used in my book *That's a Great Answer* (Maupin House, 2007). They also reference the answer frames in that book. The chapters in **Part II** are:

- **Chapter Eight—Strand A Lessons: Forming a General Understanding** provides fourteen lessons divided among A1: Main idea and theme; A2: Characters, problem/solution, and setting; A3: Summarizing; and A4: Predicting.

- **Chapter Nine—Strand B Lessons: Developing an Interpretation** provides eight lessons divided among B1: Identify or infer the author's use of structure/organizational patterns; B2: Draw conclusions about the author's purpose; and B3: Use evidence from the text to support a conclusion.

- **Chapter Ten—Strand C Lessons: Making Reader/Text Connections** provides eight lessons divided among C1: Connect the text to a personal experience, another text, or the outside world and C2: Make a personal response to the text.

- **Chapter Eleven—Strand D Lessons: Examining Content and Structure** provides ten lessons divided among D1: Examine the author's craft; D2: Extend the text; and D3: Show that you understand what was important to an author or character.

The **reflection section** at the conclusion of each chapter leaves you with points to ponder as you reflect on how the message of each chapter applies to *you*—and how you might proceed from here to teach with even greater precision and power.

The **CD** provides electronic versions of the materials needed to plan and document our work: planning templates, rubrics, charts, and cue cards, as well as many other materials that support the shared reading lessons that are not provided in the book itself. The targets, *Vocabulary Connections*, and supplemental materials for each lesson are included on the CD only. They are all provided in Word format so you can modify them as needed.

The *Planner for Shared Reading*, which is fully explained in **Part I** and which provides the structure for all lessons in **Part II**, is presented on the following page (and on the CD) as the point of departure for all that follows.

PLANNER FOR SHARED READING

Objective (strategy focus):_____

_____

How will student learning be measured at the end of the lesson? (What will count as "success?")

Text: _____ **Pages:** _____

BEFORE READING	**Establish prior knowledge, purpose, and predictions**	Prior knowledge: Predictions: Purpose for reading:
	Introduce/review vocabulary	
	Introduce the objective (How to find and use the evidence)	Making the <u>reading</u> strategic

DURING READING	**Model and practice finding evidence for the objective**	The best evidence: Model Practice
	Model and practice other strategies	Connecting? Visualizing/picturing? Wondering? Predicting/guessing? Noticing? Figuring out?

AFTER READING	**Discussion questions**	Question related to the objective: Other questions:
	Written response to text	Making the <u>writing</u> strategic
	Other follow-up activities	Oral language/fluency, vocabulary, comprehension, reading extensions, and writing extensions Oral language/fluency: Vocabulary: Comprehension: Reading extensions: Writing extensions:
	Reflect on reading and writing strategy	

PART I

Planning for RTI Tier 1 Shared Reading Instruction—One Step at a Time

CHAPTER ONE
Finding Your Starting Point: Shared Reading in Context

Before you can plan or teach any shared lesson, you need to know how the lesson will fit into the literacy block on a given day and throughout the week. In the introduction, I made a pretty big deal about having enough minutes for your reading block. I "suggested" (fairly strongly!) ninety minutes. Your reality, however, might be different. Do you have ninety minutes identified for reading? Sixty minutes? Forty minutes? Or do you have the luxury of more than ninety minutes?

First, remember that reading *block* doesn't have to mean ninety minutes (or any number of minutes) all at one time. Of course an uninterrupted session would be ideal, but that is a challenge in most schools as various "specials" must be integrated into the school day for all grades; the classroom teacher's priorities are competing with music, art, physical education, etc.

Next, don't think you need to wait until you have just the right schedule or just the right number of minutes available to you before you embark on a reading block that incorporates a strong shared reading component. You need to work with what you have now (all the while advocating for more minutes for reading). And you can do it! Below I specify how your reading block, your week, and your shared lesson will look based on the length of time you have for reading. Any of these formats could meet the requirements of RTI for explicit, systematic instruction if applied thoughtfully.

THE NINETY-MINUTE PLAN

What will reading look like if I have a ninety-minute reading block?
If you have ninety minutes, then using twenty-five to thirty of those minutes for shared reading is perfect. That leaves you with an hour (or nearly an hour) for small-group instruction—about twenty minutes per group and five minutes more or less to come together at the end of reading to reflect. Your reading block might look like this:

Daily Reading Block when You Have Ninety Minutes

Reading Component	Time
Shared reading	25-30 minutes
Three guided reading groups, independent reading, and literacy follow-up activities	60 minutes
Reflection	5-10 minutes

What will my shared reading week look like if I have a ninety-minute reading block?
If you have ninety minutes available, you can devote thirty minutes *each* day to a whole shared reading lesson. Or, at the intermediate grade level where texts (even picture books) are often longer, you can spend a couple of days completing a lesson, use a day for an extended vocabulary lesson related to a particular book, or swap shared reading once in a while for conferring with students about their independent reading. I think that for consistency, at least three days each week should be devoted to shared reading. But don't be afraid to be a bit flexible with how you use your shared reading time. There are really too many possibilities to describe, but one scenario might look like this:

Shared Reading Plan for One Week when You Have a Ninety-Minute Reading Block (One possible weekly plan for thirty-minute sessions)

Monday	Tuesday	Wednesday	Thursday	Friday
Shared reading lesson, part I	Shared reading lesson, part II	Extended vocabulary lesson for shared reading text	Shared reading (whole text)	Conferring about independent reading

What will my thirty-minute shared reading lesson look like?
Even if you're one of the lucky ones with ninety minutes available to you for reading, you need to hustle! Completing a rigorous shared reading lesson in thirty minutes requires you to stay focused and to teach efficiently. You need to stick to your game plan. Yes, there are those too-good-to-pass-up teachable moments that pop up unexpectedly. (We just *had* to visualize on this page. Or this paragraph was too perfect for making a text-to-text connection.) But don't lose track of your larger mission: explicit attention to your selected objective. If you remember that, and recognize that moving students toward independence on that objective is what is *most* important, you will see which lesson components are essential and where you can cut a few corners and still meet your goal if you are running out of time.

Realistically, you *will* need to omit a few things from the *Shared Reading Lesson Plan* (those in this book and others that you create yourself) in order to get it all in within thirty minutes. Here is what typically works for me:

Thirty-Minute Shared Reading Lesson within a Ninety-Minute Reading Block (integrated with other elements of the lesson plan)

THE SHARED LESSON

Before reading
- Discuss: Prior knowledge, predictions, purpose
- Identify and briefly introduce vocabulary words (address the words more specifically in context as you read and in a separate lesson after reading for greater reinforcement)
- Explain the objective (how to find evidence to meet the objective)

During reading
- Model and practice finding evidence for the focus objective
- Apply other strategies as appropriate

After reading
- Respond to the focus question *orally*
- Respond to other questions orally if time allows (usually time does *not* allow)
- Model a written response to the focus question if you are introducing the objective

AFTER THE SHARED LESSON

Follow-up work while the teacher is working with three small groups
- Respond to the focus question *in writing*
- Other follow-up activities
- Independent reading

Reflection (at the end of the literacy block)
- What did you learn today as a reader?
- What did you find in your independent reading that supports our objective?

THE SIXTY-MINUTE PLAN

What will reading look like if I have a sixty-minute reading block?
Some elementary schools where I have consulted have only an hour in their day designated for reading. They cite scheduling problems, personnel issues, and assorted other impediments as the reason for this. On closer examination, some of these schools actually *do* have more than sixty minutes; they just label the components of their program differently. For example, in addition to "reading," there may be a twenty-minute "skills block." They might isolate "vocabulary" as a separate part of the curriculum and teach it for fifteen minutes each day. I am skeptical about such arbitrary curriculum divisions because it tells me that there is probably a lot of whole-class instruction taking place in these schools, and that it might be based more on a variety of unrelated "programs" rather than on students' real needs.

While this is far from ideal, it is a conversation for a different day. Right now, we can't use what is not perfect as a reason not to move forward with shared reading lessons that pack a punch. And we CAN do it within sixty minutes if we have to. The biggest downfall of having only sixty minutes is not its impact on shared reading (See *Shared Reading Plan for One Week* on the following page), but its impact on small-group instruction because you realistically will not meet more than two groups each day. This seriously reduces the number of times you can see each group during a given week. Nonetheless, if you have only sixty minutes available, your reading block might look like this:

Daily Reading Block when You Have a Sixty-Minute Reading Block

Reading Component	Time
Shared reading	15-20 minutes
Two guided reading groups, independent reading, and literacy follow-up activities	35-40 minutes
Reflection	5 minutes

What will my shared reading week look like if I have a sixty-minute reading block?
You will not be able to squeeze everything into a twenty-minute shared reading lesson that you could get into a thirty-minute lesson—even if you talk fast. So, plan on dividing your lesson over multiple days. While not ideal because you ultimately teach fewer shared lessons (which means students receive less reinforcement on an objective), your actual teaching can be just as focused and explicit. Your reading week for shared reading might look something like this:

Shared Reading Plan for One Week when You Have a Sixty-Minute Reading Block (One possible weekly plan for twenty-minute sessions)

Monday	Tuesday	Wednesday	Thursday	Friday
Shared reading lesson: *before reading* and *during reading* (begin reading the text)	Shared reading lesson: *during reading* (finish reading the text)	Shared reading lesson: *after reading*	Extended vocabulary lesson related to the shared reading text	Confer with students about independent reading

What will my twenty-minute shared reading lesson look like?

The previous chart shows you one way you can carve up the shared reading lesson, addressing *before, during,* and *after* reading components on different days as needed. But what, specifically, will you address on each day? My one strong recommendation is that you make sure you get past the *before reading* part of the lesson on the first day and actually get into the text. You will lose a lot of momentum if you drag out your *before reading* instruction. (See **Chapter Two** for more on how to maximize what you do to set the stage for a shared lesson.)

**Twenty-Minute Shared Reading Lesson within a Sixty-Minute Reading Block
(integrated with other elements of the lesson plan)**

THE SHARED LESSON
Before reading (day one)
- Discuss: Prior knowledge, predictions, purpose
- Identify and briefly introduce vocabulary words (address the words more specifically in context as you read and reinforce them later in a follow-up lesson)
- Explain the objective (how to find evidence to meet the objective)

During reading (day one and day two)
- Model and practice finding evidence for the focus objective
- Apply other strategies as appropriate

After reading (day three)
- Respond to the focus question *orally*
- Respond to other questions orally (you may have more time for this in a twenty-minute-per-day, multi-day lesson as you will devote a whole session to *after reading*)
- Model a written response to the focus question if you are introducing the objective

AFTER THE SHARED LESSON
Follow-up work while the teacher is working with two small groups
- Respond to the focus question *in writing*
- Other follow-up activities
- Independent reading

Reflection (at the end of the literacy block)
- What did you learn today as a reader?
- What did you find in your independent reading that supports our objective?

THE FORTY-FIVE-MINUTE PLAN

What will reading look like if I have a forty-five-minute reading block?
This is often the scenario in middle schools or sometimes the case in elementary schools that contain just the intermediate grades (for example grades three through five). Sometimes these schools operate *as if* they were middle schools. Again, I would challenge whether this middle-school mindset of dividing the day into "periods" is best for children so young. But let's not get derailed by this issue right now. Let's see what we *can* do with our forty-five minutes.

When you have only forty-five minutes, you need to accept that your reading program will not be balanced within a given day. But it can be balanced over the course of a week. You can develop a plan to incorporate shared, guided, and independent reading over five days. The daily reading block on alternate days might look like this:

Daily Reading Block when You Have a Forty-Five-Minute Reading Block: (Days 1, 3, and 5)

Reading Component	Time
Shared reading	30 minutes (it could take all 45 minutes)
Independent reading and literacy follow-up activities	15 minutes (if time allows)

Daily Reading Block when You Have a Forty-Five-Minute Reading Block: (Days 2 and 4)

Reading Component	Time
Two guided reading groups, independent reading, and literacy follow-up activities	40 minutes
Reflection	5 minutes

What will my shared reading week look like if I have a forty-five-minute reading block?
Because the instructional format for each day varies with a forty-five-minute block (on alternate days, there is no shared lesson), the weekly plan was quite clearly outlined in the previous chart. Two features of this plan are especially significant to middle-school teachers (or to teachers of the lower intermediate grades when their day is divided into "subjects"— math, reading, science, etc.).

First, shared reading is much more than the whole class reading a novel together. (**Chapters Two** through **Seven** will clarify all the fine points of this.) Second, you need to find time for small-group instruction and independent reading on a regular basis. I am asked to visit many middle schools where teachers are dissatisfied with students' literacy performance. "What can we do about these scores?" they wonder. Then, not long into the conversation, I hear how the sixth grade has been reading *Anne of Green Gables* as a class novel for the past three months. Ouch! I personally love *Anne of Green Gables* but not for the whole class and definitely not for three months.

What I encounter too often in middle schools is that, while teachers want different results, many don't necessarily want to do things differently. They may *say* they're for change, but they have a hard time letting go of the books they love and the instructional practices they've known since they themselves were in junior high. One of the changes that is non-negotiable is that students need an opportunity to read text at their instructional level. That means we need to move away from whole-class novels, where the emphasis is on the content, into shared lessons focused on strategic reading and small-group instruction that provides strategic practice with developmentally appropriate text.

I hope a few middle-school teachers will still like me after this little tirade—and, of course, *all* middle-school teachers do not fall into the category I just described. But there's no denying that this "whole-class-teach-the-book" approach is widespread. To teach the reader rather than the reading, your weekly plan could look something like the plan that follows. Alternately, you could also teach shared reading for the first two or three days of the week, followed by two or three days of small-group instruction.

Shared Reading Plan for One Week when You Have a Forty-Five-Minute Reading Block
(One possible weekly plan for forty-five-minute sessions)

Monday	Tuesday	Wednesday	Thursday	Friday
Shared reading lesson: *before, during, and after reading*; independent reading/ follow-up activities	No shared reading; **two** guided reading groups, independent reading, and literacy follow-up activities	Shared reading lesson: *before, during, and after reading*; independent reading/ follow-up activities	No shared reading; **two** guided reading groups, independent reading, and literacy follow-up activities	Shared reading lesson: *before, during, and after reading*; independent reading/ follow-up activities

What will my shared reading lesson look like within a forty-five-minute session?
Although I am generally not in favor of shared reading lessons that extend beyond thirty minutes, this is sometimes justified—and useful—in situations where you have a forty-five-minute reading block. Note that in the chart for the *Daily Reading Block when You Have a Forty-five-minute Reading Block*, I indicated that the final few minutes of shared reading sessions would be devoted to independent reading and follow-up activities. I think it's good for *all* lessons to incorporate a hands-on component of some type for students. But I also have taught many middle-school lessons where I needed every one of those forty-five minutes just to thoroughly address the parts of my shared lesson. So I don't think you need to feel guilty about this. To be realistic, let's agree that your shared lesson in this context might range from thirty to forty-five minutes. The lesson would look as follows:

Thirty- to Forty-Five-Minute Shared Reading Lesson in a Forty-Five-Minute Reading Block (integrated with other elements of the lesson plan)

THE SHARED LESSON

Before reading

- Discuss: Prior knowledge, predictions, purpose
- Identify and introduce vocabulary words (you will have more time for introducing vocabulary in a 45-minute session)
- Explain the objective (how to find evidence to meet the objective)

During reading (day one and day two)

- Model and practice finding evidence for the focus objective
- Apply other strategies as appropriate

After reading (day three)

- Respond to the focus question *orally*
- Respond to other questions orally (you may also have more time for this in a forty-five-minute session)
- Model a written response to the focus question if you are introducing the objective

AFTER THE SHARED LESSON

Follow-up work after the shared lesson or on another day while the teacher is working with two small groups

- Respond to the focus question *in writing*
- Other follow-up activities
- Independent reading

Reflection (at the end of the literacy block)

- What did you learn today as a reader?
- What did you find in your independent reading that supports our objective?

MOVING BEYOND YOUR STARTING POINT

You might have more than ninety minutes available for reading each day. Or you might have something between the parameters I've described. You can adjust your daily and weekly plans and the composition of your shared lesson accordingly. **Chapter Two: Deciding *What to Teach (and What to Teach With*)** will help you begin your journey into shared reading by starting with a worthy objective and finding the best text possible to teach that objective. But first, contemplate these *Reflection Questions* as you consider your own starting point and how you can take the next step.

REFLECTING ON CHAPTER ONE

1. What is the length of your reading block? What components of the curriculum are you expected to incorporate during your reading block?

2. Is the reading block long enough? If not, what is standing in the way of more time for reading?

3. How much of your time each week do you currently devote to shared reading? Guided reading? Independent reading?

4. What materials do you use to teach reading? Are these mandated? Do you have some flexibility?

5. Before reading beyond this point in this book, think about what questions you hope this book will answer. In particular, how might this book help you implement RTI mandates for RTI Tier 1 comprehension instruction?

CHAPTER TWO
Deciding *What* to Teach (And What to Teach *with*)

The key to good instruction is good planning, whether it is RTI Tier 1 instruction—or *any* instruction. Lots of educators (including administrators) regard "the plan" as what is written on paper that a teacher follows from the beginning to the end of a lesson. I won't deny that the "on-paper" plan is important to the outcome of the lesson. But planning begins long before the lesson is written out, and even the most prescriptive plans are, at best, mere skeletons of the dynamic teaching that should take place. Good teaching is always much richer than any written plan suggests because good teachers know *why* they are doing what they are doing—not just *what* they are doing and *how* to do it—and are therefore able to make adjustments as they move through their lesson. They tweak the plan here and there as they teach because they understand the purpose behind each part of their lesson, and even more important, they understand the needs of their students. I can't anticipate for you the needs of the children in your class. But I can help you to "plan smart" by getting off to a solid start long before you stand before your students, text in hand.

In **Chapter Two** I highlight this portion of the *Shared Reading Planner*:

Objective (strategy focus): _____

_____
How will student learning be measured at the end of the lesson? (What will count as "success?")

Text: _____

DECIDING WHAT TO TEACH

Planning for good instruction does not begin on paper; it begins in your head. It begins with identifying an objective, turning that objective into a "target," and choosing your text. All of this thinking needs to occur long before you gather your students for the lesson you will teach. Thinking through the following questions will make your actual lesson plan a more effective tool when you teach your lesson.

Good instruction begins with a good objective

Why is it important to begin with the objective instead of the text?

The most important guideline to keep in mind in selecting a comprehension objective for shared reading is that it should be the *objective* that is the starting point of your lesson, not the *book*. I know this is not the way we typically think about lesson planning. Often, we find a book we absolutely love, and holding it close to our heart wonder, "What can I teach with this book?" On the surface, this seems to work just fine because there are many objectives that can be addressed through most books. But when we begin with the book, it is the content of the reading that becomes the centerpiece of our instruction. Rather, what we should target when we plan a lesson are the needs of the reader. That means we need to begin with the *objective*: Based on our assessment data, what is it students need to be able to understand and do better in order to become more competent, thoughtful readers?

How do I choose a comprehension objective for shared reading?

In these data-driven times, deciding what students need to "do better" involves almost no guesswork on our part. We have state assessments. We have assessments that accompany published core programs. We have fluency tests and early literacy assessments and informal inventories that help us find our students' reading levels. We have curriculum-based measures and common formative assessments that mimic the grade-level expectations of our state literacy frameworks, giving us insight into students' performance before they ever take the state test. Our heads are swimming with the data we collect from all of these instruments. RTI requires us to make sense of our data and to use it intelligently to determine what we will teach to whom in our classrooms. This works pretty well—except for comprehension. At the early literacy level, the skill progression is fairly clear where, for example, you may start with consonant sounds, progress to medial vowels, and then move on to vowel teams. For comprehension beyond basic narrative story structure, it's a matter of going broader and deeper based on the complexity of the text and the sophistication of the specific comprehension task.

Hence, to launch comprehension instruction in a manner compatible with RTI Tier 1, choose a core area of comprehension red-flagged by your data. This might be finding the main idea, understanding the author's intent, or another objective. You will work on this objective initially through a whole-class, shared reading lesson to introduce the concept (possibly using a lesson from this book as a starting point). After students have grasped the basic concept (one or two lessons), you will continue your Tier 1 instruction at the small-group level, differentiated according to different students' needs, where students will work toward mastery. Students' response to this instruction will set the stage for Tier 2 and Tier 3 interventions where needed. (See **Chapter Six** for more about this tiered support for struggling students.)

Remember that if many of the students in your class are ELLs, you will want to select objectives matched to their level of language proficiency. For students at an *entering* level, this would mean focusing on basic text features and concepts about print: cover, title, author, chapter, table of contents, etc. For those who have advanced to a *beginning* level, address narrative story elements: characters, setting, problem, solution—as well as facts and main ideas in informational text. Even at the *developing* and *expanding* levels, most ELLs will fare better with objectives that rely on literal rather than inferential thinking. For example, summarizing (A3) will be more manageable than determining what is important to an author or character (D3).

This should clarify how you select *one* objective. But you need to figure out how comprehension will look over your entire year. How will you make sure you don't miss something important along the way? Make a list of your students' comprehension priorities and incorporate them into a pacing guide. (You might want to consult your state or district curriculum or literacy frameworks, too, for the standards or benchmarks they require.) This will assure that *all* of the important objectives are covered during the course of a year—not just the ones that you "get around to."

It is not difficult to develop one of these pacing guides. Really! In workshops that I present, I often build in some time for teachers to work in grade-level groups to create a draft for a pacing chart that covers their whole year. They are amazed when they complete at least the skeleton of this plan in less than thirty minutes. I have provided a sample pacing chart on page 27 at the end of this chapter to give you a sense of what this task involves. But my chart is paced out according to focus objectives and literacy standards that are tested in *my* state (Connecticut); your chart should be organized around the standards for *your* state.

The objectives I've used for the lessons in this book are provided in a chart at the end of this chapter and also on the CD. Tips for teaching these objectives and a literature response answer frame for each objective are not included here because they are contained in my previous book, *That's a Great Answer!* (Maupin House, 2007). You will find additional suggestions in that book for teaching each objective.

How do I know if I've stated my objective appropriately?
Stating an objective clearly and concisely can be more trouble than you might think! Here are a few things to avoid when indicating your objective:

- Do not indicate that your objective is *shared reading*. Shared reading is the instructional format; it does not describe what you will be teaching or what students will be learning.

- Do not indicate that your objective is *Little Red Riding Hood*. That is the content of your lesson.

- Do not indicate that your objective is *completing a comprehension follow-up sheet on making text-to-self connections*. That is an activity that students will be able to complete if they have mastered your objective.

- Do not combine a bunch of different objectives: *Students will notice all of the important details so they can draw conclusions about the main character and picture the setting.* Do you want students to notice important details? Draw conclusions about a character? Describe the setting? Use the *picturing* strategy? There are too many things going on here. Students will be very confused and you won't know how to measure what you think you're teaching. Too many embedded objectives leads to "fuzzy" teaching without any real accountability, which is like having no objective at all.

- Do not state your objective (or post it!) in the abstract, convoluted terms of some state standards. Here's my favorite example of this from my state: *Select, synthesize, and/or use relevant information within a written work to extend or evaluate the work. (Synthesize not tested in grade 3) (Connecticut Mastery Test Fourth Generation Language Arts Handbook, page 11.)* Do you have *any* clue what students would actually be expected to *do* based on that statement? While this objective is much too obtuse for any teachers and students I know, when you read the bulleted examples below the general statement, you know exactly what is expected:

  o *Using information from the article, write a paragraph that could have appeared in the journal of _____ after _____ (event) occurred.*

  o *Imagine that you are going to write a letter to the author to find out more about _____. Write two questions you would ask that are not already answered in the story.*

  o *Imagine that you were going to give a talk to your class about _____. Using information from the passage, write **two** important ideas that you would use in your speech.*

Today's lesson should be based not on that very broad "*select, synthesize, or use...*" statement, but on one of the more targeted, concrete objectives discovered when you drill down a layer to the bulleted tasks.

So, what *should* you do when stating your objective? Make sure the objective is precise and measurable. The bulleted items above are examples of good objectives:
- They indicate what the **product** will be (*journal entry, asking questions of the author, and giving a talk to your class*)
- They instruct students how to **process** the objective (*using information from the article/passage, think about questions not already answered in the text*)
- They identify **form** and and/or **quantity** (write a *paragraph*, write *two* questions)

It will be easy to measure these objectives because both teachers and students are clear about the expectations. If you can measure it, you can manage it! You could easily create a rubric for any one of the objectives above delineating a rating scale based on the components of each objective. In fact, you *need* a rubric (or identified response criteria) to measure your objective. You also need anchor responses to guide your assessment. (See **Chapter 7** for more about scoring students' responses.)

Turning your objective into a target

What is the difference between an objective and a target?
An objective identifies a particular reading skill or strategy that may be applied to the reading

of *any* text. When we teach an objective, we ultimately intend for students to be able to apply it to the story we read today, the social studies chapter we read tomorrow, or any text for which that skill might be appropriate. A target identifies the reading skill or strategy as it is applied to one specific text. We want students to know exactly what they are supposed to do today. Here is an example of an objective from a lesson in this book and that same objective transformed into a target for the lesson.

 Objective (strategy focus): D3-b: In a short paragraph, explain how your customs are different from the customs described in this story/article. Use information from the story to support your answer.

Tell in a short paragraph why the lotus seed was so important to the grandmother in the story *The Lotus Seed*. In America, is there anything we treasure like the grandmother treasured the lotus seed? Use evidence from the story to support your answer.

How will student learning be measured at the end of the lesson? (What will count as "success?")

Notice that the objective (D3-b) could be applied to *any* text that describes customs from other cultures. The target, however, asks students to apply the concept of different customs to a particular story.

How should a target be stated?

As noted above, the critical factor in wording the target is for students to know precisely what they must produce in order to demonstrate mastery of the objective. The tiny print under the target reminds teachers that they will need to *measure* student learning: What will students be asked to do? Students will have a much clearer idea of the task if the target uses "kid language" rather than "teacher language." This is not a time for fancy, educational lingo. In fact, the simpler and more direct, the better. Begin with an action verb: *Tell, explain, compare, summarize*, etc. Try to stay away from language that sounds too formal, abstract, and complicated: *The student will be able to demonstrate an understanding of why the lotus seed was so important to the grandmother and will compare this to an American symbol.* We may have had to write "behavioral objectives" in those terms to pass student teaching, but we don't need that language for the target.

Why use a target?

Students understand the concept of a target. They know that you aim squarely for the middle—which is exactly what we want them to do when striving to meet an objective. The target also works well for me because it is easy to draw. Some teachers with much more artistic talent than I possess, create cute little critters that give the target a personality. One teacher I know drew a lovable-looking, potbellied character with the target right in the middle of his belly. His name was Mr. Target. The kids thought he was great; I did, too, but when I teach a lesson, my students have to settle for an icon that can be designed with basic geometric shapes or that I can find readymade on my computer.

How should the target be communicated to students?

Whether you draw Mr. Target or stick to something more mundane, the target should be accessible to students visually and also identified orally. Post the target in the same classroom location each day so that students know where to look for it. Say it aloud and point to it during the pre-reading portion of the lesson. Begin your target with a verb: *Explain, Identify, Tell.* Action verbs work better than passive ones such as *understand* or *know.* Also lose those little phrases they taught us to include in lesson plans when we were learning to write them in college: *The student will....* Kids are action-oriented. Cut right to the chase and state your target in a way that children will know *exactly* what you mean and *exactly* what they are supposed to *do.* (A target for each objective is included with the support materials on the CD. A sample target is included with the first lesson in Part II.)

Will I always focus *only* on my targeted objective?

At the intermediate grade level, you will probably use the same broad objective throughout the book—or at least for a good chunk of the book (A1, B2, D3, etc.)— since you are teaching for *mastery.* However, within those general categories, you will need to decide which *specific* objectives (A1-a, A1-b, etc.) your students need most. You should also, after reading, discuss questions related to other objectives, although you may not be directly *teaching* that objective. It's always useful to expose students to various ways of thinking about a text.

DECIDING WHAT TO TEACH *WITH*

Choosing your text

What kind of text should I use for a shared reading lesson?

There are so many options! Given the quality of picture books available for students of *all* developmental stages, I'd say that picture books are generally my first choice when planning a shared reading lesson. But within that domain, how do you narrow the selection? Your first challenge, not to be underestimated in either its level of importance or its difficulty, is to find a book well-matched to the objective. The "Teaching Tips" accompanying each objective in *That's a Great Answer!* will help you consider what is essential when identifying texts for individual objectives. I won't repeat all of that here. What I can tell you, though, with absolute assurance, is that you really have to get this part right or your lesson is doomed! The most careful planning can't compensate for a text that just doesn't work with the objective.

How do I avoid picking the "wrong" book?

It's not that the book you choose is inherently "wrong," it's just that there are so many aspects of book selection that you need to consider. A book that is perfect in one situation might be a very bad choice under another set of circumstances. Here are some common pitfalls to avoid:

- Don't choose a book that has very few (or no!) places for you to model the objective and have students practice it. I know this sounds obvious, but it is something teachers sometimes overlook. You can easily remedy this problem by reading the book beforehand. Mark places with sticky notes where you can model finding evidence to meet the objective and other places where you will want students to practice finding the evidence themselves. If you don't have many sticky notes sticking out of your book when you finish reading, you might as well put the book back on the shelf and keep looking.

- Don't choose a book with too much text. If the book you choose is too dense with too many words per page, plan on reading it over a couple of sessions rather than all at one time. Remember that a shared reading lesson is intended to last no more than thirty minutes. If there's too much to read, your nice lesson will turn into a read-aloud with no time to attend to the actual objective. Of course there's nothing wrong with simply reading aloud to students, but that is not the intent of shared reading.

- Don't inadvertently neglect various racial, ethnic, and cultural groups as you choose your books. Children of all races, cultures, and ethnicities need to see people who look like them when they turn the pages of a book. Gone are the days when there's a paucity of African-American characters in children's literature (except picture books for very young children which seem to primarily feature cute little white kids). Now, in fact, it's almost too easy to get caught up in themed literature related to African Americans throughout the history of our country, from slavery through the Civil Rights era, to current issues that focus on more subtle dimensions of discrimination. There are some amazing books on all of these topics, and several are used for lessons in this book or referenced as lesson extensions. But remember that "multicultural" means many different cultures. Look for books with Latino/Latina characters from various Caribbean cultures as well as from Mexico. Look for Asian and South-American characters from lots of different countries and stories that celebrate Eastern Europeans. With regard to our own history and culture, look for books about Native Americans and books that provide a realistic look at different regions of the United States. I have a particular passion for stories set in Alaska. You'll be amazed by the books you can find to support studies of particular parts of the world or our country when you really look!

- Don't select books that are clearly above or below the interest level of your students. I would say that teachers more often err on the side of choosing books that are too advanced for their students. Sometimes as teachers we look at a text and we recognize that it is an excellent piece of literature. We want so badly to share it with our students. "They'll understand this," we reason. We convince ourselves that this book will be a good fit because we want it to be so. But we learn the hard way that the text really is over the heads of those little third graders (or students of whatever grade). They don't have the background knowledge to truly comprehend the basic premise of the story. Or we need to stop six or seven times on any given page to explain the vocabulary. Remember that explicit teaching must lead to student learning if it is to make a difference; books that are too difficult make that learning harder to attain.

- Don't select books with a sensitive theme without knowing your audience. I have lots of great books that I encourage teachers to use—but there are some that I can rarely use myself. As a guest in your classroom, I need to be very careful about the books that I use to model lessons. *The Memory String* (Eve Bunting) is a wonderful book, but might be a bit intense for a student who has just lost a parent. *Mama Loves Me from Away* (Pat Brisson) is a thought-provoking story, but before using it, I would want to know if a child in my class had a parent in prison. Even books that address such themes as prejudice, bullying, and poverty imply a level of trust that *you* have with your students, but that *I* would hesitate to assume as a visitor to your classroom. Books can be a catalyst for important discussions, but it is never a good idea to rush headlong into a piece of literature that may evoke more raw feelings than you're prepared to deal with at that moment.

- **Especially for ELLs:** Make sure that the picture book you select contains illustrations that clarify rather than extend the content. English language learners will benefit from story graphics that tell in pictures what they may not be able to understand through words alone. Characters' faces should clearly communicate feelings that the text is trying to convey. Scenes should feature main ideas boldly and simply represented. Pictures that are very "busy" or contain too much detail will make it difficult for English language learners to know where to focus their attention.

These dos and don'ts are the guidelines that help me in my selection of books. The deceptive part of all this is that by the time I show up in a classroom to teach a lesson, the process required to choose the book I will use is long since finished and certainly not visible to teachers. Sometimes I think that teachers believe that the perfect book just jumps off my bookshelf into my hands. Nothing could be farther from the truth. I sit on the floor of my crowded little study pulling one book after another out of my bookcase: *No, I'll never get through this one in thirty minutes*, I conclude, *although the treatment of the topic is perfect for fifth graders. No, this one might elicit deeper personal connections than I am willing to risk*, I admit reluctantly.

"Your lesson went so well because you had the *perfect* book!" one teacher announced in the debriefing session that followed my model lesson in her classroom. Her words felt like more of an accusation than an affirmation. I try hard to show teachers that if my text is *perfect*, it's because I am willing to do the leg work ahead of time to consider how a text will be received before charging forward.

Beyond picture books, what other types of text should I consider?
The criteria I use to select picture books prevail with other texts, too. I often use poems. Depending on the length of the poem, I might use two or three poems in one lesson (all matched to the objective). The neat thing about poems is that you can *show* them using an overhead projector or interactive whiteboard, giving students visual access to the words as you read them aloud. Or you and your students can read them together. A passage from a nonfiction article or a content-area text also works well when you are applying objectives to expository materials—which you should do on a regular basis!

"What about chapter books?" teachers frequently ask. "Can those also be used for shared reading?" I have worked with one district building their curriculum and they wanted to expose students to every possible literary format, including longer text. Beginning with second grade, they incorporated longer picture books and chapter books. When you use chapter books, you will plan your lesson around the same text for several days or for as much as three weeks. Try to stay away from really long chapter books as reading the same text for four weeks or more starts to feel like a life sentence regardless of how good the book is. Another resource you will want to consider is the anthology from your core program—if you have a core program. While the selections in these books are typically beyond the reading level of many students in any classroom, they can work well for shared reading because the teacher is doing most of the reading. In fact, an advantage to incorporating stories from a core text is that students will most likely all have a copy of the text to hold in their hands. Be aware, however, that some of the selections in core program anthologies can be quite long, requiring several days to complete.

There is no question that using short text is easier than longer text. If the book you chose isn't a huge success, you are done with it in a day or two, and you can move on. With a chapter book, for example, when you and your class decide in chapter three that no one is having much fun, you may still have a hundred pages left to read. Aborting the mission mid-book is a tough decision. Still, using a few chapter books adds balance to your shared reading curriculum and allows you to engage with text that is structurally more complex than content you will access through picture books, poetry, and brief nonfiction selections.

The list of comprehension objectives that follows is quite comprehensive and should cover the objectives identified by any state—though the labeling system may be different. I have also included a list of the objectives aligned with ELL levels. The levels are based on WIDA standards (World-Class Instructional Design and Assessment), which is the framework used by many states for determining students' English language proficiency. Following the objectives is a template for a pacing guide and a sample pacing guide completed for fourth grade.

COMPREHENSION OBJECTIVES

<u>The "A" Strand: Forming a General Understanding</u>

A1: Main idea and theme
- **A1-a**: What lesson does _____ learn in this story? (fiction) [figuring out]
- **A1-b**: What is the theme of this story? (fiction) [figuring out]
- **A1-c**: What is the main idea? (nonfiction) [figuring out]
- **A1-d**: What would be another good title for this book/story? (fiction, nonfiction) [figuring out]

A2: Characters, problem/solution, setting
- **A2-a**: Using information in the story, write a brief description of how _____ felt when…. (fiction) [figuring out]
- **A2-b**: What is _____'s main problem in the story? Give details from the story to support your answer. (fiction) [noticing]
- **A2-c**: How did _____ solve his/her problem? Give details from the story to support your answer. (fiction) [noticing]
- **A2-d**: How did _____ change from the beginning to the end of the story? (fiction) [figuring out]
- **A2-e**: What is the setting of this story? Give details from the story to support your answer. (fiction) [noticing]

A3: Summarizing
- **A3-a**: Briefly summarize this story. (fiction) [figuring out]
- **A3-b**: Summarize the main things that happened in this [book]. (fiction, nonfiction) [figuring out]
- **A3-c**: Briefly summarize this article/informational text. (nonfiction) [figuring out]

A4: Predicting
- **A4-a**: Predict what will happen next in this story. (fiction) [guessing/predicting]
- **A4-b**: If the author added another paragraph to the end of the story (or article), it would <u>most likely</u> tell about _____. Use information from the story (or article) to support your answer. (fiction, nonfiction) [guessing/predicting]

<u>The "B" Strand: Developing an Interpretation</u>

B1: Identify or infer the author's use of structure/organizational patterns.
- **B1-a:** What caused _____ to happen in the story? (fiction) [noticing]
- **B1-b:** What happened at the beginning, in the middle, and at the end of the story? (fiction) [noticing]
- **B1-c:** Compare these two characters. (fiction) [noticing]
- **B1-d:** Can this part of the [story/text] be described as: a description, an explanation, a conversation, an opinion, an argument, or a comparison? How do you know? (fiction, nonfiction) [noticing]

B2: Draw conclusions about the author's purpose for choosing a genre or for including or omitting specific details in text.
- **B2-a:** Why does the author include paragraph ___? (fiction, nonfiction) [figuring out]
- **B2-b:** Why did the author write a [poem/story/nonfiction book] about this? (fiction, nonfiction) [figuring out]

B3: Use evidence from the text to support a conclusion.
- **B3-a:** Prove that [character/person] is very _____. (fiction, nonfiction) [figuring out]
- **B3-b:** Which facts show that _____? (fiction, nonfiction) [noticing]

COMPREHENSION OBJECTIVES (Cont'd.)

The "C" Strand: Making Reader/Text Connections

C1: Connect the text to a personal experience, another text, or the outside world

- **C1-a:** Make a personal connection to the *experience* in the story. (fiction) [connecting]
- **C1-b:** Make a personal connection to a *feeling* in the story. (fiction) [connecting]
- **C1-c:** Would you like _____ for a friend? Why or why not? (fiction, nonfiction) [connecting]
- **C1-d:** Using information in the story, explain whether you would ever want to _____. (fiction, nonfiction) [connecting]

C2: Make a personal response to the text

- **C2-a:** Which part of the story/article do you think was *most* important? Use information from the story to explain why you chose that part. (fiction, nonfiction) [connecting]
- **C2-b:** Which part of this [story/article] was most interesting or surprising to you? Why? (fiction, nonfiction) [connecting]
- **C2-c:** Did you like this [story/article]? Why or why not? (fiction, nonfiction) [connecting]
- **C2-d:** What was your first reaction to this text? Explain. (fiction, nonfiction) [connecting]

The "D" Strand: Examining Content and Structure

D1: Examine the author's craft

- **D1-a:** Choose [2] words from paragraph ___ that help you picture the _____. (fiction, nonfiction) [picturing]
- **D1-b:** Choose a simile and explain why the author chose that simile. (fiction, nonfiction) [noticing]
- **D1-c:** How did the author create humor in paragraph _____? (fiction) [noticing]
- **D1-d:** Give an example of personification in paragraph ____. (fiction) [noticing]
- **D1-e:** Do you think the author made this story believable? Why or why not? (fiction) [figuring out]

D2: Extend the text

- **D2-a:** What two questions would you like to ask the author that were not answered in this text? (fiction, nonfiction) [wondering]
- **D2-b:** Imagine you are going to give a talk to your class about _____. What two points would you be sure to include in your speech? (nonfiction) [figuring out]
- **D2-c:** Using information in the text, write a paragraph that could have appeared in _____'s journal after _____ occurred. (fiction, nonfiction) [figuring out]

D3: Show that you understand what was important to an author or character

- **D3-a:** How does the author/character show that _____ is important to him/her? (fiction, nonfiction) [noticing]
- **D3-b:** How are your customs different from the customs described in this story/article? (fiction, nonfiction) [figuring out]

COMPREHENSION OBJECTIVES MATCHED TO ELL LEVELS
(Levels based on WIDA* standards)

Level 1: Entering
- Identify concepts about print and text features

Level 2: Beginning
- Identify facts and explicit messages including story elements
    - o **A2:** Who are the characters? (fiction) [noticing]
    - o **A2-b:** What is _____'s main problem in the story? Give details from the story to support your answer. (fiction) [noticing]
    - o **A2-c:** How did _____ solve his/her problem? Give details from the story to support your answer. (fiction) [noticing]
    - o **A2-e:** What is the setting of this story? Give details from the story to support your answer. (fiction) [noticing]

Level 3: Developing
- Sequence pictures, events, processes
    - o **B1-b:** What happened at the beginning, in the middle, and at the end of the story? (fiction) [noticing]
    - o **A3-a:** Briefly summarize this story. (fiction) [figuring out]
    - o **A3-b:** Summarize the main things that happened in this [book]. (fiction, nonfiction) [figuring out]
    - o **A3-c:** Briefly summarize this article/informational text. (nonfiction) [figuring out]
- Identify main ideas
    - o **A1-c:** What is the main idea? (nonfiction) [figuring out]
    - o **A1-d:** What would be another good title for this book/story? (fiction, nonfiction) [figuring out]
- Use context clues to determine meanings of words
    - o **A5:** Determine word meanings from context.

Level 4: Expanding
- Interpret information or data
    - o **A1-a:** What lesson does _____ learn in this story? (fiction) [figuring out]
    - o **A1-b:** What is the theme of this story? (fiction) [figuring out]
    - o **A2-a:** Using information in the story, write a brief description of how _____ felt when…… (fiction) [figuring out]
    - o **A2-d:** How did _____ change from the beginning to the end of the story? (fiction) [figuring out]
    - o **A4-a:** Predict what will happen next in this story. (fiction) [guessing/predicting]
    - o **A4-b:** If the author added another paragraph to the end of the story (or article), it would <u>most likely</u> tell about _____. Use information from the story (or article) to support your answer. (fiction, nonfiction) [guessing/predicting]
    - o **B1-a:** What caused _____ to happen in the story? (fiction) [noticing]
    - o **D1-a:** Choose [2] words from paragraph ___ that help you picture the _____. (fiction, nonfiction) [picturing]
    - o **D1-b:** Choose a simile and explain why the author chose that simile. (fiction, nonfiction) [noticing]

- o **D1-c:** How did the author create humor in paragraph _____? (fiction) [noticing]
- o **D1-d:** Give an example of personification in paragraph ____. (fiction) [noticing

- Find details that support….
  - o **B1-c:** Compare these two characters. (fiction) [noticing]
  - o **B3-a:** Prove that [character/person] is very _____. (fiction, nonfiction) [noticing]
  - o **B3-b:** Which facts show that _____? (fiction, nonfiction) [noticing]
  - o **D3-a:** How does the author/character show that _____ is important to him/her? (fiction, nonfiction) [noticing]

Level 5: Bridging
- Draw conclusions from implicit and explicit text
  - o **B1-d:** Can this part of the [story/text] be described as: a description, an explanation, a conversation, an opinion, an argument, or a comparison? How do you know? (fiction, nonfiction) [noticing]
  - o **B2-a:** Why does the author include paragraph ___? (fiction, nonfiction) [figuring out]
  - o **B2-b:** Why did the author write a [poem/story/nonfiction book] about this? (fiction, nonfiction) [figuring out]
  - o **C1-a:** Make a personal connection to an *experience* in the story. (fiction) [connecting]
  - o **C1-b:** Make a personal connection to a *feeling* in the story. (fiction) [connecting]
  - o **C1-c:** Would you like _____ for a friend? Why or why not? (fiction, nonfiction) [connecting]
  - o **C1-d:** Using information in the story, explain whether you would ever want to _____. (fiction, nonfiction) [connecting]
  - o **C2-a:** Which part of the story/article do you think was *most* important? Use information from the story to explain why you chose that part. (fiction, nonfiction) [connecting]
  - o **C2-b:** Which part of this [story/article] was most interesting or surprising to you? Why? (fiction, nonfiction) [connecting]
  - o **C2-c:** Did you like this [story/article]? Why or why not? (fiction, nonfiction) [connecting]
  - o **C2-d:** What was your first reaction to this text? Explain. (fiction, nonfiction) [connecting]
  - o **D1-e:** Do you think the author made this story believable? Why or why not? (fiction) [figuring out]
  - o **D2-a:** What two questions would you like to ask the author that were not answered in this text? (fiction, nonfiction) [wondering]
  - o **D2-b:** Imagine you are going to give a talk to your class about _____. What two points would you be sure to include in your speech? (nonfiction) [figuring out]
  - o **D2-c:** Using information in the text, write a paragraph that could have appeared in _____'s journal after _____ occurred. (fiction, nonfiction) [figuring out]
  - o **D3-b:** How are your customs different from the customs described in this story/article? (fiction, nonfiction) [figuring out]

*WIDA: World-Class Instructional Design and Assessment

YEAR-LONG PACING TEMPLATE FOR COMPREHENSION OBJECTIVES

<u>Sept.</u>
1.

2.

<u>Oct.</u>
1.

2.

<u>Nov.</u>
1.

2.

<u>Dec.</u>
1.

2.

<u>Jan.</u>
1.

2.

<u>Feb.</u>
1.

2.

<u>March</u>
1.

2.

<u>Apr.</u>
1.

2.

<u>May</u>
1.

2.

<u>June</u>
1.

2.

SAMPLE PACING GUIDE FOR COMPREHENSION OBJECTIVES: GRADE 4

Based on current needs as identified by assessment data

Sept.

1. Review A2: text elements (especially A2-d: where the character changes and A2-b: identifying the problem)
2. A3: summarizing fiction and nonfiction

Oct.

1. A1: theme and main idea (especially A1-b: theme in fiction and A1-c: main idea in nonfiction)
2. C1: personal connections (especially C1-a: connecting to an experience and C1-b: connecting to a feeling)

Nov.

1. B3: identifying evidence to support a conclusion
2. C2: personal response/reaction to text (especially C2-a: most important part and C2-b: most interesting/surprising part)

Dec.

1. D2: extending the text (D2-c: journal entry)
2. D2: extending the text (D2-a: ask the author questions, D2-b: give a talk to your class)

Jan.

1. B1: text structures (especially B1-c: compare/contrast and B1-d: can this part of the text be described as…?)
2. B2: author's purpose for selecting a particular genre/including particular details

Feb.

1. D3: author's/character's customs or values
2. D1: evidence of author's craft (especially D1-e: do you think this story is believable? and D1- b: similes)

March

State assessment: no objectives addressed this month

Based on anticipated needs at the next grade level

April

1. extend A1: main idea/theme
2. extend A3: summarizing

May

1. extend C1 and C2: personal connections and personal reactions
2. extend B2: author's purpose for selecting a particular genre/including particular details

June

1. extend D2: extending the text
2. extend D1: author's craft

REFLECTING ON CHAPTER TWO

1. What assessment data and resources do you use to choose your comprehension objectives? Do you feel you can adequately pinpoint your students' comprehension needs based on your available data and resources? Explain.

2. How closely do the objectives on the list on pages 22-23 in this chapter align with your objectives? Are there others that you should also include?

3. How do you choose your texts for shared reading? Are they chosen for you, or do you choose them yourself?

4. How much short text do you presently use for shared reading? Where could you find additional short text?

5. What objectives at your grade level are especially troublesome for students?

6. How could you better meet the needs of the ELLs in your classroom, or how could you collaborate more effectively with the ESL teacher to meet ELLs' comprehension needs?

7. Something to try: With a grade-level partner, create a year-long pacing guide that incorporates all of your essential objectives. Use the blank template on page 26 and the sample pacing guide on page 27 to get you started.

8. Something to try: Try to convert an objective to a target for a particular text. How could you help a colleague to do this?

CHAPTER THREE
Supporting Readers before Reading

Teachers sometimes do not think of the *before reading* part of the lesson as "reading instruction" because there is no actual "reading" involved. I disagree. What a teacher does to get students ready to read, before opening the book, has a great deal to do with the student learning that will occur by the end of the lesson. In fact, this *before reading* component may be the most important part of all for struggling students. Three instructional elements need to be addressed before reading: Establish prior knowledge, purpose, and predictions; introduce/review vocabulary; and introduce the focus strategy (how to find and use the evidence).

In **Chapter Three** I highlight this portion of the *Shared Reading Planner*:

Establish prior knowledge, purpose, and predictions	**Prior knowledge:** **Predictions:** **Purpose for reading:**
Introduce/review vocabulary	
Introduce the objective (How to find and use the evidence)	**Making the <u>reading</u> strategic**

To fill in this part of the planner meaningfully, you will need to be able to answer the following questions.

ACTIVATING BACKGROUND KNOWLEDGE

How do I help students establish prior knowledge, set a purpose, and make predictions?
   Establishing prior knowledge:

- When you first introduce the text, review or extend students' knowledge of the genre and the author (as well as the topic or theme), if appropriate.

- Make sure the background knowledge you activate is important and relevant: Will students need this knowledge to understand the text?

- If the lesson extends for more than one day, after the first lesson, activating background knowledge should mostly be reviewing the learning from the day before and *briefly* summarizing what was read.

- Keep it short—two or three minutes (avoid too many personal connections from students).

- **Especially for ELLs:** Remember that much prior knowledge is based upon one's culture. Try to anticipate what your ELLs might not be familiar with based on their cultural background (going to the beach, visiting the Statue of Liberty, names such as Martin Luther King or George Washington, issues around Civil Rights, etc.). In such cases, you will need to *build*, not just *activate*, prior knowledge.

MAKING PREDICTIONS

- For fiction: Students should make predictions about what the story will be about based on the title, front cover, back cover, and possibly one or two illustrations inside the book. Avoid a lengthy picture walk since this gives too much away and consumes too much time.

- For nonfiction: Students should make predictions about what they will *learn* based on any available text features. Also make predictions based on the title, cover illustration, and blurb on the back of the book if available.

- Keep it short—one or two minutes. Sometimes, in fact fairly frequently, it is impossible to predict the content of a text based on available information before you read. This is particularly true with poems or short stories that do not have accompanying illustrations. When you can't make sense of the title (*Probuditi!* by Chris Van Allsburg) or when it is clearly misleading (*Spaghetti* by Cynthia Rylant), fishing for predictions only wastes time!

SETTING A PURPOSE

- The purpose for reading should match the objective and the target.

- This should be made absolutely clear to students: "Today we will work on…"; "At the end of today's lesson I will ask you to…."

- Say the objective/target orally and show students where the target is posted so they can refer to it. This meets the needs of both auditory and visual learners.

- Keep it really short; you are just telling students *what* to do at this point, now *how* to do it—about one minute.

INTRODUCING VOCABULARY

How should I introduce vocabulary to students?

- The best vocabulary words to choose are those that are important to the text *and* can be useful to students' speaking and writing vocabularies beyond the context of the book. Very technical terms, even though they may be important to the text (and should be briefly explained during the reading), are not the words you want students to practice. (There is lots of research that supports this. See books by Isabel Beck for more information about research-based vocabulary instruction.) An example of a good word to teach in *The Honest-to-Goodness Truth* by Patricia McKissack (Lesson A1-a: What lesson does this story teach?) might be *trudged* because that is a word that might fit nicely into a story students would write or use within their speaking vocabulary: "I *trudged* home after school, knowing my mom would not be happy with my report card." Another word that is also in this book but would probably not serve students well after this book was finished is *sashayed*. It's an archaic term that people seldom use today, so just a brief explanation in context might be sufficient.

- When it comes to vocabulary, less is more. Intermediate-grade students can't really learn more than about two words per day if the instruction is to be thorough, and if you intend to provide opportunities for follow-up review and practice on subsequent days. You can identify several words for a particular book, and you can briefly introduce them, but don't try to work on them all at once.

- After providing a simple definition of the word and an example of the word used in a sentence, ask *several* students to use the word in an *oral* sentence. There should be more student talk than teacher talk during vocabulary instruction.

- Be sure to *write* the word as well as say it. Although vocabulary instruction and spelling instruction are not the same, you can also point out interesting features regarding the way the word looks.

- Something else that doesn't work: copying definitions from a dictionary—as dictionary definitions typically explain words with other words children don't know. Also, it's hard to really see how a word is used just by knowing its definition. Additionally, it is inefficient to ask students to copy *your* definitions during instruction as this distracts them from more actively using the words themselves.

- Unless you return to the same words later or on subsequent days for additional practice, your initial instruction will have been for naught. In order to "own" a word, students need to use it in a context meaningful to them many times.

- Resist the urge to turn every shared reading lesson into a vocabulary lesson by stopping constantly during your reading to explain new words in depth.

- Make sure that when you pre-teach a word before reading a text you are using it the same way it is used in the text. (This type of error reveals a glaring lack of teacher planning.)

- Pre-reading vocabulary instruction should only take about five minutes. If it takes much longer than that, you are most likely trying to teach too many words at once.

- Note that each lesson in this book contains a *Vocabulary Connections* activity (on the CD). This will be useful for reinforcing or even assessing the words later in the week after they have been introduced and practiced. This activity is explained more thoroughly in the introduction to Part II of this book. A sample *Vocabulary Connections* activity is included in the first lesson plan (for objective A1-a).

EXPLAINING THE OBJECTIVE

How do I introduce the objective? (How to find and use the evidence)
If there is one part of a shared reading lesson that is more misunderstood or more neglected than other parts, this is it! Many teachers are not even aware that they *should* be introducing the objective explicitly—or what this means. This is unfortunate because this is the portion of the lesson that makes the biggest difference to Tier 1 instruction. The goal of Tier 1 instruction is to get as many students to mastery as possible so you don't have to deal with Tiers 2 and 3.

To be *explicit* means to *explain clearly*, and the objective, above all else in a lesson, needs to be explained clearly. What you are explaining in this case is how to find the evidence to meet a particular objective. Every objective requires a different strategy for unlocking the meaning within. For example, if you're expected to make a personal *connection* to a feeling in a story, how do you go about doing that? If you are *figuring out* a theme, what kind of evidence would prove that you have found that central idea? Teachers acknowledge the importance of teaching students a set of metacognitive strategies to improve their comprehension but seldom get past those random connections or inferences that often lead nowhere. Being a strategic reader means knowing *what* strategy is the best fit for the objective at hand, *when* to activate that strategy, and most important, *how* to tease out the required evidence for meeting the objective. In short, efficient reading is about *being* strategic, not *having* a strategy. To accomplish all of this you need to:

- Explain to students how to find the evidence for a particular objective; for example, how to find the theme of a story. This is easier said than done because, as skilled readers ourselves, we have been finding the themes of stories (or locating other evidence) for so long, we now do this virtually automatically with little or no intentional strategizing. That is not the case for our students, however, who are less experienced in the fine art of finding evidence for an objective. So, appraise your process: What do you do first? What do you do next? Are there other steps in this process, too? Break the process down into a few logical steps. Students will understand a few simple steps; they will not understand a process if it contains too many steps or if it sounds complicated to them.

- Make the process as simple as possible—even though many of these objectives concern complex higher-level thinking. You need to use language that students in your grade will understand—no small feat when you are not used to explaining the concept of "theme" or "author's values" to eight-year-olds! This will require you to plan ahead. Think about how you will say what you want to say before you stand up in front of your class to begin your lesson. It is doubtful that the perfect words will simply tumble out of your mouth without forethought. Fortunately, perfection is not required here; all you need are a few helpful hints to get students started. Tomorrow you can add a few more hints for students as you pay close attention to how you and they approach the current objective.

- **Especially for ELLs:** When you are reviewing with students how to find the evidence for a particular objective, don't forget to call on your English language learners who are capable of responding: *What do we do first when we want to summarize a story? Or How do we figure out the main idea?* Of course you may need to support them as they formulate their oral sentence, but then ask them to repeat it until they can say it fluently—certainly not to the point of embarrassing them, but to show them that *they* can succeed with this, too.

- Persevere! When you first begin to include this explanation of the objective into your reading instruction, it may feel awkward and you will worry that you are not doing it "right." You may not even get very helpful help from the reading specialist in your school if you ask for assistance because this may be a new concept to him, too. But don't give up! This part of the lesson is so important to students' success that you need to work at it until you can see that the hints you provide are giving kids more efficient access to the evidence they need to meet an objective. When you no longer have to tell them (with a sigh) to "go back and find the evidence for your answer," you will know that this part of your lesson is making a difference.

Unfortunately, when you omit this explanation of the objective and how to find the best evidence, you won't realize it until it's too late. Fast forward to *after* reading, when you ask students a question related to your objective, and they write some superficial response that lacks specifics from the story. You then tell them, "Go back and find the evidence to support your answer." The truth is, if they knew what evidence they were looking for, they most likely would have found it in the first place! If they have no idea what they are looking for, simply going back to re-read will make little difference.

Remember that the CD accompanying this book contains suggestions for how to explain each of the objectives as part of the support materials for each lesson. These explanations have even been written out on a *Target Template* so you can apply them immediately to your lesson. As you think of additional helpful hints to share with students about how to find evidence for a particular objective, add your bulleted items to the list that I've provided.

A blank *Target Template* is included on the next page for you to use when teaching objectives that may not be contained in this book, or when you want to vary the explanation to better meet the needs of the students you teach.

Before moving on to **Chapter Four**, use the reflection questions at the end of this chapter to think about how you support readers *before* reading and how you might strengthen this portion of your lesson, especially the way you explain an objective.

How to hit the target:

REFLECTING ON CHAPTER THREE

1. How do you typically get students ready to read a text? How long does this part of the lesson generally take? Should you shorten the time you spend on *before reading* activities?

2. When you introduce a text, do you get "bogged down" in any area of pre-reading? Which one(s)? How could you modify your instruction to keep students on track?

3. One of the areas of pre-reading that teachers sometimes neglect is activating students' prior knowledge related to the genre or structure of the text. How could discussing the genre/structure improve students' comprehension?

4. How would it help students to understand how to find the evidence for meeting a comprehension objective? (Think about some students in your class who might have shown better progress if you had explained such strategic thinking to them before reading.)

5. How do you incorporate vocabulary? About how many words do you introduce at once? What do you do with the words once they've been introduced? What could you try that would enhance your students' learning of new words?

6. Something to try: Explaining how to find evidence to meet an objective can be tricky at first. Choose an objective and think about how you would explain to students in your grade how to be successful with that objective. Use the *Target Template* on page 34 to record your bulleted points.

CHAPTER FOUR
Supporting Readers during Reading

You might think to yourself, "How hard could this be?" During reading you *read*. Well, yes—and no! The thing that distinguishes shared reading from a garden-variety read-aloud is *how* you read. During a basic read-aloud, you read the text all the way through, possibly stopping here and there to check students' understanding by asking a key question or two.

Your stopping points during a shared lesson are much more intentional and are chosen because they match the lesson objective. For example, if you're working on the A4-a objective, *making predictions*, you will stop at points where you can anticipate the next move of a character based on the events of the story so far and your knowledge of the character's motives. You should not plan to stop for passages related to the setting, the theme of the story, the plot structure, etc., although a few spontaneous applications of other strategies (too perfect to pass up) would be fine. Remember, your goal is to make students *strategic* as they apply the day's objective. As noted in the previous chapter, recent research about comprehension strategy instruction makes the point that it's not so much about *having* a strategy (picturing, wondering, etc.) as it is about *being* strategic: engaging differently with the text depending on your purpose for reading. The time for reading the text, divided between modeling and practicing, should be approximately fifteen minutes, with the percentage of time devoted to practice increasing for follow-up lessons.

In **Chapter Four** I highlight this portion of the *Shared Reading Planner*:

Model and practice finding evidence for the objective	The best evidence: Model
	Practice
Model and practice other strategies	Connecting? Visualizing/Picturing? Wondering? Predicting/Guessing? Noticing? Figuring out?

Here are some questions to resolve for modeling and practicing the focus strategy and incorporating other strategies, too.

MODELING HOW TO FIND THE BEST EVIDENCE

How do I model finding evidence for the objective?

- Read the text yourself before reading it with the class, and use those little sticky notes to mark the places you want to pause to think aloud about how you are applying the objective. You'll know if this is a suitable book for your objective if you have plenty of sticky notes sprinkled throughout your text when you finish planning your lesson.

- Tell students before you begin reading that you will start by modeling *your* thinking. Then, after a short while, you will pause and prompt them to share *their* thinking. Eventually you will want them to raise their hand to share their thinking even without your prompting, but that may or may not happen in the first lesson of a lesson sequence. This sequence follows that gradual release model. It also lets students know how they will be accountable throughout the lesson and *exactly* what you are expecting of them.

- When you model, make sure you refer to your objective: "Remember that today we are making predictions. This is a good place to stop and predict because the character is about to make a decision. I think she will decide to _____ because _____." Notice that you are clarifying to students *why* you are making a prediction in this particular spot. You are also justifying your prediction based on prior information in the text.

- Allow students to share their thinking when they express an interest in doing so. That's your best indicator of when to move from modeling to practicing. Students may, however, need a little "nudge" to begin to take a more active role in finding evidence themselves.

- Unless you have a special reason for doing so (giving students an overall sense of the imagery a poem evokes, the rhythm of the piece, etc.), do NOT read the text through one time and then go back to the places where you want to demonstrate your thinking. Your students will not do this when they read (read it once and then go back and re-read to gain meaning), so don't model your own reading that way. This is the single most common problem I observe when I watch a teacher teaching a shared reading lesson; they don't take advantage of those teachable moments *while* they are reading.

- **Especially for ELLs:** When you're reading a story, be dramatic! Of course all students enjoy listening to stories where the reader uses lots of expression and changes her voice to sound like different characters in the book. But this is especially crucial for English language learners who will note your voice changes and recognize that the speaker in the story is changing. With regard to nonfiction text, take the time to go back and re-read key sections that are important, emphasizing the words to which you want students to pay close attention: *I'm going to read this part again. Listen to which words I accent and try to tell me afterward which words you think are the most important.*

- Know when enough is enough! Sometimes teachers go way overboard in the *modeling* department.

PRACTICING HOW TO FIND THE BEST EVIDENCE

How should students practice finding evidence?

- Even when an objective is brand new to students, give them the opportunity to try it for themselves. After a while, even a short while, just watching gets boring. Teachers perceive that students are not simply "watching;" they are "observing"—which means their minds are more fully engaged. As I visit shared lessons and "observe" students, I think we need to recognize this situation for what it is: without the chance to talk about their *own* thinking, many students will rapidly lose interest in *your* thinking.

- Maintain high standards. Too many teachers accept any contribution students make and praise them for their thinking. "Great!" we say. "Thanks for sharing." We don't want to hurt their feelings, and besides, this may be a kid who rarely participates; we certainly don't want to discourage him from raising his hand again. BUT, the way something is practiced is ultimately the way it is learned. Every child in the class hears you tell little Tommy that his answer was "great," so now they will do their best to produce a response just like Tommy's. Start with something positive about what Tommy said: "You picked a great place to make a prediction. But let's think harder about what the character is likely to do here. What did he do the last time the class bully bothered him?"

- Pay attention to who's "getting it" and who isn't. As your instruction moves from shared reading to small-group instruction, you will need to know who is ready to move forward with the objective and where additional reinforcement on the basics is needed. When teachers don't gather this information during a lesson, this missed opportunity turns classroom order into classroom chaos. "I don't get it," whine too many students. In addition to reading the text, teachers need to read their audience.

- **Especially for ELLs:** Again, you aren't doing ELLs a favor when you give them a "pass" on participating. They need to be as accountable as every other kid in the class—in a way that is respectful of their level of language proficiency. "Turn-and-talk" is a good technique for ELLs because they will respond orally to just one other child, rather than fearing the embarrassment of talking (and possibly making mistakes) in front of an entire roomful of their peers.

PRACTICING THE USE OF OTHER READING STRATEGIES

What about other strategies?

- Remain flexible in the use of multiple strategies. Good readers use many different strategies to construct meaning from text. While our lesson may focus on strategic thinking specific to a particular objective, the reality is that, as skilled readers, we cannot and should not overlook opportunities to apply other strategies when those strategies are likely to enhance our understanding and appreciation of the text. Imagine as you are reading along, you encounter a passage that creates such an elaborate picture in your mind you just have to stop and savor it for a moment before moving on. It's okay to note that "picturing" to students, and it's okay if one of your students stops you to point out a picture in her mind or a connection or to ask an important question about the text. The difference between this and the modeling and practicing of your lesson objective is that you won't necessarily *plan* to apply these strategies. You'll just let them happen as you and your students construct meaning together.

- Don't allow random strategy applications to overtake your lesson. First, you need to be mindful of the time available for shared reading. When you start adding additional lesson elements, your thirty-minute lesson inches upward toward forty minutes or more. Also, the more attention you devote to strategies other than your focus strategy, the more attention you will divert from your lesson's real objective. Your "fuzzy teaching" will show up later in students' less-than-desirable learning outcomes.

- For a more thorough examination of the six comprehension strategies noted here (connecting, picturing, wondering, guessing/predicting, noticing, and figuring out) see my book, *Constructing Meaning through Kid-friendly Comprehension Strategy Instruction* (Maupin House, 2004).

Use the questions on the next page to reflect on the way you model strategic thinking and the way you then turn over some of this responsibility for strategic thinking to your students, so they can practice this strategic thinking themselves.

REFLECTING ON CHAPTER FOUR

1. When you are modeling a think-aloud, how do you know when it is time to move on to student practice?

2. About how much modeling is appropriate?

3. How do you monitor who is "getting it" and who isn't during shared reading?

4. How do you keep students engaged during shared reading—especially during the modeling portion of the lesson when you are doing most of the talking?

5. How do you (or could you) incorporate other thinking strategies as you read? Which strategies typically offer opportunities for inclusion with any text?

6. Something to try: Choose a picture book that you have not taught before. Make sure it is a good match for the objective you wish to teach. Using two different color sticky notes, mark the text—for example, pink sticky notes where you will model and yellow sticky notes where students will practice. How many sticky notes are affixed to your book in all? What is the proportion of teacher modeling to student practice?

CHAPTER FIVE
Supporting Readers after Reading

The deceptive thing about the *after reading* instructional components is that they do not all occur within the context of the shared lesson. You will pose the discussion questions at the conclusion of the shared lesson and the written response might be modeled then as well. But the follow-up activities will be addressed later, during the workshop portion of the reading block while the teacher is conferring with students individually or meeting with small groups. Students will most likely reflect on the reading and writing strategy at the very end of the literacy block. The time needed for discussing follow-up questions and conducting an initial model of the written response will be about ten minutes.

Chapter Five focuses on this portion of the *Shared Reading Planner*:

Discussion questions	**Question related to the objective** **Other questions**
Written response to text	**Making the <u>writing</u> strategic**
Other follow-up activities	**Oral language/fluency:** **Vocabulary:** **Comprehension follow-up activities:** **Reading extensions:** **Writing extensions:**
Reflect on reading and writing strategy	

Consider the following points in order to support readers effectively after reading.

DISCUSSING THE RESPONSE TO THE OBJECTIVE (AND OTHER QUESTIONS)

What should I discuss with my students after reading the text?

- Ask a question related to the lesson objective *first* because this will help you gauge how well students have learned what you think you taught them. The question should match the objective. In fact, it will mimic the target precisely.

- Give several students an opportunity to respond to the question—even if the first child answers correctly. You want many students to rehearse their response orally, not just for the content of their answer, but for the use of language structures and conventions. This helps them figure out the following: "How will I turn the question into an answer stem? How will I make my words flow together so they sound right? What transition words will I use as signals for someone hearing (or reading) my response?" If students can "talk" the answer to the question, there's a much better chance that they'll be able to write it later. This part of the lesson might more accurately be termed "oral rehearsal" rather than "oral discussion." Such "rehearsal" is key to English language learners' comprehension of text. But you will quickly discover that taking the time for this enhances the learning of many students who struggle to put their thoughts into words.

- Prepare some additional questions, too, in case you have a few minutes to discuss points about the text that were not part of today's lesson objective. You do not need to ask *all* of these questions. But asking one or two of them will expose students to additional ways of thinking about a text. Even limited exposure to different forms of literary thinking will be better than no exposure at all and can set the stage for an objective you might teach next week or next month. Additional questions also serve as good review of past objectives.

WRITING A RESPONSE TO A QUESTION RELATED TO THE OBJECTIVE

How do I move from oral reflection to written response?

- Ask *one* question for written response, which again should mimic the day's target. The days of handing students a whole sheet (or packet) of written questions about a text are gone—I hope! Instead, ask several questions orally if time permits, but treat written response like any writing genre: a written form that needs to be learned and practiced to the point of independence. [For guidance on how to teach the art of written response effectively, see my two books on this topic, *Teaching Written Response to Text*, (Maupin House, 2002) and *That' a Great Answer* (Maupin House, 2007).]

- Model the response to the question when you first introduce it. However, even on that first day, I eventually take my model away and ask students to write the response themselves, usually with evidence of their own that I have charted for this purpose. This lets them know, right from the start, that they will be accountable for producing their own response. Do *not* ask students to copy your model or to write the question.

- Do not model the response on subsequent days. If your follow-up lesson involves a picture book, you will need to chart the evidence so students can refer to it as they write their responses. By the time they are reading text themselves in order to respond (by the third stage of instruction—see page 53), they should be responsible for locating their own evidence and, of course, for writing their response without a model.

- Beware of creating over-dependence on graphic organizers. Both of my books, *Teaching Written Response to Text* and *That's a Great Answer*, offer many graphic supports, both answer organizers and answer frames, that can support students as they are learning how to respond to a question for a particular objective. But until you take those scaffolds away, you will not know if your students are truly *independent* in their capacity to respond. Don't wait until the day of some high-stakes assessment to find this out the hard way. From the very first day you distribute the graphic aid, let your students know that they will be allowed to use it today and tomorrow (or however long you think is reasonable), but by Friday, you will expect them to be able to write their answer on a plain piece of paper with no support.

- **Especially for ELLs:** Begin with the answer frame (rather than the answer organizer) in *Teaching Written Response to Text*. Or even better, use the answer frame in *That's a Great Answer* (which is usually shorter and simpler than the frame in *Teaching Written Response to Text*.) Answer frames provide the language structures that English language learners need. Allow ELLs sufficient time with the frame before moving them to more independent responses. But *do* monitor their progress and nudge them toward independence when they are able, or they will fall short of mastery when they need it most—on your state assessment.

APPLYING THE READING TO OTHER AREAS OF LITERACY

What other follow-up literacy activities are appropriate for students?
The activities that follow do not take the place of independent reading, which should be a part of all students' literacy work every day. Independent reading and the way it integrates with shared and guided reading is big enough and important enough to be the topic of its own book and cannot be examined here with the depth it deserves. Here's the central concept, however: Independent reading is not SSR. It should be a regular, consistent part of students' reading program, along with its two close cousins, shared reading and guided reading. It should have a focus—the very same one addressed in the day's shared lesson—which is followed up in small-group instruction. There needs to be some teacher monitoring and student accountability. This "triple threat" approach to teaching a comprehension objective is what gives Tier 1 comprehension instruction the best chance of succeeding with the most children. These three components—shared, guided, and independent reading—need to be at the "core" of any core curriculum.

While some programs and literacy initiatives believe that the *only* thing students should do during reading is *read*, I have a different view. I think that teachers need to look more deeply into factors that may be standing in the way of students' reading proficiency and then assure that these factors are addressed through the curriculum in specific and differentiated ways. The following kinds of text-related activities included within the lesson plans in this book will meet the needs of students in the intermediate grades in key areas of literacy development. Note that these are only suggestions; add your own creative ideas:

- **Oral language:** Activities include giving speeches, role playing, performing skits, participating in debates, and conducting interviews. We tend to think of "oral language" as a necessary part of primary-grade instruction but don't pay much attention to it as a curriculum component beyond the early grades. Big mistake. *All* students—not just ELLs—need to fine-tune and extend their speaking skills.

- **Fluency:** Activities include choral reading; re-reading text passages for attention to accuracy, rate, expression, punctuation, and phrasing; and reader's theater. Remember, the goal here is not just speed and accuracy, but phrasing and expression.

- **Vocabulary:** Although students could engage in many activities to enhance their use of new vocabulary, a *Vocabulary Connections* activity is included for each lesson in this book (only on the CD). This activity provides a sentence with the word in context (often from the text—or a sentence I created if the text sentence wasn't helpful.) Talking about that sentence first will help students define the word. The interactive part of the activity is a question that requires students to respond by connecting the word to their own lives. This is a favorite vocabulary activity of mine because students must really understand the word in order to apply it meaningfully, and it also encourages the use of complete sentences. The *Vocabulary Connections* activity may be done orally or in writing. Add other vocabulary activities as you see fit.

- **Comprehension follow-up activities:** Follow-up activities to reinforce strategic thinking could be obtained through many sources. However, activities for the lessons in this book are matched to my book, *Constructing Meaning through Kid-Friendly Comprehension Strategy Instruction* (Maupin House, 2004) with specific page references. Some of these activities reinforce multiple strategies while others are targeted to a specific strategy (connecting, picturing, wondering, etc.).

- **Reading extensions:** These include books by the same author or books on the same theme or topic as the book used for the lesson. They correlate the lesson to other texts in some way.

- **Writing extensions:** These activities provide suggestions for connecting reading and writing through a variety of writing genres: letters, journal entries, stories, news articles, etc.

What do you mean *reflect* on the reading and writing strategy?

- Save time for this! The greatest deterrent to reflecting on learning is that we just don't get to it. Suddenly it's time for lunch and we are in a frenzy to get kids out the door. Talking together about what we've learned today as readers and writers is low on our list of priorities when everyone is scrambling to wrap up the morning work and head to the cafeteria. But we should make this a much higher priority. If we want our students to be able to apply what they learned today to what they will do tomorrow, they will need to articulate their thinking: What was hard? What was easy? How would you explain what we worked on today to a child who was absent? What do you think we should do tomorrow?

- Ask the *students* to reflect, rather than providing the closure yourself. Again, in our zeal to get the job done quickly, it's often the *teacher* who sums up what was learned today, not the students.

Before turning to the next chapter, reflect on essential insights from **Chapter Five**:

REFLECTING ON CHAPTER FIVE

1. How do you make sure that all of your students are prepared to write a written response?

2. What kind of *after reading* activities do you typically provide for your students?

3. How much discussion generally follows the reading of a text in your classroom?

4. Have you ever included a time for *reflection* at the end of your reading or literacy block? Explain how this looks in your classroom.

5. How do you incorporate independent reading into your reading curriculum? Is your independent reading aligned with your comprehension objective? How do you hold students accountable for this?

6. Something to try: For a period of one week (or several consecutive days), treat your oral discussion after reading as "oral rehearsal," giving many students the opportunity to reply to a question—supporting them as needed. Did this impact students' written responses? How? Which students were helped the most by oral rehearsal?

7. Something else to try: For a period of one week (or several consecutive days), include a time for *reflection* at the end of your reading/literacy block. What kind of evidence do you notice by the end of the week regarding students' improved capacity to articulate their thinking about their own reading and writing processes?

CHAPTER SIX
Getting Students to Independence with Comprehension Objectives in an RTI Classroom

First of all, let's be clear that *all* classrooms are RTI classrooms—from pre-kindergarten through high school (and even beyond that for some students with specialized needs). This is a federal mandate that "makes official" what good teachers have known all along: all regular education and special education students are entitled to instruction founded on research-based practices and progress monitoring. And students will respond positively to instruction when that teaching is appropriately differentiated—with different students receiving different kinds of support based on their very different needs.

Easier said than done? It's not as hard as you might think. The instruction described in this book, and which is modeled in the lessons that follow, explains how to implement those instructional components that get your Tier I teaching of comprehension off to a solid start with shared reading.

You would continue Tier 1 instruction through follow-up, differentiated, small-group instruction that reinforces the same comprehension objective with developmental-level text and provides scaffolding according to students' different needs that you diagnosed during your Tier 1 shared lessons. You would further follow up at the Tier 1 level with independent reading matched to the objective.

Students' performance at both the small-group and independent levels would be regularly monitored and assessed. The very good news here is that, with powerful Tier 1 teaching, eighty percent of your students (theoretically) should need no additional interventions; focused Tier I instruction should be "just what the doctor ordered" and should produce efficient learning for most children most of the time to get them to independence—in this case, independence in the area of comprehension.

First, let's look at what "getting to independence in comprehension" will look like for the majority of your students, the ones for whom your good teaching will make it unnecessary to move to Tier 2 and Tier 3 interventions. Then we will see what the model looks like for students who struggle.

GETTING STUDENTS TO INDEPENDENCE WITH TIER 1 INSTRUCTION

Getting students to independence on a reading comprehension objective is a process with four predictable stages for students who do not require further instructional interventions. If you only need one lesson for each stage, your students are doing very well indeed. However, it is likely that two or more lessons will be needed by at least some students during some stages of the lesson sequence. (This would still be considered *Tier 1 instruction*.) The chart below illustrates how instruction should change from one stage to the next as students work toward independence. The section that follows describes these four stages and explains how and why moving beyond the first couple of stages means moving from a whole-class lesson to small-group instruction, even at the Tier 1 level.

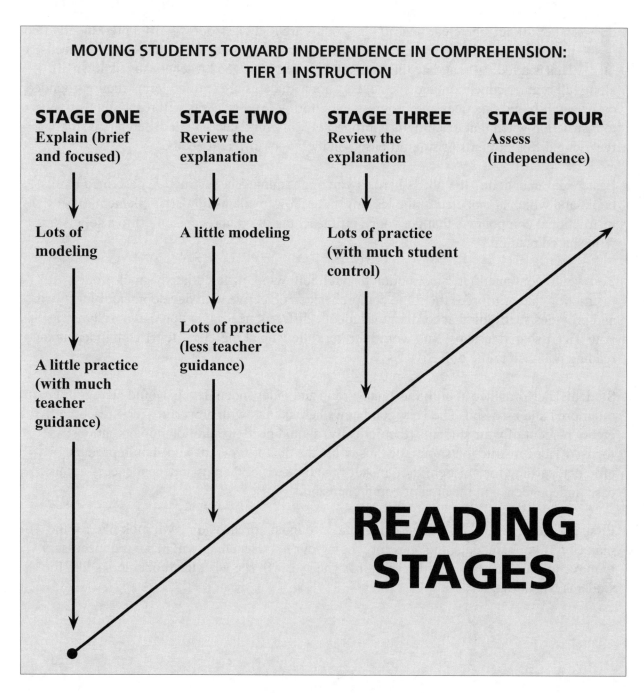

MOVING STUDENTS TOWARD INDEPENDENCE IN COMPREHENSION: TIER 1 INSTRUCTION

STAGE ONE
Explain (brief and focused)

↓

Lots of modeling

↓

A little practice (with much teacher guidance)

↓

STAGE TWO
Review the explanation

↓

A little modeling

↓

Lots of practice (less teacher guidance)

↓

STAGE THREE
Review the explanation

↓

Lots of practice (with much student control)

↓

STAGE FOUR
Assess (independence)

READING STAGES

Meeting the criteria for each instructional stage

Generally, only the first two stages of Tier 1 instruction are appropriate for whole-class (shared) lessons. By the third stage, students should be working on the objective with text they can read themselves—which means the instruction should take place in small, developmental-level groups or individually as it might happen in a workshop-based classroom. Note that with each succeeding stage there is less teacher-explanation and modeling and more student practice, until finally (by Stage Four) students meet the objective without any teacher input whatsoever. It is at this point, when students *should* be independent, that their responses should be considered an "assessment." Hint: You need to be intentional and a bit aggressive about getting students to the point of independence.

Independence does not "happen" on its own. In fact, as long as you continue to hand out answer organizers and frames, students will be more than happy to take them from you. Supplying these graphic aids at the beginning of the learning process is appropriate and useful. Supplying them indefinitely does not lead to independence; it leads to dependence and learned helplessness! Hence, right from the start you will need a plan and a sense of when students in your class should be able to meet an objective independently. Remembering that you will need to address *many* objectives over the year, sooner is better than later for getting students to the point of independence on any particular objective! See below for the goal of each instructional stage and what your teaching should look like during each stage.

What is the goal of Stage One instruction?
The goal of the first lesson is to introduce students to the objective. The lessons in **Part II** of this book have been designed to *introduce* each objective. Students are not expected to be independent at the end of this first lesson. However, your teaching needs to establish the foundation that will lead students to independence as efficiently as possible. You will read the text aloud—perhaps a picture book, another short text, or a passage from a longer text. That means you may select a text that is above students' reading level but well within range of their interests and cultural and linguistic backgrounds. That means that your lesson will incorporate all of the components included in the lesson planners in this book and described in **Chapters Three** through **Five**.

By the end of the first lesson, students should understand the objective and know how to find evidence to meet the objective. They should have observed you as you model finding evidence to meet the objective three to four times (through about half of the text). They should have practiced finding evidence in the shared text when prompted by you. They should have helped you write a written response to a question based on the lesson objective or written their own response to that question following your model. Additionally, it is important that students feel good about the progress they have made on the objective so far. In order for students to put forth their best effort tomorrow, they need to feel that they have achieved success today.

Although most students will need lots more practice to truly master the objective, you should not need a complete "do over" of this first lesson. If students are totally confused at the end of this lesson with no understanding of the objective, you need to re-assess your teaching to determine where your instruction might have gone off track. You will need to change your *teaching* before you can hope to change students' *learning*.

What is the goal of Stage Two instruction?

The goal of this second instructional stage, which should begin with your second lesson, is to give students more control over the process of meeting the objective, while structuring the experience to (as closely as possible) guarantee their success. That means you will again use a picture book or another appropriate shared text that fits the same description as the text used for your introductory lesson. This time, however, you will not tell students how to find evidence to meet the objective; you will ask *them* to tell *you*. (You can certainly help them along as they try to articulate their thinking.) You should ask several students to explain this process—not only the quick study who gets his hand in the air first; you want students to know that they are *all* accountable for the learning your first lesson should have generated.

You might begin your reading with one or two examples of finding evidence for the objective—which you can model. But you should move quickly from your modeling to student practice. It is okay to prompt students a bit, but try not to "lead the witness" too directly. In other words, you could tell your students, "When I come to a place in the text where I notice evidence for meeting our objective, I will pause and hope that one of you will jump right in with your observations about evidence without me even asking you. Even better, I would love it if *you* would tell *me* to pause when you find places in the text yourself where you notice evidence. That will show me that you are really getting good at this objective." Now students are very clear about what you expect of them and what counts as success.

It is during the second instructional stage that you will notice markedly different levels of student competence. Some students will thrive on the challenge of noticing and reporting on the evidence themselves. Some students will be reluctant to identify relevant stopping points but will accurately find evidence when *you* pause and ask *them*. And some students will barely be able to tell you anything about the evidence, even with lots of instructional hand-holding. You will take careful mental notes about all of this as you move on to the next stage of instruction. But right now, you need to give all students the tools they need to write a written response following the reading as, this time, you will not be modeling it for them.

Remember that during Stage Two instruction you are again reading the text *to* students; they will most likely not have their own copy of the text. If you expect them to retrieve specific textual evidence to defend their response, they will need access to that evidence. So, as you find the evidence during your reading, you will need to chart it. Sometimes, I do this myself. Sometimes I ask a student in the class to record it on either a whiteboard or an overhead transparency. Depending on the text, I sometimes chart as I read. Or, sometimes I finish the book and then create the chart (with student input).

Although some students will be much more adept than others at locating the evidence at this point, *all* students should be able to tell you orally at the end of the reading what details from the text they will use to respond to the question related to the objective. Again, give *many* children the opportunity to respond to the question. It's fine to bring out the answer frame related to the objective (included in *That's a Great Answer* or *Teaching Written Response to Text*). Don't actually model the response in writing, but help students to practice orally the way they will begin their answer, referring to the format on the answer frame. Many struggling readers and English language learners are so insecure about finding the right words to get started with their response that they choose not to start at all. Remember that practicing the response first *orally* gives these reluctant writers the confidence to pick up their pencil and *write* their response.

The tricky thing about this second stage of instruction, though, is that while all students will hopefully succeed with the written response, they will have gotten to this point with vastly different levels of support from you. That is why Stage Three instruction will need to move from whole-class (shared) instruction to guided instruction in small groups.

What is the goal of Stage Three instruction?
The goal of Stage Three instruction is for students to be able to produce a high-quality response to a question related to the objective after reading a text *themselves*—with less and less help from you! For many students, this stage will require more than one lesson in order for them to gain competence and confidence but should not go on indefinitely. It's hard to provide an absolute number of lessons that would be realistic, but try to complete this stage within a week, if possible. (If it takes longer than that, students may be experiencing some other kind of road block that will require some Tier 2 attention.)

Because the students in your class have different needs, you will need to differentiate your instruction. Mere mention of the word "differentiate" causes many teachers to hyperventilate. Do not panic! You can do this! Based on the work of Carol Ann Tomlinson, who has done much in the area of differentiated instruction, there are only three components that can be differentiated in instruction: process, product, and content. Let's look at what these mean to your teaching of comprehension for the students in your classroom:

- Your top students: These high flyers are ready to charge forward. They are skilled readers and should apply the objective to appropriately complex text. (This is the *content* of the lesson.) It might be reasonable for these students to read a text *above* grade level. Furthermore, they already "get it" and are able, all by themselves, to locate places in the text that provide the evidence they need for meeting the objective. That means you should hold them accountable for doing this. They should monitor their understanding themselves. The *process* for these students should be to read an assigned text silently and independently without designated stopping points determined by you, to mark places in the text where they notice details that support the objective, and then answer the related question as independently as possible, preferably without the help of a graphic organizer. Their independent written response is the *product* they will generate, and they may be able to produce it even without oral rehearsal. The teacher's role in all of this will be to find a suitable text, review with students in their small group before reading the kind of evidence they are looking for, and to practice just enough to make sure they are on track. Then send them back to their seats to complete the reading and the written response (though a written response may not be required every day). The lesson the next day will begin with a discussion of the previous day's reading, including evidence students found that was related to the objective.

- Your middle students: These students appear to understand the objective but are inconsistent in retrieving evidence. And they lack confidence. At the start of Stage Three, they need nudging from you in the form of prompting to pick up on the clues that the author is providing. You might need to do some modeling at the beginning of your lesson, saying something like: "Right here I'm noticing that the author is giving us evidence we could use to answer our question. Does anyone see what that evidence is?" The instructional *process* for these students is more guided than independent at first but should gradually move toward more independence with less prompting in each successive lesson. Although you might need to prompt (and even model) at first, they should read the text silently themselves during group time and ultimately locate their own evidence. You may want to talk with them before they read about pausing periodically to monitor thinking: "If you have read several paragraphs and haven't found any evidence, you might want to go back and re-read to see if you missed something." You could also designate a few stopping points for them: "Pause at the end of the second paragraph and again at the bottom of page 3." The *content* for these students should be text that they can decode easily. You do not want word identification problems to undermine comprehension—and that is exactly what will happen if students are struggling with fluency as well as understanding at the same time. The *product* for middle students should be a well-constructed written response, but it is likely that they will initially still need a graphic organizer to help them. They will also benefit from oral rehearsal of their response before committing it to paper. They should always have the opportunity to evaluate their responses after they are written to determine whether they meet the criteria and how they might improve them to reach the target score.

- Your lowest students: These students still do not really grasp the objective and thus have much difficulty even knowing what evidence to look for. As for the written response, they barely know where to begin. The *process* for these students might at first look like a combination of shared and guided reading where the teacher models reading a short chunk of text in which she finds useful details for the objective, prompts students in the next short text chunk, and asks them to find their own evidence in a third chunk. The *process* should be very controlled and carefully monitored with low readers. They will need several Stage Three lessons. Each one should require a little bit more independence; for example, slightly longer chunks to read with less modeling and prompting. The *content* (the text itself) must be manageable, which in some cases will mean below grade level. The *product*, or written response, will probably require some shared writing at first where students work together with you to create a good answer. Although you are doing this lesson with intermediate-grade students, you might initially want to follow more of a primary "interactive writing" model where you and the students actually "share the pen" to create your answer on chart paper or a transparency using the answer frame, explicitly showing students *why* the response is organized in the manner prescribed on the graphic organizer. While the logic of this organization might be apparent to you, it will not be apparent to them! This is the way you will *begin* your Stage Three instruction. Remember that by the end of this stage, the goal for your lowest students is also *independence*, though they may be achieving that independence with easy text. As you assess written responses with these students, you will see that they are often too general, without sufficient text-related details, or (once you have abandoned the answer frame), repetitive, confusing, and perhaps even inaccurate. They may also demonstrate substantial written language problems that make their responses difficult to read. Be honest with your assessment, but be sure to begin with what they have done *well*, and show them specifically what they would need to do (and how easy it is!) to obtain a higher score. As classroom teachers we always need to meet students "where they are." But we also need to recognize that it really isn't okay for students to be reading below grade level. The final portion of this chapter, "A perplexing assessment dilemma that impacts Tier 2 and Tier 3 interventions," addresses this issue in greater detail.

What is the goal of Stage Four instruction?
The goal of Stage Four instruction is not really *instruction* at all; it is assessment. Regardless of how long it takes students at any level to reach this stage, they must eventually reach it. If not, lower-performing students will fall farther and farther behind, while quicker students zoom ahead—which will cause the achievement gap to widen rather than narrow. At this stage, the goal for all students is to write a response to a question related to an objective without reminders about what constitutes "evidence" for the objective, without modeling or prompting during reading, without oral rehearsal of the response after reading, and especially, without an answer frame to guide the response. Of course the goal is for all of this to occur swiftly and efficiently ("Just follow these simple steps…."), but there will be some students whose progress is anything but swift and efficient. Despite your absolute best Tier 1 efforts and instruction that is worthy of reporting on the television nightly news, there will be some students who simply aren't making the progress they need to make. With interim Tier 1 progress monitoring, you generally know this before they even reach this final stage of your instructional sequence. What should you do for these students? You intervene with additional, targeted support at the Tier 2 and possibly the Tier 3 level.

SUPPORTING STRUGGLING READERS WITH TIER 2 AND TIER 3 INTERVENTIONS

Let's set the scene: You are currently working with your fourth graders on *summarizing a problem-solution narrative* because test data from multiple sources confirm that this is a skill that these kids desperately need. You have introduced and reinforced this objective in two shared whole-class lessons using great picture books. After only two (Tier 1) shared lessons, eight of your students now appear to be "off and running." Their Tier 1 small-group instruction will offer much opportunity for applying this skill independently to challenging text. Another group of six students is also off to a solid start on this objective but still needs close guidance. They have trouble separating big, important events from the little details in a story. You know that if you take the time to plan carefully and work with them on grade-level text that is not too complex and that has clearly depicted story elements, they should get to the desired goal, too, with no further intervention needed.

Then there are your "famous five!" These kids, though their fluency is adequate, rarely contributed their thinking during your shared *summarizing* lessons and when prodded, struggled to recall even basic story events. It was nearly impossible for them to retell the events in sequence. These struggling students continue to be part of your "Tier 1 responsibility," too, and you are prepared to meet their needs as best you can by dividing a very easy text into tiny chunks and guiding them ever so slowly through it, reminding them to monitor their understanding throughout so they can put the pieces together at the end. This seems reasonable to you, but after several lessons you feel like you're getting nowhere— and you have a fistful of mediocre written summaries to validate your gut feeling. In fact, it is becoming increasingly clear that these kids can't even identify essential story elements (characters, setting, problem, etc.). No wonder they can't summarize!

They need additional small-group time, all five of them, to build foundational knowledge: How do we identify the *problem* in the story? What do we mean by *setting*? This more intense small-group instruction targeted to finely delineated prerequisite skills is Tier 2 intervention. You find twenty to thirty minutes (approximately) to meet with this group two to three times a week for about eight to twelve weeks, or maybe your school literacy specialist meets with the group. Either way, you should consult with the specialist and collaborate about the kinds of teaching strategies and materials that will offer the precise support these students need to get them back on track.

Let's hope that everyone in your Tier 2 group masters the concept of story elements and is released from this additional support. In theory, you will meet the needs of an additional five to fifteen percent of the students in your class at the Tier 2 level. In fact, you have data that show that four of your five students *did* respond well to your intervention—everyone but Tommy. Tommy still doesn't get it! Rather than just sighing and hoping next year's teacher has better luck with Tommy, move to a Tier 3 intervention with this student. Now Tommy will get one-on-one tutorial help—he could work with another student or two with the identical need if such a student had also been identified—to dig deeper into the reason behind all the trouble he is having with understanding the parts of a story.

Now the literacy specialist works with Tommy (for as much as forty-five minutes per day, for up to twenty weeks) because she has the certification and the skills to reach deeper into the assessment data and provide the kind of clinical assessments and prescriptive interventions required by students who struggle most profoundly. In this case, the literacy specialist is able to tell you after a few sessions that the real problem here is Tommy's lack of vocabulary. He is missing the meaning of so many content words that it is virtually impossible for him to make meaning as he reads. Tommy's short-term Tier 3 intervention is centered on vocabulary strategies that will help him help himself when he encounters a word he doesn't understand. Tommy may be one of the fortunate two to five percent of students in your class who will respond favorably to Tier 3 intervention and be able to return to the regular Tier 1 core instruction with his classmates. If not, a referral may be in order for more intensive assessments that could lead to special education services.

The chart on pages 57-59 provides an at-a-glance picture of what RTI means to shared, guided, and independent reading and clarifies how the lessons in **Part II** of this book support the initial step of your Tier 1 instruction.

WHAT RTI *IS*—AND IS *NOT*—FOR COMPONENTS OF COMPREHENSION INSTRUCTION

	Tier 1	Tier 2	Tier 3
Shared (whole class)	**Is:** consistency and fidelity to core practices for *all* students based on universal screening. (e.g., systematic teaching of a year-long continuum of comprehension objectives based on assessments such as DRA and state literacy tests) **Is:** explicit, incorporating the gradual release of responsibility **Is:** provided by the classroom teacher **Is not:** reading books to/ with students and asking random questions you feel are appropriate based on the content of the text (e.g., read-aloud or whole-class reading of a novel) **Is not:** using *only* state- or district-generated benchmarks or grade-level expectations (these are *necessary*, but not *sufficient*, because they do not take into account assessed student needs) **Is not:** a core anthology— although an anthology can be a resource used to deliver Tier 1 instruction (a "program" is NOT a curriculum!!!)	**Is not:** whole-class instruction; Tier 2 interventions are addressed with small, homogeneously-based groups of students	**Is not:** *ever* whole-class instruction

	Tier 1	Tier 2	Tier 3
Guided (small group)	**Is:** a follow-up to shared/Tier 1 instruction and is **differentiated** according to data obtained by monitoring students' performance during Tier 1 (e.g., students working on the same objective identified through Tier 1 but with materials at different instructional levels based on students' reading level and varied instructional processes matched to students' needs) **Is:** provided by the classroom teacher **Is:** going to work for about 80% of your students (if solid shared- and guided-reading practices are in place) **Is not:** students reading in leveled texts—with no clear objective for the lesson **Is not:** students reading the next chapter or few pages in a book and answering end-of-chapter questions	**Is:** a short-term, small-group intervention with no more than 5 students with the same needs that addresses prerequisite skills and knowledge that are preventing the mastery of the current Tier 1 objective(s) (e.g., although the teacher is currently addressing *personal connections* with the class as a whole in both shared and guided reading for Tier 1 instruction, assessment data have indicated that a small group of students can't achieve this goal because they are unable to determine the "big idea" or theme of a text; this must be addressed first before these students will be able to make significant personal connections **Is:** more focused than Tier 1 instruction in its analysis of deficiencies and subsequent specifically targeted instruction **Is:** provided two to three times per week in the classroom **in addition to** Tier 1 instruction—by the classroom teacher with support from a specialist or by a specialist **Is:** the final tier for students who respond positively to the Tier 2 intervention **Is not:** a "program" that is "followed;" need to follow the child **Is not:** regular small-group instruction that every student receives; this is **extra** **Is not:** a year-long plan with a pre-test in September and a post-test in June; data should be obtained every few weeks **Is not** necessarily focused on comprehension; might address word recognition, fluency, vocabulary, etc. if that is the demonstrated need	**Is not:** *typically* conducted in small groups

	Tier 1	Tier 2	Tier 3
Independent/ Individual	**Is:** focused application of the Tier 1 comprehension objective addressed in both shared and independent reading to self-selected, "just right" text that students can read with ease **Is:** monitored by the teacher with some kind of student accountability **Is:** a consistent (daily) part of the literacy curriculum **Is not:** SSR **Is not:** something to do when your other work is finished	**Is not:** *typically* delivered to students individually	**Is:** delivered individually (most of the time) or in groups of up to three students with identical, very specific needs **Is:** customized to highly precise needs through weekly progress monitoring and data collection **Is:** delivered by someone with specialized skills (such as the school literacy specialist) **Is:** monitored weekly **Is:** usually conducted outside the classroom **Is:** a short-term intervention of several weeks **Is:** the final tier of intervention if the student responds positively **Is:** the last stop before a special education or other evaluation is considered if the student still does not respond/ show needed progress **Is not:** your first line of defense when students are experiencing problems **Is not:** a "dumping ground" for chronically below-level students

MAKING SMARTER TIER 2 INTERVENTION DECISIONS

While you will, of course, use your Tier 1 progress monitoring data to define your Tier 2 comprehension interventions, I have noticed that some comprehension objectives "layer" logically on others. If you notice that your students in their Tier 1 small-group instruction are struggling with an objective you feel they should be able to grasp based on your shared Tier 1 lessons (and which other students seem to be handling with no difficulty in their small groups), consult the chart below and consider an intervention that targets the layer beneath the one you are currently addressing in your Tier 1 small groups—or possibly even the layer beneath that. I'm not much of a mountain climber, but the analogy seems to work: Begin at the base. Keep climbing. Reach the summit.

LAYERING COMPREHENSION OBJECTIVES

Layer 1: Begin at the Base

The objectives below lay the groundwork for all objectives that follow. However, there is no prescribed order for the objectives *within* this layer.

- **A1 objectives (main idea and theme):** Although this may seem at first like higher-level thinking, I am recognizing more and more as I visit classrooms that, until students can identify the "big idea" or gist of a text, it is nearly impossible for them to work with other objectives such as making personal connections or understanding what is important to an author or character. It is even difficult to summarize a text if you don't understand the "big idea" that the author is trying to convey. So, address A1 objectives early, and come back to them often—even as a follow-up to other objectives.

- **A2 objectives (text elements):** These objectives leading to basic construction of meaning are a logical starting point since they relate to foundational understanding of characters, setting, problem, and solution. Students *must* understand these text elements before we can expect them to master other objectives because all objectives ultimately build on an understanding of basic text elements.

- **A4 objectives (making predictions):** You probably don't need to spend a huge amount of time on this objective with most intermediate-grade students, even those who struggle a bit. But it *will* be important to return to this and reinforce it explicitly with students who have a hard time monitoring their understanding during their reading.

- **B3 objectives (drawing conclusions based on text evidence):** Lots of students need to begin here. They are not inclined to read closely enough to retrieve evidence for *any* objective. Until students see this as a personal priority—and learn to collect that evidence *as* they read—higher-level comprehension objectives will be beyond their reach.

Layer 2: Keep Climbing

The objectives below require an understanding of concepts and skills students should have learned in Layer 1. Note once again that there is no prescribed order of objectives *within* this layer.

- **A3 objectives (summarizing):** Until students can identify text elements, how realistic is it that they will be able to summarize text? Furthermore, without the ability to summarize a text, how likely is it that students will be able to think critically about it? Even when it's not the main objective, *always* ask your students to briefly summarize what they have read to make sure they have the foundation they need to move forward into other objectives.

- **C1 objectives (personal connections to a text):** Notice that this objective is not in the first learning layer. The reason teachers get such superficial personal connections from students is because they ask them to derive these connections before they are sure students can construct basic meaning and comprehend the "big idea." Until students can identify text elements and summarize a story or nonfiction passage, or tell you the theme or main idea, it is doubtful they will be able to make a very powerful personal connection to it. So, additional practice on this objective in a Tier 1 intervention will not be of much use to students unless you retrace your steps and work on A1 and A3 first.

- **C2 objectives (personal response/reaction):** A personal reaction to a text requires that students see straight to the heart of the matter. That means, again, that knowledge of the "big idea" (A1) is crucial and that students know how to find evidence (B3) to support their opinion.

- **D1 objectives (author's craft):** Those wonderful author's crafts that make writing interesting and engaging are not typically the *first* thing we address in a piece of writing. But this is the objective that connects reading and writing, so we want to use what students know about noting evidence (B3) and build on it to enhance both their reading and their writing. Determining whether a story is believable is especially dependent on noticing the right evidence.

> **Layer 3: Reach the Summit**
> The objectives below require an understanding of concepts and skills students should have learned in both Layers 1 and 2. Note once again that there is no prescribed order of objectives *within* this layer.

- **B1 objectives (text structure):** The concept of beginning-middle-end within this set of objectives is more of a foundational-level understanding. But beyond that, identifying text structure (cause/effect, sequence, compare/contrast) challenges children to integrate many things that they know about reading, especially how to summarize it (A3).

- **B2 objectives (author's reason for including particular details or selecting a particular genre):** As in the objective above, it is often more appropriate to ask *why* the author included certain information after you've constructed basic meaning. Lots of times a reader doesn't really appreciate the significance of a particular detail until he recognizes the author's intent for the story in general (A1) and can connect to it (C1).

- **D2 objectives (extending the text):** These are the objectives most closely aligned with critical and creative thinking. The specific objectives within this category (asking questions of the author, creating a journal entry, giving a speech) all require synthesis and insights that draw upon multiple comprehension objectives and are seldom achieved with superficial reading.

- **D3 objectives (understanding the author's or character's values and customs):** As with D2 above, objectives that ask students to consider the personal values and cultural beliefs of an author or character require a pretty thorough understanding of the text—and the ability to "get inside the head" of the author or character.

A perplexing assessment dilemma that impacts Tier 2 and Tier 3 interventions

I want to address one final point about assessing students' performance on comprehension objectives because it has significant implications for students reading below grade level. When students receive their Tier 1 differentiated instruction, they are instructed with text that is matched to their reading level, just as they should be. With this easy text, they often succeed quite well. We congratulate them: "Hooray! You did it! You mastered the objective."

Then along comes THE STATE TEST—with passages to read that are on or above grade level, way beyond the readability of some of our strugglers. The outcome of the state assessment looks much different from our formative assessment, and that is disheartening for both teachers and students.

This point invariably comes up when I am doing workshop or conference presentations: "If giving students text to read at their developmental level is so important, then why do state assessments include passages beyond the fluency level of so many of our kids?"

"I feel your pain," I tell teachers. I know how discouraging it is to work long and hard with students on an objective and still have them fail where it counts most—on the state test. Still, we can't really dispute the logic of the grade-level state standard. Without it, it would be nearly impossible to gauge who is making appropriate progress, and who is not. A fourth grader who reaches goal on a comprehension assessment at the grade four level is in a very different place academically from a fourth grader who achieves mastery with text written at a grade two level.

But there is a larger issue here. Although the instructional focus in this case was comprehension, the fact that some students required text two years below grade level in their Tier 1 classroom small-group instruction in order to meet that objective should have signaled the need for other interventions long before the state test delivered the bad news to us.

When a student is reading two years (or even one year) below grade level, the issue is frequently fluency (or even word recognition or phonemic awareness), not merely comprehension. Someone needs to administer the kind of assessments that will pinpoint exactly what those deficiencies are, and then intervene to correct these problems before the student falls even farther behind.

Some Tier 2 interventions and probably most Tier 3 interventions will not address comprehension at all—even if the difficulty diagnosed initially was the students' inability to perform some specific comprehension task. When we provide students with the appropriate assessments, we may learn that their inability to comprehend is actually a function of their inability to decode, their lack of sight words, or their limited vocabulary. Powerful Tier 2 and Tier 3 interventions will address the *cause* of the problem, not merely its *symptom*.

Hence, we need multiple assessment measures—those that evaluate students against their peers using a common benchmark and others that are aligned to our curriculum. When low-performing readers achieve success on comprehension objectives with below-level text, but not with text written for students in their own grade, we can say with some assurance to ourselves (and to parents) that the problem is not really a comprehension problem; it is a fluency problem. Unless we give students the opportunity to respond to text they can adequately decode, we will not really know whether the problem relates to comprehension or word identification. When students continue to score poorly on grade-level passages, we know that we must do more to help them become fluent readers—and to read that text independently. That will require an intervention that accelerates as well as remediates.

The final chapter in **Part I** examines assessment more closely. But before turning to that chapter, reflect on all you have learned in this chapter about getting students to independence—with or without the need for Tier 2 and Tier 3 interventions.

REFLECTING ON CHAPTER SIX

1. What are the challenges of getting some students to independence on comprehension objectives?

2. What are the challenges you face as you move from shared reading to small-group instruction with a particular objective?

3. How does your small-group instruction change based on the level of students in a particular group?

4. What do you do when your Tier 1 small-group instruction doesn't work? What kind of collaboration could you seek to better meet the needs of struggling students?

5. What kinds of interventions do your lowest-performing students need? What assessments could be used to provide evidence of these needs?

6. This book doesn't really address independent reading, but how could your independent reading assist your students as they pursue independence on an objective?

7. Something to try: Now that you've been introduced to all components of the *Planner for Shared Reading* (provided on page xix of this book and also on the CD), complete the planner for an objective of your choice. If you and one or two grade-level partners each write one lesson, you can share them and you will have two or three good lessons!

CHAPTER SEVEN
Assessing Students' Response to Instruction

There will probably be some interim assessments along the way, but at the end of our Tier 1 instruction—after we've introduced a comprehension objective to our whole class in a couple of shared lessons, after we've reinforced the same objective in our differentiated small groups for a few days, and after students have had sufficient opportunity to practice the objective independently in their own "just right" texts—we need to know who has responded well to our instruction and who has not.

In the case of reading comprehension, this is pretty straightforward: we ask a question! We ask a question matched to our objective, which students will answer in writing. It's the same kind of question we've been asking since we began working on this objective. The difference this time is that children will have to answer the question, without the benefit of our guidance, for a text they haven't seen before. We won't explain how to find the evidence. We won't model our thinking. We won't prompt them to locate their own details in the text or show them how to organize their written response. We won't to do any of these things for them today because our explicit teaching before this point taught them how to do all this. And now they will be asked to do it by themselves.

How did students respond to our instruction? We will determine that based on how well they answer our question. There may be a few students we didn't catch during the course of our Tier 1 shared, guided, or independent reading that show up now as "non-responders." Our data will become the evidence we need to get them the Tier 2 support they need now. The students we already identified for Tier 2 or Tier 3 interventions may still be receiving those services and might not yet be ready to show us their learning.

We can't entirely trust our assessment data, however, without making sure that there is validity both in the questions we ask and our scoring of students' answers. Scoring students' answers to open-ended comprehension questions is tricky business. Teachers tend to be tough critics when it comes to their students' written answers to comprehension questions. "Better safe than sorry!" they philosophize: Better to score them low on classroom and district questions and whip them into shape now before they have to respond to questions on the real deal—the high-stakes state assessment. But scoring too hard is no more helpful than inflating students' scores—and that happens, too! How do you decide how many points your students should receive on a particular question? Consider the answers to these questions.

VALID QUESTIONS

How do I make sure that my questions are valid?
Before we consider the response, we need to consider the question: You need the "right" question, one that truly measures the objective! In those statistics courses we all took in college, we learned that to be a worthy means of accountability, a measure needs to be both valid and reliable. It must assess what it intends to assess (validity), and if we asked the same question again (or used an alternate form of the assessment measure), we'd get basically the same level of performance (reliability).

This is another one of those matters that seems oh-so-obvious: How could a question be "wrong?" A question is "wrong" when it isn't a good match for the objective. Even better, make sure your objective matches your target because your target is matched to both the objective and the text—and it is stated in a way that students at your grade level can easily understand. The following examples show the correlation between the objective, the target, and the question that will assess the objective.

Good alignment
Objective: A1-a: What lesson does _____ learn in the story?
Target: Figure out the lesson that the first two pigs learn in the story *The Three Little Pigs*.
Question to assess the objective: Explain in writing the lesson that the first two pigs learn in the story *The Three Little Pigs*. Use evidence from the text to support your answer.

The alignment here is good because there's a one-to-one match between the objective, the target, and the question. Students have been learning about figuring out the lesson learned in a story, and now they must put that understanding to the test (literally) by responding to a "lesson" question in writing.

Poor alignment
Objective: A1-a: What lesson does _____ learn in the story?
Target: Figure out the lesson that the first two pigs learn in the story *The Three Little Pigs*.
Question to assess the objective: What was the main problem of the first two little pigs in the story *The Three Little Pigs*? Use evidence from the text to support your answer.

The alignment here is poor because the assessment question is not entirely matched to the objective and target. The question is *related* but assumes that, if students can identify the problem in the story, they can then determine the lesson. While this might work for capable students, it would probably confuse less competent students.

VALID SCORING

How do I make sure my scoring is valid?

No matter how much we try to clarify and simplify the scoring of students' responses, scoring is a messy process. I can give you some guidelines that will apply to teachers everywhere. But each state has its own quirky way of evaluating its literature responses, so you will want to consult the game-plan for your state in addition to what I tell you here.

The rating scale varies from state to state. Some states use a four-point scale. Some states grade on as much as a six-point scale. In Connecticut, we score 2, 1, 0. Truthfully, it almost doesn't matter what the scale is for the highest- and lowest-performing students. A great answer will get full credit, and a completely deficient answer will receive whatever the lowest point value is (usually 0, sometimes 1). It's that "gray area" in the middle where things get sticky. Take a look at the scale below to get a feel for scoring criteria.

Score = 2 (or highest rating; goal)

A great answer is accurate, well organized, elaborated with sufficient, specific text references, and fluent enough to be read or understood easily. It is also completed *independently* by the student.

Score = 1 (or middle rating; may include several score points; may or may not be considered a goal response)

A middle-of-the road response is typically correct in terms of the information it contains. However, the elaboration may be a mix of generalities and specifics, with too little evidence directly from the text. The fluency of the response is basically adequate, though you may be tempted to take out your red pen. In my state, anything under a 2 is below goal, but if the rating scale in your state contains enough points, some scores beneath "perfect" may also qualify as "passing." Although the score is mid-range, the expectation, again, is that students complete the task independently.

Score = 0 (or lowest rating; substantially below goal)

A very poor answer is sometimes inaccurate, too sparse to show much organization at all, or poorly organized with redundant information or circular reasoning. There is seldom any elaboration beyond the most general level, and the response may contain so many language errors, that it is difficult to make sense of it. The student attempts to complete the response independently but with completely unacceptable results.

It's difficult to provide a clear picture of scoring by speaking only in generalities. Each lesson plan in **Part II** contains a set of anchor responses scored 2, 1, or 0 for the identified objective in order to demonstrate more clearly what you should look for when assessing students' responses.

Additionally, a template is provided at the end of this chapter for teachers to practice developing their own anchor responses for a particular text and objective. (You may need to modify it based on your state's rating scale.) You will also find at the end of this chapter and on the CD a rubric clarifying literature response criteria (helpful for teachers) and a chart which simplifies the criteria for easy student use. And finally, there is a checksheet for tracking student progress on all of the comprehension objectives identified in this book. This sheet has been organized for a school year divided into three marking periods. You can modify it if your academic year is divided differently. A completed student checksheet is also provided as a sample. A page containing the objectives is included, too—for easy electronic copying and pasting.

JUST ADD CHILDREN

By now you should have a solid grasp of the *what, how,* and *why* of planning for shared reading that will meet the rigorous requirements of RTI Tier 1 reading comprehension instruction. And you have some guidelines to help you navigate beyond shared instruction into Tier 1 small-group instruction and independent reading. You even have a few principles to help you traverse the much more difficult terrain of interventions in Tiers 2 and 3 and a few thoughts to keep in mind as you assess your students' response to the instruction you've provided. As you apply this understanding to the actual *teaching* of the lessons in **Part II** of this book, please remember that the lessons I wrote are probably more thorough than any plan you would ever need to put down on paper.

"You expect me to write all *that*?" some teachers cry out in dismay when they look at the length of the plans I bring when I model a lesson in their classroom.

"No," I assure them. I am trying to be extra thorough here to demonstrate as many facets as possible of a good lesson. I tell them that, as long as what I hear them *say* as they teach covers all of the necessary elements of good instruction, I am not all that fussy about what they *write* in their plan. What gets written down is between you and your principal. I do, however, believe that some kind of written plan should exist because even a well-delivered lesson should not be random; it should be one piece of a logical progression of lessons that addresses students' needs in a systematic way.

So, here are all of those lessons you've been asking for. I've done my best to capture the elements of good teaching and to get them down on paper in a way that makes sense and makes learning fun. These lessons have not been subjected to the rigors of experimental research with samples, control groups, and the like, but they are most definitely founded upon expert opinion, well-reasoned theories, and direct evidence through extensive field testing (which I and other teachers conducted at length!).

Just add children in order to activate the "fun" part! I wish you could have come with me to the many classrooms I've had the opportunity to visit as I wrote (and rewrote) these lessons. I've tried them out in classrooms from kindergarten through eighth grade (though only intermediate-grade lessons appear in this book). Kids are comical, profound, and full of insights that remind me over and over why it is that I still love teaching.

As I was packing up my books after a session in one third grade, a little boy named Martin ran up to me and grabbed my hand: "That was a great lesson," he announced, as if it was his job to evaluate the quality of my instruction. But then again, perhaps it *was* his job. It is *every* student's responsibility to expect the best from his teachers.

"Thank you, Martin," I smiled, hoping that my lesson had been worthy of such critical acclaim. While the lessons in this book are surely not perfect, I hope they will at least provide a place for you and your students to begin as you guide them toward more strategic reading comprehension.

Before you turn to the lessons, take a few minutes to reflect on the questions at the end of this chapter.

HOW AM I DOING ON WRITTEN RESPONSE?

Name: _____ **Date:** _____

Question: _____

I think my score on this question would be _____

☐   My answer is <u>correct</u>. The information came right from what I read.

☐   My answer is <u>organized</u>. It makes sense when I read it. It has a good order.

☐   My answer has plenty of <u>details</u>. It has examples or other evidence from the text.

☐   My answer is <u>written</u> so people can read it easily. I didn't leave words out. I tried to spell carefully. I remembered capitals and periods.

The best thing about my answer is _____

_____ .

I still need to work on _____

_____ .

RUBRIC FOR ASSESSING STUDENTS' ORAL AND WRITTEN RESPONSE TO COMPREHENSION QUESTIONS

Name: _____ Date: _____

Question: _____

	0 Deficient	1 Developing	2 Excellent
Accuracy	The answer is clearly inaccurate and is well below the range of developmental-level expectations. It does not indicate that the student has constructed basic meaning from the text, either as explicitly-stated information or as inferred relationships among ideas. The answer may point to problems that go deeper than comprehension—perhaps insufficient word-identification skills.	The answer is partially accurate. It shows some confusion about events or information described in the text, and inferences may be far fetched or not tied directly to the content of the reading.	The answer is completely accurate. It is clearly based on events in the text that really happened, correctly represents factual information, and formulates reasonable inferences.
Organization	The answer has no organizational framework and is well below the range of grade-level expectations. It may be too sparse to provide a sense of organization; it may be very long and repetitive, saying the same thing over and over in a variety of ways; or it may be largely incoherent with no sense of direction.	The answer is marginally organized. It may begin in a logical fashion but loses its focus, or the parts may all be present but are not well-sequenced.	The answer is logically organized. It follows the steps specified in the response criteria or uses another sequential structure that makes sense to the reader.
Thoroughness	The answer is vague and/or irrelevant and is well below the range of grade-level expectations. It may be so general, far fetched, or loosely tied to the text that it is hard to tell whether the student has even read the text.	The answer is more general than specific. It contains some details and elaboration, but the student has missed or has neglected to include enough evidence from the text to sufficiently support a general statement or main idea.	The answer is thorough according to grade-level expectations. It meets all criteria for details and elaboration specified for the response to a particular question. The details show a close, careful reading of the text.
Fluency	The answer is nearly incomprehensible because of written language deficits and is well below the range of grade-level expectations. It shows extreme lack of skill in communicating ideas in writing and may signal the need for interventions beyond the scope of written-response instructional supports.	The answer sounds somewhat "choppy." It is generally able to be read and understood but may show more carelessness or lack of proficiency in the use of grammar, usage, writing conventions, vocabulary, and language structure than is appropriate for a student at this grade level.	The answer flows smoothly. It demonstrates grade-level-appropriate competence with grammar, usage, writing conventions, vocabulary, and language structure.

Greatest strength: _____

Next steps: _____

ANCHOR RESPONSES

The objective: _____

_____

The text: _____

Sample response for this objective that would receive a score of 2

_____

_____

_____

_____

_____

_____

_____

Sample response for this objective that would receive a score of 1

_____

_____

_____

_____

_____

_____

_____

Sample response for this objective that would receive a score of 0

_____

_____

_____

_____

_____

_____

_____

COMPREHENSION CHECKSHEET: INTERMEDIATE GRADES

Name: _____ **Date:** _____

Teacher: _____

Please record student's score in the appropriate box using the following scale:

3 = Exceeds expectations: Demonstrates remarkable insight into text based on this objective; text may be above grade level

2 = Proficient at grade level: Grasps the objective adequately in order to comprehend text*

1 = Developing: Grasp of the objective is inconsistent and/or superficial based on grade-appropriate text*

0 = Not evident at this time: Insufficient grasp of the objective with any text

Note that a score of 2 represents grade-level expectations. Reserve a **score of 3** for students who clearly excel.

* If the student masters an objective with **below-level text**, this should be noted with a [ ], and the student should be considered for a Tier II intervention to accelerate learning.

Objectives/Indicators of Mastery for Comprehension for Grade _____	1	2	3
1.			
2.			
3.			
4.			
5.			
6..			
7			
8.			
9.			
10.			
11.			
12.			
13.			

Marking Period

Notes for MP 1: _____

_____

Notes for MP 2: _____

_____

Notes for MP 3: _____

_____

COMPREHENSION OBJECTIVES

*****Copy and paste these objectives into the checksheet according to when they are introduced at your grade level.

FORMING A GENERAL UNDERSTANDING

A1: The student will determine the main idea in an informational text or select a new title for a text.

A2: The student will identify or infer important characters, settings, problems, events, relationships, and details within a text.

A3: The student will summarize a narrative or informational text.

A4: The student will predict what will happen next or what the author might include if adding another paragraph to a text.

A5: Vocabulary: identifying word meanings from context

DEVELOPING AN INTERPRETATION

B1: The student will identify the author's use of structure/organizational pattern.

B2: The student will identify the author's reason for including certain information or choosing a particular genre.

B3: The student will use stated or implied evidence from the text to draw and support a conclusion.

MAKING A PERSONAL CONNECTION TO A TEXT

C1: The student makes a personal connection to a text.

C2: The student reacts to the text.

EXAMINING THE CONTENT AND STRUCTURE

D1: The student will analyze and evaluate the author's craft including word choice and whether or not the story is believable.

D2: The student will produce a journal entry, identify the most important part of a text, or ask two questions of the author not answered in the text during an oral discussion or through a written response.

D3: The student will demonstrate an awareness of author's or character's values, customs, and beliefs included in a text.

SAMPLE COMPREHENSION CHECKSHEET: INTERMEDIATE LEVEL

Name: _____ **Date:** _____

Teacher: _____

Please record student's score in the appropriate box using the following scale:

3 = Exceeds expectations: Demonstrates remarkable insight into text based on this objective; text may be above grade level

2 = Proficient at grade level: Grasps the objective adequately in order to comprehend text*

1 = Developing: Grasp of the objective is inconsistent and/or superficial based on grade-appropriate text*

0 = Not evident at this time: Insufficient grasp of the objective with any text

Note that a score of 2 represents grade-level expectations. Reserve a **score of 3** for students who clearly excel.

* If the student masters an objective with **below-level text**, this should be noted with a [ ], and the student should be considered for a Tier II intervention to accelerate learning.

	Marking Period		
Objectives/Indicators of Mastery for Comprehension for Grade <u>5</u>	**1**	**2**	**3**
1. A5: Vocabulary	1	2	2
2. A3: The student will summarize a narrative or informational text.	1	1	2
3. A1: The student will determine the main idea in an informational text, or determine the theme/lesson, or select a new title for a narrative text.	1	2	1
4. C1: The student makes a personal connection to a text.	1	2	2
5. C2: The student reacts to the text.	1	2	3
6. D2: The student will produce a journal entry, identify the most important part of a text, or ask two questions of the author not answered in the text during an oral discussion or through a written response.	1	2	2
7. B2: The student will identify the author's reason for including certain information or choosing a particular genre.		1	2
8. B1: The student will identify the author's use of structure/organizational pattern.		2	2
9. D3: The student will demonstrate an awareness of author's or character's values, customs, and beliefs included in a text.		2	3
10. D1: The student will analyze and evaluate the author's craft including word choice and whether or not the story is believable.		2	2
11. B3: The student will use stated or implied evidence from the text to draw and support a conclusion.		2	3

Notes for MP 1: _____

_____

Notes for MP 2: _____

_____

Notes for MP 3: _____

_____

REFLECTING ON CHAPTER SEVEN

1. What are some of the issues you face when scoring students' written responses that make scoring challenging?

2. What kinds of questions seem to give your students the biggest problems? Why?

3. How many students in your class *should* make goal on district or state literacy assessments that require written response? How many students *do* make goal? How can you address this discrepancy?

4. Do you ask students to reflect on their own or their peers' written responses to assess them? How does that process look in your classroom? Does it help students? How?

5. Something to try: Using the scoring template on page 71 of this chapter, create your own anchor responses scored 2, 1, or 0 for answers to a particular question matched to a shared reading text. How does creating a set of anchor responses help you assess student work? (You may use a rating scale other than 2, 1, or 0 if you prefer.)

PART II

Shared Reading Lessons

Part II Introduction

Now that you've thought about the *why* and *how* of comprehension instruction, the lessons that follow should need no further explanation. I do want to explain a bit more about the support materials for each lesson, some of which you will find only on the CD, not in the book itself. Other supports are included in the book and precede each lesson.

IN THE BOOK

The following materials precede each lesson and are included in the book:

Objective: The same coding system is used for this book that was used in *That's a Great Answer* so that the two books may be easily coordinated. It would certainly be possible to teach other comprehension objectives, but these forty objectives cover a broad range of skills needed by good readers everywhere.

Title and Author of the Book: Selecting the books to use for these lessons was one of my favorite parts of this project—an excuse to linger over some of the most wonderful books in my personal library. I hope I've chosen some books that you treasure, too, and that I have introduced you to a few books you are meeting for the first time.

Introduction to the Book: This is a brief summary of the book so you will know what it contains even before reading it from cover to cover.

Why This Is a Good Book for Teaching This Objective: This explains why the book is a good match for the particular objective—so that you may look for similar attributes when selecting your own resources to reinforce the same objective.

Other Objectives That May Be Addressed by Re-reading This Book: I hope you will consider these books "mentor texts" for teaching objectives other than just the one designated for the lesson itself. When you do revisit the same text, these "other objectives" would also be good matches for this book.

Other Books Matched to This Objective to Lead Students toward Independence: To help you select other texts suitable for this same objective, I make three book suggestions for each objective—along with annotations. Many of these books are as wonderful as the book selected to teach the lesson. I recommend them for your school or classroom library if you desire to augment your current collection.

Scoring Students' Responses: Anchor responses are provided based on a simple rating scale of 2, 1, or 0, along with a brief explanation of why the response would be scored in this manner. Please remember that these are just suggested scores. Your district or state may have different scoring standards or criteria, so of course you should abide by those.

ONLY ON THE CD

These materials support each lesson but are found only on the CD. (Samples are included in the book for the first lesson for objective A1-a: *What lesson does this story teach?* for the book *The Honest-to-Goodness Truth*.)

Target: The page with the target icon contains the information (stated in kid-friendly language) that you will want to share with students about how to find the evidence for the lesson objective. This is generally the same information provided in the *Before Reading* part of the lesson plan labeled *Introduce the objective (How to find and use the evidence)*. The only difference is that while the explanation in the lesson plan is sometimes applied specifically to one particular book, the points on the Target sheet are generic and may be applied to the study of this objective for *any* book you wish to use. This sheet is a good visual reference and a useful extension of your oral explanation—which visual learners desperately need. I post this target where students can easily see it. I also physically bring the target sheet to the small group and place it on the table in front of students, a clear and very concrete reminder that the same objective we introduced during shared reading will now be reinforced in guided reading. It keeps all of us focused!

Vocabulary Connections: This is a follow-up activity for the vocabulary words introduced during the lesson. You will want to introduce some words *before* reading the text and also point them out *while* you read. But the most serious vocabulary work will most likely occur *after* reading when you can take the time to get students to interact with the words—over and over. The *Vocabulary Connections* activity is a good culmination of text-related word study and is easily differentiated:

- For high-performing students: Ask them to complete written responses to all of the questions independently after the words have been introduced and practiced in various ways. Their response should begin with appropriate words from the question, should use the vocabulary word correctly in the context of the sentence, and should include not only a subject and verb, but sufficient elaboration.

- For average learners: Ask them to write responses to *some* of the questions (fewer vocabulary words; you decide how many). Their responses should meet the same standards for good language use as those of the most capable students. You might need to spend more time, however, reviewing word meanings orally and having these students respond orally to the questions before putting their responses on paper.

- For ELL students and students with language difficulties: Ask them to orally rehearse their response to one or two questions over and over until they are comfortable with the structure of their sentence. When you (and they) are confident that they've "got it," guide them to write their response. Support their use of written language conventions (spelling, grammar, punctuation, etc.). Ask students to read their written responses orally for further reinforcement. Working on one word per day in this fashion during small-group instruction will do much to enhance the language development of English language learners and other students who struggle with oral and written language.

OTHER WAYS TO ORGANIZE YOUR TEACHING

The lessons in this book are classified according to objectives that fall within different thinking strands (A, B, C, D). While this was the most straight-forward way of packaging these lessons, your curriculum may be organized differently—perhaps around themes or topics, genres or text structures, or particular authors. Because I tried to represent many different authors, there are not enough lessons here by any one author to constitute an "author study." However, you could easily fit these lessons into curriculum that revolves around theme/topic or genre/text structure. The chart on the following page offers some suggested categories and also shows how these books represent many different text types and topics.

THEME/TOPIC	GENRE/TEXT STUCTURE
Character Traits/Self-Esteem • *The Honest-to-Goodness Truth* • *Melissa Parkington's Beautiful, Beautiful Hair* • *Eggbert, the Slightly Cracked Egg* • *Momma, Where Are You From?* • *The Princess and the Pizza* • *Silver Packages* • *Uncle Jed's Barbershop* • *Snowflake Bentley* • *Pebble*	**Realistic Fiction** • *The Honest-to-Goodness Truth* • *Melissa Parkington's Beautiful, Beautiful Hair* • *The Raft* • *Uncle Jed's Barbershop* • *Something Beautiful* • *One Green Apple* • *The Other Side* • *Four Feet, Two Sandals* • *Heroes*
Growing Up/Connecting to Personal Experiences • *The Raft* • *Heroes* • *Something Beautiful* • *Weslandia* • *Four Feet, Two Sandals*	**Fairytales/Folk Tales** • *The Princess and the Pizza* • *Extra! Extra! Fairy-Tale News from Hidden Forest* • *The Empty Pot*
Civil Rights Era • *Momma, Where Are You From?* • *This Is the Dream* • *As Good as Anybody* • *Remember* • *The Other Side* • *Goin' Someplace Special*	**Personal Narrative/Memoir** • *How I Learned Geography* • *Silver Packages* • *The Chocolate Pilot* • *Goin' Someplace Special* • *Pictures from Our Vacation* • *Going Home*
Other Cultures • *One Green Apple* (Middle East) • *Four Feet, Two Sandals* (Middle East) • *Going Home* (Mexico) • *Planting the Trees of Kenya* (Africa) • *Beatrice's Goat* (Africa) • *The Empty Pot* (Asia) • *The Lotus Seed* (Asia)	**Informational Text** • *A Platypus, Probably* • *The Flag We Love* • *Water Dance* • *Will We Miss Them?* • *So You Want to Be President*
The Environment • *A River Ran Wild* • *Water Dance* • *The Seashore Book* • *Will We Miss Them?* • *Dear World*	**Historical Fiction/Narrative Nonfiction** • *A River Ran Wild* • *Beatrice's Goat* • *This Is the Dream*
World War II/Holocaust • *How I Learned Geography* • *The Chocolate Pilot* • *Heroes*	**Fantasy** • *Dear Mrs. LaRue* • *The Wretched Stone* • *The School Nurse from the Black Lagoon* • *Weslandia* • *Extra! Extra! Fairy-Tale News from Hidden Forest*
Animals • *A Platypus, Probably* • *Dear Mrs. LaRue*	**Biography** • *Planting the Trees of Kenya* • *As Good as Anybody* • *Snowflake Bentley*
America/Patriotism • *The Flag We Love* • *So You Want to Be President*	**Photo Journal** • *Remember*
	Descriptive Narrative • *The Seashore Book* • *Water Dance*
	Allegory • *Eggbert, the Slightly Cracked Egg* • *Pebble*
	Poetry • *Dear World*

And now…the lessons. From my heart to your classroom.

Chapter Eight

STRAND A LESSONS

Forming A General Understanding

OBJECTIVE

A1-a: What lesson does _____ learn in this story?

BOOK

The Honest-to-Goodness Truth by Patricia McKissack

INTRODUCTION TO THE BOOK

In this story, young Libby is caught telling a fib to her mom. She vows she will never again tell a lie, and she is true to her word—even when the truth hurts someone's feelings. For example, she tells her friend Ruthie Mae that she likes her dress but then informs her she has a hole in her sock. Life continues in this painfully true manner for several days, and Libby can't understand why she's losing all her friends. Nothing changes until someone tells a similar "truth" to her. Only then does Libby learn that sometimes it's best to "sweeten the truth with a little love." The lesson here is about having good manners.

WHY THIS IS A GOOD BOOK FOR TEACHING THIS OBJECTIVE

This book is perfect for this objective because the lesson learned is simple and direct and is the kind of issue children struggle with in their own lives. The text is also appropriate for students in the younger grades—where this objective is often taught.

OTHER OBJECTIVES THAT MAY BE ADDRESSED BY RE-READING THIS BOOK

- **A3-a:** Briefly summarize this story.
- **A4-b:** If the author added another paragraph to the end of the story, it would <u>most likely</u> tell about _____. Use information from the story to support your answer.
- **C1-a:** Make a personal connection to an experience.
- **D1-e:** Do you think the author made this story believable? Why or why not?

OTHER BOOKS MATCHED TO THIS OBJECTIVE TO LEAD STUDENTS TOWARD INDEPENDENCE (Remember to chart the evidence when you use a picture book so that students may provide specific details from the text)

In each of these books, a character learns an important lesson:

- *Keepers* **by Jeri Hanel Watts**
  In this tender story, a little boy buys himself a new baseball glove with the money he had saved to get his grandmother a present for her ninetieth birthday—and is then ashamed that he did such a thoughtless thing. He finds a way to make Grandma's birthday special, despite his lapse in judgment, so all's well that ends well.

- *Aunt Chip and the Great Triple Creek Dam Affair* by **Patricia Polacco**

  In this fantasy, Polacco shows how disastrous the results can be when everyone in a town stops reading and only watches TV. Fortunately, Aunt Chip who was formerly the town librarian saves the day when she teaches one young boy to read. The town survives as other children learn to read and teach their parents. Oh, the power of books!

- *A Bad Case of Stripes* by **David Shannon**

  Camilla Cream develops a nasty case of stripes when she abandons her sense of self and instead flip-flops to be just like her friends. Eventually she recognizes that she needs to be true to herself—even if that means admitting she likes lima beans.

SCORING STUDENTS' RESPONSES

 A1-a: What lesson does Libby learn in this story?

Score = 2

In this story, Libby learns that telling the truth is important, but you have to be careful not to hurt people's feelings. At the beginning of the story she told her friend that she had a hole in her sock. Later she also tattled on her friend when he didn't do his homework. At the end Libby sees what she has been doing to her friends when someone says something mean about her horse. It may be true, but it didn't have to be said.

> (This is an excellent answer. The reader correctly identifies the lesson and provides two examples from the beginning of the text that illustrate Libby's behavior *before* she learned her lesson. The reader also clarifies the event at the end of the story that taught Libby her lesson.)

Score = 1

In this story, Libby learned to be kind when she told the truth. At the beginning of the story, she lied, and then she told the truth, but she was mean.

> (This reader accurately identifies the lesson, but does not seem clear about the storyline that follows. Also, there are no specific examples that *show* Libby's behavior.)

Score = 0

In this story a girl lied and got in trouble with her mother. So she didn't lie anymore.

> (This reader missed the point of the story. Yes, it is wrong to lie. But that is not the lesson the character learns. No score for this response.)

PLANNER FOR SHARED READING

Objective (strategy focus): <u>**A1-a:**</u> What lesson does [_____] learn in this story?

◎ <u>Figure out what lesson Libby learns in this story.</u>

    How will student learning be measured at the end of the lesson? (What will count as "success?")

Text: *The Honest-to-Goodness Truth* by Patricia McKissack   **Pages:** <u>Whole book</u>

<table>
<tr>
<td rowspan="3">BEFORE READING</td>
<td>Establish prior knowledge, purpose, and predictions</td>
<td>Prior knowledge: Is it important to always tell the truth? (Ask for examples) Would there ever be a time that telling the truth would not be a good idea?
Predictions: Based on the title, what do you think this story will be about? What do you think the author might mean by "the honest-to-goodness truth?"
Purpose for reading: As we read today, let's try to figure out the lesson the character learns about telling "the honest-to-goodness truth."</td>
</tr>
<tr>
<td>Introduce/review vocabulary</td>
<td>glare   trudged   glumly   hurtful   victims</td>
</tr>
<tr>
<td>Introduce the objective (How to find and use the evidence)</td>
<td>Making the <u>reading</u> strategic
To try to figure out what the lesson is that some learned, we should see how they are acting at the beginning of the story, and then see how they are acting at the end of the story. Be sure you can explain what caused them to change.</td>
</tr>
<tr>
<td rowspan="2">DURING READING</td>
<td>Model and practice finding evidence for the objective</td>
<td>The best evidence:
<u>Model:</u>
pp. 1-2: Libby told a lie and got in trouble for it, so she promised to tell the truth forever more.
p. 7: Libby told Ruthie Mae that she had a hole in her sock.
p. 12: Libby told her teacher that Willie didn't do his homework.
<u>Practice:</u>
p. 14: Daisy forgot her Christmas speech and cried in front of the parents.
p. 15: Charlesetta stole peaches and got a spanking; Thomas didn't have lunch money.
pp. 20-21: Miz Tusselbury's garden looked like a jungle.
Mama says that sometimes the truth is told at the wrong time or in the wrong way and can be hurtful.
p. 24: V. Washington insulted Libby's horse.
p. 15: Libby thought back to her own truth telling.
p. 27: Libby apologizes to her friends.</td>
</tr>
<tr>
<td>Model and practice other strategies</td>
<td>Connecting? Did anyone ever hurt your feelings by being truthful?
Visualizing/Picturing? Picture someone looking glum, trudging, glaring
Wondering? Wonder why Libby didn't figure her problem out sooner.
Predicting/Guessing? Predict what might happen next. (What will happen next time she tells the truth?)
Noticing? Notice details about the setting of this story.
Figuring out? Figure out the lesson. (Tell the truth in a way that is not hurtful.)</td>
</tr>
</table>

AFTER READING	**Discussion questions**	**Question related to the objective** • **A1-a:** What is the lesson that Libby learned in this story? **Other questions** • **C1-c:** Would you like Libby for a friend? Why or why not? • **A4-b:** If the author added another paragraph to this story, what do you think it might say?
	Written response to text	**Making the <u>writing</u> strategic** • See *That's a Great Answer*, p. 52, or *Teaching Written Response,* pp. 105-106, for a template matched to this objective. • Model the response using the template. • Remove your response and ask students to write the response themselves using the template—choosing their own evidence if possible
	Other follow-up activities	**Oral language, fluency, vocabulary, comprehension, reading extensions, writing extensions** **Oral language/fluency:** This story contains lots of dialogue between different characters that calls for good expression. Practice reading one of the *Quotes for Fluency Practice* (on the CD) until your voice sounds like that of the character. **Vocabulary:** See *Vocabulary Connections* activity on the CD **Comprehension:** These follow-up activities may be found in *Constructing Meaning through Kid-Friendly Comprehension Strategy Instruction*: I'm Connected, p. 159; Picture This, p. 164; True or False, p. 171; A Message from the Author, p. 186. **Reading extensions:** The following books relate to manners: • *The Golden Rule* by Ilene Cooper • *Have You Filled a Bucket Today?* by Carol McCloud • *My Mouth Is a Volcano* by Julia Cook **Writing extensions:** Imagine that you are Libby. Write a letter of apology to one of the people whose feelings you hurt by telling the truth. What did you learn from this experience?
	Reflect on reading and writing strategy	• How do you figure out the lesson in a story? • Why do you think authors write stories where a character learns a lesson?

A1-a: What lesson does _____ learn in this story?

How to hit the target:

- Notice the "bad behavior" at the beginning of the story. (What is "bad" about this?)

- Notice how the character's or person's behavior changes. (How does the person act at the end of the story? Where do you first notice the change?)

- Figure out what lesson the character or person learned that changed bad behavior to good behavior.

VOCABULARY CONNECTIONS

The Honest-to-Goodness Truth

glare	trudged	glum	hurtful	victims

1. Ruthie Mae **glared** at Libby because she was so mad at her.

2. Libby **trudged** slowly up her steps, wondering why Ruthie Mae was mad at her.

3. Libby felt **glum** when her friends wouldn't speak to her.

4. Sometimes it can be **hurtful** when you tell the truth in the wrong way or at the wrong time.

5. Libby apologized to all of the **victims** whose feelings she'd hurt.

1. What would make you feel **glum**?

_____

_____

2. When would you feel like **glaring** at someone?

_____

_____

3. What might cause you to **trudge** home?

_____

_____

4. If someone said something **hurtful** to you, how would you handle it?

_____

_____

5. What might make you feel like a **victim**?

_____

_____

THE HONEST-TO-GOODNESS TRUTH
QUOTES FOR FLUENCY PRACTICE

Mama asked:

"Libby Louise Sullivan, I'll ask you once more and again: Did you feed and water Ol' Boss?"

Libby answered:

"I was gon' do it soon as I got back from jumping rope with Ruthie Mae."

Libby said:

"Morning, everybody. Morning, Ruthie Mae. I like your outfit. It's real pretty. . . but you've got a hole in your sock."

Libby asked Ruthie Mae to walk home with her:

Ruthie Mae: "No, no, and no again!"

Libby: "What'd I do?"

Ruthie Mae: "You told the world I had a hole in my sock."

Libby: "It was the truth."

Ruthie Mae: "It was plain mean!"

Libby answering her teacher in the classroom:

Libby: "Me, Miz Jackson, me, me, me, Miz Jackson! Willie don't got his geography homework."

Miz Jackson: "Doesn't have his homework."

Libby: "No, ma'am, he don't."

Willie: "Why'd you tell on me?"

Libby: "All I did was tell it like it is. So there!"

Libby talking to Miz Tusselbury:

Miz Tusselbury: "What's that sad look you wearing on such a pretty day?"

Libby: "Can the truth be wrong?"

Miz Tusselbury: "The truth is never wrong. Always, always tell the truth!"

Libby: "That's what I thought."

OBJECTIVE

A1-b: What is the theme of this story?

BOOK

Eggbert, the Slightly Cracked Egg by Tom Ross

INTRODUCTION TO THE BOOK

Eggbert is a happy egg, well-respected by his companions in the fridge (other eggs, vegetables, and bottles of this and that)—until it is discovered that he is slightly cracked! He is told that he must leave. Poor Eggbert spends most of the rest of the story trying to fit in by disguising his crack. But it is no use. His crack is always discovered, and so many rejections make him feel completely worthless. Then one day he sees that there are some magnificent cracks that actually enhance the world's beauty: the Grand Canyon, clouds, even volcanoes. Eggbert decides that being cracked might not be such a bad thing after all. He paints beautiful post cards of these cracks and sends them home to his friends in the fridge.

WHY THIS IS A GOOD BOOK FOR TEACHING THIS OBJECTIVE

This is a little story with a big message. Actually, there are a couple of themes at work here: For Eggbert—accepting yourself the way you are, and for his friends—the need to be open and kind to people who are different from you. Although the concept of theme is often difficult for students, both of the themes present in this book are concepts that are part of children's day-to-day lives; they can relate. The fact that this is quite a short little book with whimsical cartoon watercolor illustrations makes it even more engaging.

OTHER OBJECTIVES THAT MAY BE ADDRESSED BY RE-READING THIS BOOK

- **A2-a:** Using information in the story, write a brief description of how Eggbert felt when his friends from the refrigerator treated him badly because he was cracked.

- **B2-a:** Why does the author include the information on page 21 about Eggbert's discovery of "wonderful cracks?"

- **A4-b:** If the author added another paragraph to the end of the story in which it is discovered that another egg is cracked, how might the other foods in the refrigerator have responded this time?

- **C1-c:** Make a personal connection to a feeling in this story. (Think about the feeling(s) the author wants you to think a lot about.)

OTHER BOOKS MATCHED TO THIS OBJECTIVE TO LEAD STUDENTS TOWARD INDEPENDENCE (Remember to chart the evidence when you use a picture book so that students may provide specific details from the text)

Other allegorical books that tell a very simple story in order to deliver an important message might be:

- *Pebble* by Susan Milord

  This, too, is an allegory. The "pebble," looking for its place and significance in the world, is not so different from you or me. We are all trying to figure out who we are in the grand scheme of things, and Pebble uncovers an answer that will be quite transparent to students.

- *Is There Really a Human Race?* by Jamie Lee Curtis

  In this book, Jamie Lee Curtis asks a series of provocative questions that encourage readers to consider whether they are inadvertently part of the "Human Race" where they aim for their goal competitively or collaboratively: How will *you* make the world a better place?

- *The Paper Crane* by Molly Bang

  In this modern retelling of a Japanese folktale, Molly Bang shows how one person's generosity reaps unanticipated rewards—and the gift just keeps getting better. This book encourages readers to consider the value of giving with the added notion that one can always give more.

SCORING STUDENTS' RESPONSES

 A1-b: Explain the theme of *Eggbert, the Slightly Cracked Egg*

Score = 2

The theme of *Eggbert* is that you shouldn't let other people put you down and make you feel like you are not worth anything. At first this is what happened to Eggbert. When his friends told him to leave because of his crack, he hunched his shoulders together so his crack would disappear. He also tried to paint himself to look like a flower so no one would see his crack. In the end he figured out that cracks are beautiful (like the Grand Canyon) and he was proud that he had a crack.

> (This response includes a clearly stated and accurate theme as well as specific details that support the theme. The response also indicates what the character learned in relation to the theme.)

Score = 1

The theme of *Eggbert* is that you should be happy the way you are. Also, other people shouldn't put you down just because you are not perfect.

> (This response is accurate and, in fact, references both of the possible themes in this text. Unfortunately, no details are provided to supply evidence.)

Score = 0

Eggbert was an egg who lived in a refrigerator until he cracked. Then he got kicked out. He was really sad. His friends were mean to him.

> (This is more of a summary than a description of the theme. It relates very general information about the plot but does not specify the message that the author was trying to convey.)

PLANNER FOR SHARED READING

Objective (strategy focus): <u>A1-b:</u> <u>What is the theme of this book?</u>

◎ <u>Explain the theme of *Eggbert, the Slightly Cracked Egg*.</u>
   How will student learning be measured at the end of the lesson? (What will count as "success?")

Text: *Eggbert, the Slightly Cracked Egg* by Tom Ross   **Pages:** <u>Whole book</u>

BEFORE READING

<table>
<tr>
<td rowspan="5" style="writing-mode: vertical-lr;">BEFORE READING</td>
<td>Establish prior knowledge, purpose, and predictions</td>
<td>Prior knowledge: What kind of story uses animals as characters in order to teach a lesson to people (fables)? The story we will read today is kind of like a fable. It appears to be about an egg, but it really offers a message about people in general.
Predictions: Based on the title, what do you think this book might be about?
Purpose for reading: As we read this book, let's try to figure out the theme: the author's message about people in general.</td>
</tr>
<tr>
<td>Introduce/review vocabulary</td>
<td>hunched (his shoulders)   discouraged   glimmer   regret   amazed</td>
</tr>
<tr>
<td>Introduce the objective (How to find and use the evidence)</td>
<td>Making the <u>reading</u> strategic
When you try to figure out the theme of a story, you need to think about what it says about people in general. What message is the author sending you that could be helpful in your own life?

So, as we read this story, notice places where the author provides details about the main character (Eggbert). Think about what he learns. Think about what you could learn from Eggbert to make your own life happier.

If you can figure out this "message to the world," you have figured out the theme.</td>
</tr>
</table>

DURING READING	**Model and practice the focus strategy**	**The best evidence:** Read the entire story all the way through without stopping. At the end, ask students what they think it says about people in general: People should like themselves just the way they are and should not try to be something they are not. After students have identified the probable message, ask hem to go back and find specific evidence to prove the theme they identified. Model a couple of examples before students practice. **Model:** **p. 5:** Slightly cracked eggs had to leave (Some people are not open to anyone who isn't perfect) **p. 6:** Eggbert hunched his shoulders, made his crack disappear (He felt embarrassed because he wasn't perfect) **p. 8:** Eggbert tried to find someplace to fit in (People need to fit in) **Practice:** **p. 10:** Painted himself to look like things around him (Go to great lengths to fit in) **p. 11:** Potato plant told him to leave (People can be mean when you are different or not perfect) **p. 15:** Bee told Eggbert to leave (Mean again) **p. 19:** Cat told Eggbert to leave (Mean again) **p. 20:** Eggbert started to sob because he realized he couldn't hide who he was (When you don't like yourself, you feel so sad) **p. 21:** Cracks can be beautiful (began to accept himself for who he was) **p. 24:** Famous cracked sights (You can be beautiful and perfect just the way you are)
	Model and practice other strategies	**Connecting?** How could this message apply to you? Has there ever been a time when you wanted to be like someone else but then decided you were just fine exactly as you are? **Visualizing/Picturing?** What scene could you picture especially clearly in your mind? **Wondering?** What other details could the author have included to make the message even stronger? **Predicting/Guessing?** Could you predict how this story would end? Why or why not? **Noticing?** What details did you find were the *best* examples of the way people really act? **Figuring out?** Why did the author write this story? Why did he choose an egg as the main character?

AFTER READING	**Discussion questions**	**Question related to the objective:** **A1-b:** Explain the theme of *Eggbert, the Slightly Cracked Egg* using evidence from the text. **Other possible questions:** **A3-a:** Briefly summarize this story. **C1-a:** Make a personal connection to this text. **C2-c:** Did you like this story? Why or why not? **D1-e:** Do you think the author made this story believable? Why or why not?
	Written response to text	**Making the <u>writing</u> strategic** • See *That's a Great Answer*, p. 55, for the template matched to this objective. • Model the response using the template. • Remove your response and ask students to write the response themselves using the template-choosing their own evidence if possible.
	Other follow-up activities	**Oral language, fluency, vocabulary, comprehension, reading extensions, writing extensions** **Oral language/fluency:** Find a page in this book that shows Eggbert's feelings. Practice reading the page until you *sound* just like Eggbert *felt*. Some possible pages might be: p. 6 (where Eggbert waves goodbye to his friends); pp. 9-10 (where Eggbert decided to paint himself to look like his surroundings); p. 17 (where Eggbert sees the stars); p. 21 (where Eggbert first notices the beautiful cracks in the world). **Vocabulary:** See *Vocabulary Connections* activity on the CD **Comprehension:** These follow-up activities may be found in *Constructing Meaning through Kid-Friendly Comprehension Strategy Instruction*: Prove It, p. 174; Character Study, p. 185; A Message from the Author, p. 186 **Reading extensions:** Read another book where the character learns to accept himself or herself just the way s/he is. Create a Venn diagram showing text-to-text connections. Some possible picture books might be: • *A Bad Case of Stripes* by David Shannon • *Odd Boy Out: Young Albert Einstein* by Don Brown • *Hewitt Anderson's Great Big Life* by Jerdine Nolen • *Tacky the Penguin* by Helen Lester **Writing extensions:** Pretend that you are Eggbert. You have just discovered another cracked egg in the refrigerator. Write a paragraph giving this egg advice. Be sure to include lots of details based on your own experience.
	Reflect on reading and writing strategy	• How do you identify *theme* in a book? • Was this a good book to use in order to identify a theme? Why? • What kinds of texts will probably have important themes?

▶ OBJECTIVE

A1-c: What is the main idea of this text?

BOOK

A Platypus, Probably by Sneed B. Collard III

INTRODUCTION TO THE BOOK

This is an informational book that provides insight into one of the world's most unique creatures—the platypus. The author describes how a female platypus hunts for food, finds a mate, builds a shelter, and cares for her pups. Sidebars in smaller print reveal additional details about this strange, Australian mammal.

WHY THIS IS A GOOD BOOK FOR TEACHING THIS OBJECTIVE

When you are teaching objectives using nonfiction, half of the battle is using text that students find interesting. This book surely qualifies. Students are fascinated by this strange Australian water creature. Alluring illustrations and just enough text make it a good choice for focusing on main idea. Furthermore, this book is representative of many texts that students will read for the purpose of identifying a main idea and supporting details: There are no subheadings or boldfaced words to guide the way. The same principle, however, suggested for teaching main idea with this book may also be applied to social studies or science texts that *do* provide helpful organizational features to assist students.

OTHER OBJECTIVES THAT MAY BE ADDRESSED BY RE-READING THIS BOOK

- **B1-d:** Can this part of the text be described as: a description, an explanation, a conversation, an opinion, an argument, or a comparison? How do you know?
- **B3-b:** Which facts (details) show that _____?
- **C2-b:** Which part of this book was most interesting or surprising to you? Why?
- **D2-a:** What two questions would you like to ask the author that were not answered in this text?

OTHER BOOKS MATCHED TO THIS OBJECTIVE TO LEAD STUDENTS TOWARD INDEPENDENCE (Remember to chart the evidence when you use a picture book so that students may provide specific details from the text)

- *Platypus* by Joan Short, Jack Green, and Bettina Bird
  This nonfiction book provides an appropriate amount of information about the platypus for intermediate-grade students. In very short chapters (one or two pages) the author describes the habits, habitat, and physical characteristics of the platypus. Color photographs and drawings enhance the treatment of the topic.

- ***Platypus!* by Ginjer Clarke**
  This "Step Two" Step-into-Reading book is filled with facts that even older struggling readers would find informative.

- ***If My Mom Were a Platypus: Animal Babies and Their Mothers* by Dia Michels**
  This book is great for older or more capable readers and offers fascinating information not just about the platypus, but about the babies of thirteen different kinds of animals. In this book, *you* are the baby!

SCORING STUDENTS' RESPONSES

 What is the main idea of *A Platypus, Probably*? What details support this main idea?

Score = 2

The main idea of *A Platypus, Probably* is that a platypus is an animal that has many characteristics that make it different from most other animals. First, although it is a mammal and has lungs for breathing, not gills, it spends its life in the water. Also, this mammal lays eggs, which most other mammals don't do. Finally, it has a bill sort of like a duck's bill, and it doesn't have teeth.

> (This answer would receive a score of 2 because it correctly identifies the main idea and provides ample support for this main idea with relevant details. In fact, only two or three details would probably be necessary. This answer includes four details.)

Score = 1

The main idea of *A Platypus, Probably* is that a platypus is weird. It is a funny looking animal and it was even around in the time of the dinosaurs.

> (This answer would receive a score of 1. The student has the general idea [weird animal], but one detail is very general [funny looking animal] and the other detail [lived during the time of the dinosaurs] is not really relevant to the main idea.

Score = 0

The main idea of *A Platypus, Probably* is about a platypus. A platypus lives far away in Australia and I have never seen one, but I would like to see one sometime because I think they are interesting and maybe scary, too.

> This student is confusing *topic* [platypus] with *main idea* [what is the big idea that the author wants us to understand about the platypus?]. Also, this student is mostly giving general information about a platypus [lives far away] and then makes a weak connection [I would like to see one; they are interesting and maybe scary].

PLANNER FOR SHARED READING

Objective (strategy focus): <u>A1-c:</u> <u>What is the main idea of this text?</u>

 <u>What is the main idea of *A Platypus, Probably*? What details support this main idea?</u>
How will student learning be measured at the end of the lesson? (What will count as "success?")

Text: <u>*A Platypus, Probably* by Sneed Collard III</u>   **Pages:** <u>Whole book</u>

<table>
<tr>
<td rowspan="3" style="writing-mode:vertical">BEFORE READING</td>
<td>Establish prior knowledge, purpose, and predictions</td>
<td>Prior knowledge: What do you know about the platypus? Where does it live? What does it look like?
Predictions: (Look through the book.) Do you predict that this book will tell you a story or give you information? What kind of information do you think you will get from this book?
Purpose for reading: Let's read to figure out the main idea of this book and some of the details that support this main idea.</td>
</tr>
<tr>
<td>Introduce/review vocabulary</td>
<td>***Note that there are many technical terms in this book that were not selected for vocabulary instruction because students will be unlikely to apply them readily within their speaking and writing vocabularies. However, they may be addressed incidentally as you read the book to students.

ancient   ancestors   bill   paddles   dense   squabble</td>
</tr>
<tr>
<td>Introduce the objective (How to find and use the evidence)</td>
<td>Making the <u>reading</u> strategic
When you are looking for the main idea, sometimes it is easier to find the details first and then figure out the main idea. Notice lots of details as you read. You could list them on a chart or place a small sticky note on the page to remind you of each detail. When you have finished reading, look over all of your details and decide how they all "add up." What are all of your details mostly about? If you can figure that out, you will have figured out the main idea.</td>
</tr>
</table>

		The best evidence:
DURING READING	**Model and practice finding evidence for the objective**	**Model:** **p. 4:** Platypus ancestors lived when dinosaurs roamed the earth. **p. 6:** The platypus's bill is shaped like a duck's but is soft like leather. It is very sensitive to the touch. **p. 7:** The platypus uses its bill to know when to attach. **p. 8:** The platypus stuffs its food (mussels, shrimp, tadpoles, etc.) into its cheek pouches. **p. 9:** The platypus doesn't have teeth; it crushes its food on grinding pads inside its bill. **p. 9:** The platypus is a mammal, even though it spends its life in the water. It can't breathe under water. **Practice:** **p. 11:** Platypus fur is even denser than polar bear fur, and the platypus cleans it a lot so it stays waterproof. **p. 15:** A platypus has webbed front and hind feet, just like a duck. **p. 16:** A platypus has a spur with venom on each hind leg. It uses this to attack its enemies. **p. 19:** Before giving birth, the female platypus digs a nesting burrow up to 60 feet long and then seals herself inside. **p. 20:** The mother platypus (unlike almost any other mammal) lays eggs. **p. 22:** Platypus babies (pups) finally hatch and slurp milk from their mother's belly. Platypuses don't have nipples like other mammals.
	Model and practice other strategies	**Connecting?** Have you ever seen any animals that you consider "unique?" In what ways were they like the platypus? **Visualizing/Picturing?** What could you really visualize as we read this book? **Wondering?** What else would you still like to know about the platypus? **Predicting/Guessing?** What do you predict might happen to the platypus in the future? Do you think it will continue to survive? Why or why not? **Noticing?** What details did you notice about the platypus that someone else might have missed? Why might they be important? **Figuring out?** In what ways might the platypus be considered an *important* animal?

AFTER READING	**Discussion questions**	**Question related to the objective** **A1-c:** What is the main idea of *The Platypus, Probably*? What details support this main idea? [Something like: A platypus is a very unique mammal with many interesting characteristics.] **Other questions** **B3-b:** Which facts (details) show that a platypus is unlike most other mammals? **C2-b:** Which part of this book was most interesting or surprising to you? Why? **D2-b:** Imagine you are going to give a talk to your class about _____. What two points would you be sure to include in your speech?
	Written response to text	**Making the <u>writing</u> strategic** • See *That's a Great Answer*, p. 59, or *Teaching Written Response*, pp. 81-82, for a template matched to this objective. • Model the response using the template. • Remove your response and ask students to write the response themselves using the template—choosing their own evidence if possible.
	Other follow-up activities	**Oral language, fluency, vocabulary, comprehension, reading extensions, writing extensions** **Oral language/fluency:** Practice reading one or two pages in this book until you sound like an authority on the topic of platypuses. Read these pages to the class, sounding like a world-famous platypus scientist. **Vocabulary:** See *Vocabulary Connections* activity on the CD **Comprehension:** These follow-up activities may be found in *Constructing Meaning through Kid-Friendly Comprehension Strategy Instruction*: Visualize Vocabulary, p. 166; Questions… Questions…Questions, p. 170; Good Questions to Ask, p. 195; I'm a Word Watcher, p. 197 **Reading extensions:** Here are some additional platypus books. • *Platypus* (a Step into Reading book) by Ginjer Clarke • *If My Mom Were a Platypus: Animal Babies and Their Mothers* by Dia Michels • *Platypus* by Joan Short, Jack Green, and Bettina Bird **Writing extensions:** Imagine that you are a platypus. Write about yourself: What do you want people to know about you? Why should they appreciate you? What makes you more special than any other animal?
	Reflect on reading and writing strategy	• How do you go about finding the main idea of a nonfiction text? Which should you identify first, the main idea or the details? Why? • What is difficult about figuring out the main idea in nonfiction reading?

A1-d: What would be another good title for this book?

BOOK

How I Learned Geography by Uri Shulevitz

INTRODUCTION TO THE BOOK

This post-World War II story describes a childhood memory of the author whose family flees Poland after the Warsaw Blitz for the city of Turkestan in central Asia in what is now Kazakhstan. The family has no money and food is scarce. Imagine their disbelief, then, when their father returns from the market and, instead of the bread he was sent to purchase, brings home a map of the world. But the map adds color to an otherwise dreary home, and gazing at the names of all those faraway places mentally transports the author to some of these magical lands where he is able to dream of a happier and more hopeful future.

WHY THIS IS A GOOD BOOK FOR TEACHING THIS OBJECTIVE

This is a great book for this objective because the title of the book, while adequate, and in some ways clever, doesn't really capture the essence of this story. The author does learn a bit about geography as he studies the map. But the map symbolizes a bigger idea students should also appreciate through reading this story: It is important to feed the soul as well as the body. I am always intrigued by the new titles students choose for a story because they are often more creative than anything that occurred to me. (Titles are not exactly my forte; I agonize over the title of every book I write.) One strategy I use in introducing this objective to students is to refrain from telling them initially what the book title is. Then they are more imaginative. When they know the title, that tends to shut down their creativity; their new title doesn't stray far from the one the author has chosen.

OTHER OBJECTIVES THAT MAY BE ADDRESSED BY RE-READING THIS BOOK

- **A2-e:** What is the setting of this story?
- **C1-b:** Make a connection to an important feeling in the story.
- **D2-c:** Using information in the text, write a paragraph that could have appeared in _____'s journal after _____ occurred. (Good points for a journal entry: The night that Father brings the map home; after the map has been on the wall for a while.)
- **D3-a:** What is important to the author? Use details from the text as evidence.

OTHER BOOKS MATCHED TO THIS OBJECTIVE TO LEAD STUDENTS TOWARD INDEPENDENCE (Remember to chart the evidence when you use a picture book so that students may provide specific details from the text)

These stories reveal big ideas that allow for creativity in choosing a new title.

- ***Small Beauties: The Journey of Darcy Heart O'Hara* by Elvira Woodruff**
  This story, as well as the illustrations, will melt your heart. Darcy lives in a small Irish village in 1845 at the height of the Potato Famine. Darcy wasn't so quick to get her chores done, but she was a great *noticer*—a dew-covered spider web, clouds that look like castles, an acorn, a pebble, a butterfly's wing. And she'd carry many of her treasures home in the hem of her skirt. But when the potato blight made it impossible for Darcy's family to pay the rent, they had to leave their beloved Irish homeland for America. Now instead of tiny cottages there were tall buildings and nothing felt like home—that is until Darcy removed all those small beauties from her hem once again—vestiges of the memories her family held most dear. Bring a box of tissues when you read this one! And don't forget to read the author's note at the end of the book—an interesting text-to-world connection. While the title of this book really does capture the big idea of the story, students enjoy trying out their own good titles.

- ***Harvesting Hope: The Story of Cesar Chavez* by Kathleen Krull**
  This is actually a really clever title for this biographical account of the life of Cesar Chavez. Students will probably not be quite as clever, but they should be able to recognize the big idea that emerges in this book: Chavez rose from the humblest of beginnings and fought diligently to improve working conditions not just for himself, but for all migrant farm workers.

- ***Fishing Day* by Andrea Davis Pinkney**
  While the topic of this story is fishing, the message goes much deeper. Reenie, a little African-American girl, and her mama go fishing on the "Jim Crow River" and succeed in catching many fish. Meanwhile, another little boy (Caucasian), who can't seem to catch anything, attempts to ruin Reenie's good time by throwing rocks into the water to frighten the fish away. Reenie takes pity on the boy and helps him catch some fish, too. Attitudes seem to change after that act of kindness. Will students be able to see past the fishing trip to reel in another good title?

SCORING STUDENTS' RESPONSES

 A1-d: What would be another good title for this book?

Score = 2

I think a good title would be Imagining a Better World after World War II. This would be a good title because this book is mainly about how hard it was to have a normal life in that time with no food and bombed out houses. But the map gave the boy hope. He saw the names of places far away and it helped him dream about a happier life.

> (This response would receive full score because it offers a plausible title, references the big idea, and provides specific evidence from the story.)

Score = 1

I think a good title would be Traveling to Places in Your Mind. That is what the boy in the story did when he was sad after the war. His father brought home a map instead of bread.

> (This response would receive partial credit. The title is fine. But the reader doesn't convey any clear connection between the title and the big idea of the story. The detail, while appropriate, is not really connected either.)

Score = 0

I think a good title would be Countries of the World. That's what the boy looked at when he saw the map and he liked the map a lot.

> (This answer is not adequate. The reader does focus on the countries and the map, but why is this title a good one?)

PLANNER FOR SHARED READING

Objective (strategy focus): <u>**A1-d:**</u> <u>What would be another good title for this book?</u>

◎ <u>Decide on a good title for this story.</u>

How will student learning be measured at the end of the lesson? (What will count as "success?")

Text: <u>*How I Learned Geography* by Uri Shulevitz</u>   **Pages:** <u>Whole book</u>

<table>
<tr>
<td rowspan="4" style="writing-mode: vertical-lr">BEFORE READING</td>
<td>Establish prior knowledge, purpose, and predictions</td>
<td>Prior knowledge: What do you know about World War II? What happened to many of the countries in Europe after this war? (Read the author's note on the last page of this book before reading the story in order to build prior knowledge.)
Predictions: (Do not show students the book title or cover prior to reading this story.) Based on what we read in the author's note, what do you expect this story to be about?
Purpose for reading: Today when we read, we will try to decide on a good title for this book. Then I'll show you the title the author chose and you can decide which you like best—yours or the author's.</td>
</tr>
<tr>
<td>Introduce/ review vocabulary</td>
<td>devastate   scarce   triumphantly   apologetically
meager   savored   transported   enchanted</td>
</tr>
<tr>
<td>Introduce the objective (How to find and use the evidence)</td>
<td>Making the <u>reading</u> strategic
When you are deciding on a new title for a book, think about what the text is mainly about as you read. When you finish reading, make sure you can identify the big idea. Ask yourself: Why did the author write this? Once you've figured out the big idea, decide how to capture that idea in a single word or a short phrase. Some ways you can do that are:
<ul>
<li>Use a character's name for the title if the character is really important to the big idea (Shiloh, Frog and Toad).</li>
<li>Use the topic of the text (How to Dig a Hole to the Center of the Earth).</li>
<li>Use a few words that you think capture the big idea (Small Beauties).</li>
<li>Use the name of the place where the story took place if that was really important (Weslandia).</li>
<li>Use a phrase that you found right in the book if you think it sums up the meaning of the story (A Platypus, Probably; Something Beautiful).</li>
</ul></td>
</tr>
</table>

DURING READING	**Model and practice finding evidence for the objective**	**The best evidence:** **Model:** **pp. 1-2:** War devastated the land and people lost everything. **pp. 3-5:** The family moved to a Mideastern country far away and lived in a small, dark room with no books or toys and almost no food. **pp. 9-12:** Father went to the bazaar to buy bread but came home with a map instead. His family was angry. **Practice:** **p. 13:** The map made the room look cheery. **pp. 14-27:** The little boy was transported to many exotic places in his mind, which he really enjoyed. **p. 28:** The child admitted that his father was right after all.
	Model and practice other strategies	**Connecting?** Connect to a place where you would like to be transported in your mind. **Visualizing/Picturing?** Which place described by the boy can you see most vividly in your mind? What do you see? **Wondering?** Wonder what else the father could have brought home from the bazaar. **Predicting/Guessing?** At what point in the story could you predict that the little boy was glad he had the map? **Noticing?** What details did you notice that helped you figure out the big idea of this text? **Figuring out?** (After students have devised their own titles) Figure out why the author might have chosen this title.

AFTER READING	**Discussion questions**	**Question related to the objective** **A1-d:** What would be a good title for this story? **Other questions** **A2-a:** Using information in the story, write a brief description of how the little boy felt when his father returned home from the bazaar with a map instead of bread. **A2-e:** What is the setting of this story? Give details from the story to support your answer. **C2-a:** Which part of the story/article do you think was *most* important? Use information from the story to explain why you chose that part.
	Written response to text	**Making the <u>writing</u> strategic** See *That's a Great Answer*, p. 61, or *Teaching Written Response*, pp. 86-87, for a template matched to this objective. Model the response using the template. Remove your response and ask students to write the response themselves using the template—choosing their own evidence if possible.
	Other follow-up activities	**Oral language, fluency, vocabulary, comprehension, reading extensions, writing extensions** **Oral language/fluency:** Make a list of cities and countries all over the world that have exotic-sounding names. Practice saying these names until you can say them quickly, accurately, and smoothly. **Vocabulary:** See *Vocabulary Connections* activity on the CD **Comprehension:** These follow-up activities may be found in *Constructing Meaning through Kid-Friendly Comprehension Strategy Instruction*: One Word, p. 160; Picture This, p. 164; Reading with All of My Senses, p. 168; A Message from the Author, p. 186. **Reading extensions:** These books all relate to the devastating effects of World War II on the countries of Europe: • *Mercedes and the Chocolate Pilot* by Margot Theis Raven • *One Thousand Tracings: Healing the Wounds of World War II* by Lita Judge • *Boxes for Katje* by Candace Fleming **Writing extensions:** Research a place where you would like to be transported in your mind. Write a paragraph about this place and draw your special place with details that show what you visualize.
	Reflect on reading and writing strategy	• What should you think about as you read if you want to decide on a new title for a book? • What kinds of things can you choose for a new title (character's name, setting, phrase from the book, etc.)

A2-a: Using information in the story, write a brief description of how _____ felt when _____.

BOOK

Heroes by Ken Mochizuki

INTRODUCTION TO THE BOOK

This is a book about racial profiling. The story takes place after World War II and describes a situation between Donnie, a Japanese-American child, and his American friends. Whenever they play war, Donnie is forced to play the "bad guy." He objects, telling his buddies, "My dad was in our army and he fought in Italy and France. And my Uncle Yosh was in Korea." But his friends are not convinced and the tormenting continues. At last Donnie's dad and uncle see for themselves the humiliation Donnie is suffering. They arrive at his school the next day at dismissal time—in full military attire, adorned with many medals. As the story ends, the boys are playing football together. Donnie observes, "This time, they were following me instead of chasing me."

WHY THIS IS A GOOD BOOK FOR TEACHING THIS OBJECTIVE

Many books suitable for elementary readers feature characters' feelings. I chose this one because I believe that we can't remind children often enough about the hurt that results when someone is the victim of discrimination. In this case, the discrimination was racially motivated and mirrors similar profiling issues that we hear about far too frequently through the news media. Look for books that showcase other forms of discrimination, too, such as physical and mental disabilities.

OTHER OBJECTIVES THAT MAY BE ADDRESSED BY RE-READING THIS BOOK

- **A3-a:** Briefly summarize this story.
- **B1-a:** What caused _____ to happen in the story?
- **C2-a:** Which part of the story do you think was *most* important? Use information from the story to explain why you chose that part.
- **D1-e:** Do you think the author made this story believable? Why or why not?

OTHER BOOKS MATCHED TO THIS OBJECTIVE TO LEAD STUDENTS TOWARD INDEPENDENCE (Remember to chart the evidence when you use a picture book so that students may provide specific details from the text)

These books all feature racial/ethnic discrimination and the negative feelings that result:

- ***The Yellow Star: The Legend of King Christian X of Denmark* by Carmen Agra Deedy**
  This is the story of a wise king who diffused Nazi terror in his country by finding a most creative solution to a Nazi order that all of the Jews in Denmark must wear a yellow star. Ever mindful of the feelings of *all* of his people, King Christian's solution was both smart and compassionate.

- ***Sister Anne's Hands* by Marybeth Lorbiecki**
  This story set in the 1960s describes an incident where a student in a parochial school displays overt prejudice against his African American teacher. For the rest of the year, students in this class learn lessons that go way beyond reading and writing as they begin to open their hearts and acknowledge the feelings of people who may look different from themselves.

- ***One Green Apple* by Eve Bunting**
  New to this country from the Mideast. Farah feels like the loan green apple amid a whole bushel of red apples: she just doesn't fit in. At first her classmates seem to thrive on making her feel like an outsider. But gradually her different language, different clothing, and different customs seem less important than the teamwork involved in making cider with other members of her class.

SCORING STUDENTS' RESPONSES

◎ **A2-a:** How did Donnie feel when his friends always made him play "the bad guy" when they played war?

Score = 2

I think Donnie felt humiliated when he always had to be the bad guy. When he and his friends played war, they always made him be the enemy because he was Japanese. That made him feel like he had done something terrible, but he hadn't done anything bad. The kids were thinking that Donnie must be like the people who bombed Pearl Harbor. Donnie finally proved that he didn't deserve this treatment because his father and uncle came to school with medals for fighting in the war with the Americans.

> (This is a great answer because it describes Donnie's feelings with a very specific word and also includes lots of relevant details from the text that support this feeling.)

Score = 1

I think Donnie felt bad when he always had to be the bad guy. His friends played war and they shot him. Donnie's family came from Japan and that's what his friends didn't like.

> (This student has the basic idea right but isn't clear enough about *why* Donnie's friends felt this way based on his Japanese-American heritage. Also, a more precise word than "bad" could have been used to identify Donnie's feelings.

Score = 0

Donny was mad that his friends always made him be the enemy. Then he was happy when his dad and uncle came to school with their army medals.

> (This reader doesn't provide any context for Donnie's feelings—and it's the context that is the whole point of this story: *Why* was Donnie "mad" and then "happy?")

PLANNER FOR SHARED READING

Objective (strategy focus): <u>**A2-a:**</u> <u>Using information in the story, write a brief description of</u> <u>how [   ] felt when [   ].</u>

◎ <u>How did Donnie feel when his friends always made him play "the bad guy" when they</u> <u>played war?</u>
    How will student learning be measured at the end of the lesson? (What will count as "success?")

Text: <u>*Heroes* by Ken Mochizuki</u>   **Pages:** <u>Whole book</u>

<table>
<tr>
<td rowspan="3" style="writing-mode: vertical;">BEFORE READING</td>
<td>Establish prior knowledge, purpose, and predictions</td>
<td>Prior knowledge: What do you know about Japan during World War II? Why were Americans so angry with Japan? What is a hero? How do you become a hero?
Predictions: Based on the title and the cover, what do you think might happen in this story? Who might be a hero?
Purpose for reading: As we read this book, let's think about how the main character is feeling and why he's feeling this way.</td>
</tr>
<tr>
<td>Introduce/ review vocabulary</td>
<td>enemy   medal   commanded   protested   veteran   brag   panic   yanked</td>
</tr>
<tr>
<td>Introduce the objective (How to find and use the evidence)</td>
<td>Making the <u>reading</u> strategic
When you're trying to figure out how a character feels, make sure you find the parts of the text that describe the event that created these feelings: What happened? Notice things that the character said or did or thought that shows how he or she feels. Also look at the pictures, especially at the expression on the character's face. What does the character's expression show about his or her feelings? Think of a specific word to name the feeling. Stay away from overused words like happy and sad.</td>
</tr>
</table>

DURING READING	**Model and practice finding evidence for the objective**	**The best evidence:** **Model** **p. 2:** Kids pretended to shoot at Donnie; stared; wanted his dad to drop him off for school down the street (embarrassed) **p. 3:** Donnie had to be the enemy because he looked like "them." (frustrated) **p. 5:** Friends didn't believe that Donnie's father served in the U.S. army; friend said, "There wasn't anybody looking like you guys on our side." Donnie played with these boys so he would have friends. (frustrated, conflicted) **p. 7:** Donnie knew his dad had been a hero in the war. He had medals. (proud) **Practice:** **p. 11:** Donnie hated being the enemy so much that he hid. **p. 15:** Donnie ran when his friends tried to capture him in the war game. **p. 19:** Donnie cried that he wasn't the bad guy and ran to his dad. **p. 24:** Donny's friends called him *sissy* and *daddy's boy*; chased him down the hall **p. 25:** Donnie's dad and uncle appeared with their army medals and military uniforms and hats. **p. 26:** Now everyone was following Donnie, not chasing him.
	Model and practice other strategies	**Connecting?** Have you ever felt discriminated against for any reason? Explain. Can you make any text-to-world connections about stories you've heard in the news about racial profiling? **Visualizing/Picturing?** What words did the author use to help you picture the boys playing war? **Wondering?** Consider why the author wrote this book? **Predicting/Guessing?** Predict what might happen if the author added another page. **Noticing?** What details did you notice that were examples of prejudice? **Figuring out?** Why do you think Donnie's friends reacted to him the way they did? How could this have been avoided?

	Discussion questions	**Question related to the objective** **A2-a:** How did Donnie feel when his friends always made him play "the bad guy" when they played war? **Other questions** **A3-a:** Briefly summarize this story. **B2-a:** Why does the author include the last line of the story, "This time they were following me instead of chasing me"? **D2-c:** Using information in the text, write a paragraph that could have appeared in Donnie's journal after his friends chased him back to his dad's garage. **D3-a:** What do you think was important to the author? Why did he write this book?
	Written response to text	**Making the <u>writing</u> strategic** • See *That's a Great Answer*, p. 63, for a template matched to this objective. • Model the response using the template. • Remove your response and ask students to write the response themselves using the template, preferably using a different word to describe Donnie's feelings and different evidence from the book.
	Other follow-up activities	**Oral language, fluency, vocabulary, comprehension, reading extensions, writing extensions** **Oral language/fluency:** Practice reading a page with dialogue (different speakers) and sound effects ("rat-a-tat-tat" and "pow" for guns). **Vocabulary:** See *Vocabulary Connections* activity on the CD **Comprehension:** These follow-up activities may be found in *Constructing Meaning through Kid-Friendly Comprehension Strategy Instruction*: Active Reader Report, p. 155; I'm Connected, p. 159; Important Words, p. 180. **Reading extensions:** These books all focus on Japanese-Americans following World War II: • *Baseball Saved Us* by Ken Mochizuki • *Passage to Freedom: The Sugihara Story* by Ken Mochizuki • *The Bracelet* by Yoshiko Uchida **Writing extensions:** This story describes a practice called "racial profiling." That means that some people make decisions about the kind of person you are based on what they *think* they know about other people of that race. Write an essay about why you think racial profiling is dangerous and hurtful. Be sure to include a main idea statement, three reasons, and plenty of details.
	Reflect on reading and writing strategy	• How do we identify characters' feelings in a story? • Why is it important to think about how a character feels?

A2-b: What is _____'s main problem in the story? Use evidence from the story to support your answer.

BOOK

Melissa Parkington's Beautiful, Beautiful Hair by Pat Brisson

INTRODUCTION TO THE BOOK

This is the story of a little girl who has always been known for her beautiful hair. Although she has enjoyed the attention she received for her hair when she was younger, she decides she would like to be known for something other than "something that just grew out of her head." She attempts to be come a great athlete and then a great artist—but doesn't succeed at either. She then decides she will be extra kind to people. This is somewhat gratifying—that is, until she visits the mall with her mother one day. She passes a beauty salon with a sign in the window that says "Share Your Hair." Right then she decides that she will donate her hair to a needy child so that someone else may enjoy her beautiful, beautiful hair. There is a touching ending to this story as Melissa's father puts her to bed the night after her hair has been cut.

WHY THIS IS A GOOD BOOK FOR TEACHING THIS OBJECTIVE

This is a good book for introducing this objective because the problem is very clear and is repeated over and over throughout the beginning of the story. Also, the text is a fairly simple one and is appropriate for students in the lower intermediate grades where this objective is often addressed. I have even taught this lesson in several second grades with much success.

OTHER OBJECTIVES THAT MAY BE ADDRESSED BY RE-READING THIS BOOK

- **A3-a:** Briefly summarize this story.
- **B3-a:** Prove that the character was very [kind]. Use evidence from the story for support.
- **Dc-c:** Using information in the text, write a paragraph that could have appeared in [Melissa's] journal after [she got her hair cut].

OTHER BOOKS MATCHED TO THIS OBJECTIVE TO LEAD STUDENTS TOWARD INDEPENDENCE (Remember to chart the evidence when you use a picture book so that students may provide specific details from the text)

These stories all have clearly defined problems that are relatively easy for students to identify:

- *My Rows and Piles of Coins* **by Tololwa Mollel**
  This story set in Tanzania is about a little boy who dreams of owning a bicycle so he can help his mother carry goods to market. Although he saves "rows and piles" of coins, the problem is that he never has quite enough money to purchase the bicycle he longs for. When his father buys a motor bike, he offers to sell his son his old bike—for exactly the amount of money the boy has saved. But then the father returns the money as a reward for all the help the little boy offers his family.

- *Boxes for Katje* **by Candace Fleming**
  Katje's village in Holland has been destroyed by World War II and now her family is very poor with little food or clothing. Across the ocean in America, a little girl in Indiana sends a goodwill package to ease the suffering in Europe and Katje receives that package. A beautiful friendship grows from this act of kindness as many more boxes and letters traverse the Atlantic. This story is based on true experiences and shows how even one little child can help to solve a big problem.

- *The Story of Ruby Bridges* **by Robert Coles**
  The problem is that schools in the South in 1960 are segregated, and Ruby Bridges is the first African-American child to enter the William Frantz Elementary School in New Orleans. Ruby is the target of much discrimination and many hostile acts, all signs that this problem is extreme. The afterword on the final page of the book contains information about Ruby's life after her first difficult days in a desegregated school—a resolution of sorts.

SCORING STUDENTS' RESPONSES

◎ What is Melissa's main problem in this story? Use details from the story to support your answer.

Score = 2

Melissa's main problem was that she wanted to do something spectacular and she wanted something better than gorgeous hair. First she tried being an artist or an athlete, but she wasn't spectacular at those things, so that didn't solve her problem. Eventually she donated her hair so that a sick child could have beautiful hair and that made her feel good inside, and her problem was solved.

> (This response would receive the full score because it identifies both the problem and the failed attempts to solve the problem. It also indicates the solution, which is not really necessary, but does provide nice closure.)

Score = 1

Melissa wanted to get her hair cut so that a sick child could have pretty hair. That was very nice of her and that solved her problem.

> (This response shows some understanding of the problem but not the circumstances that led Melissa to donate her hair. In this case, the "back story"—Melissa's desire to do something spectacular—is critical to recognizing the essence of the problem.)

Score = 0

Melissa' problem is that she tried to be an artist or an athlete, but she wasn't good at those things. Then she got her hair cut and gave it away.

> (It is questionable whether this reader has understood the story. The problem was not that Melissa wasn't a good artist or athlete, but that her ability in these areas didn't address her problem: being spectacular. Also, this reader doesn't seem to make the connection between Melissa's initial problem and the reason she got her hair cut.)

PLANNER FOR SHARED READING

Objective (strategy focus): <u>A2-b:</u> <u>What is [   ]'s main problem in the story? Use evidence from the story to support your answer.</u>

◎ <u>What is Melissa's main problem in this story? Use evidence from the story to support your answer.</u>
      (How will student learning be measured at the end of the lesson? (What will count as "success?")

Text: <u>*Melissa Parkington's Beautiful, Beautiful Hair* by Pat Brisson</u>   **Pages:** <u>whole book</u>

<table>
<tr>
<td rowspan="3">BEFORE READING</td>
<td>Establish prior knowledge, purpose, and predictions</td>
<td>Prior knowledge: What makes someone "spectacular" (or fabulous)?
Predictions: Based on the title and the cover, what do you think this story will be about?
Purpose for reading: Today when we read, we're going to look for the main problem that the character faces.</td>
</tr>
<tr>
<td>Introduce/ review vocabulary</td>
<td>gorgeous   stunning   spectacular   fabulous   donate salon</td>
</tr>
<tr>
<td>Introduce the objective (How to find and use the evidence)</td>
<td>Making the <u>reading</u> strategic
The problem in a story is something that someone wants to change. It is usually explained close to the beginning of the story, unless the author wants you to know what life was like before the problem happened. Sometimes the author needs to give you some information first so that you will understand more about the problem. After you see what the problem is, then read to find evidence that it is still a problem. The problem in a story almost never gets solved right away.</td>
</tr>
</table>

DURING READING	**Model and practice the focus strategy**	**The best evidence:** **Model:** **pp. 1-3:** Everyone loves Melissa's hair. (This is what life was like for Melissa *before* the problem.) **p. 4:** Melissa wanted people to notice her for something she *did*, not just for her pretty hair. (This is the problem!) **pp. 5-12:** Melissa tried to get good at basketball and art but didn't succeed. (The problem isn't solved yet.) **Practice:** **pp. 14-20:** Melissa decided to be kind to everyone. (This made her feel a little better, but didn't solve the problem completely.) **pp. 21-26:** Melissa decided to have her hair cut to give it to a child who needed hair. She was willing to give away something special to her in order to make someone else happy. (This solved her problem.)
	Model and practice other strategies	**Connecting?** Any connection to someone who gave away something they prized to help someone else? **Visualizing/Picturing?** Which scene from this story could you picture even if there were not pictures on the page? **Wondering?** Wonder about what you could do to be kind in the way Melissa was kind. **Predicting/Guessing?** Predict the reaction of Melissa's classmates when she goes to school the next day. **Noticing?** What did you notice about Melissa as a person? **Figuring out?** How would you describe Melissa? Choose a word.

AFTER READING	**Discussion questions**	**Follow-up to objective:** **A2-b:** What was Melissa's problem in this story? Use evidence from the story to support your answer. **Other questions:** **C1-c:** Would you like Melissa for a friend? Why? **B-2a:** Why did the author include the part about art and basketball in this story? **D-3a:** What do you think was important to this author? What does she value?
	Written response to text	**Making the <u>writing</u> strategic** • See *That's a Great Answer*, p. 66, or *Teaching Written Response*, pp. 61-62, for a template matched to this objective. • Model the response using the template. • Remove your response and ask students to write the response themselves using the template—choosing their own evidence if possible.
	Other follow-up activities	**Oral language, fluency, vocabulary, comprehension, reading extensions, writing extensions** **Oral language/fluency:** The part of the story where Melissa decides to get her hair cut is very important and should be read with great expression. Practice reading this part (see excerpt on the CD) until your voice shows lots of emotion. **Vocabulary:** See *Vocabulary Connections* activity on the CD **Comprehension:** These follow-up activities may be found in *Constructing Meaning through Kid-FriendlyComprehension Strategy Instruction*: I Have a Connection, p. 158; Friends I Might Have Known, p. 12; Picture This, p. 164; Character Study, p. 185. **Reading extensions:** The following books also demonstrate a character's generosity: • *Thank You, Mr. Falker* by Patricia Polacco • *The Paper Crane* by Molly Bang • *One Thousand Tracings: Healing the Wounds of World War II* by Lita Judge **Writing extensions:** Make a list of things you could donate or give to someone that would make their life happier. What would you give? Who would you give it to? How would your gift make this person's life better? But there's a catch: Whatever you give can't cost anything!
	Reflect on reading and writing strategy	• Where do you usually find the problem in a story? • How do you decide what the problem is? • What kind of evidence do you look for as you read?

OBJECTIVE

A2-c: How did _____ solve his/her problem?

BOOK

Planting the Trees of Kenya: The Story of Wangari Maathai by Claire Nivola

INTRODUCTION TO THE BOOK

This is the story of Wangari Maathai, winner of the 2004 Nobel Peace Prize, who changed the fate of her land by teaching the citizens of Kenya to care for it. After spending five years in America to attend college, Maathai returned to Kenya to discover that the beautiful trees and former way of life in her country had disappeared. Devastated, she wondered how she alone could bring back the trees and restore the gardens and the people. This inspiring story describes how the determination and resourcefulness of even one person can solve a big problem!

WHY THIS IS A GOOD BOOK FOR TEACHING THIS OBJECTIVE

Nearly all stories offer up some kind of problem that needs to be solved. But this is the story of a *real* person who solves a *real* problem. Hopefully, Wangari Maathai's mission to replant the trees of Kenya will help students recognize their own potential to bring about change—not necessarily on the grand scale described in this story but at least within the context of their own lives.

OTHER OBJECTIVES THAT MAY BE ADDRESSED BY RE-READING THIS BOOK

*   **A1-c:** What is the main idea of this story?
*   **B1-b:** What happened at the beginning, middle, and end of this story?
*   **C2-b:** Which part of the story was the most interesting or surprising to you?
*   **D3-a:** What is important to the main character? Find evidence to support your answer.

OTHER BOOKS MATCHED TO THIS OBJECTIVE TO LEAD STUDENTS TOWARD INDEPENDENCE (Remember to chart the evidence when you use a picture book so that students may provide specific details from the text)

These books describe how "everyday people" have solved real-life problems—sometimes with a bit of help.

*   *How I Learned Geography* by Uri Shulevitz
    The real-life problem in this book is personal poverty, and it is overcome by the power of the imagination. The result: Hope prevails as the soul is nourished.

- *One Hen: How One Small Loan Made a Big Difference* by Katie Smith Milway
  A little boy from Ghana turns a small loan into a thriving farm and substantial income. He buys a single hen and, a year later, has twenty-five hens. His business grows from there. This book is a great example of how a little help can make a big difference.

- *Beatrice's Goat* by Page McBrier
  A very poor family in Africa begins to thrive after receiving the gift of a goat from Heifer Project International. For Beatrice, the new goat in the family means not only more milk for her and her siblings to drink, but as baby goats are born and then sold to other villagers, Beatrice is able to achieve her dream of attending school. Her family then moves to a sturdier home. This is the story of how one small gift transforms a family and their future.

SCORING STUDENTS' RESPONSES

 In this story, how did Wangari Maathai solve her problem?

Score = 2

In this story, Wangari Maathai solved the problem of the destruction of trees in Kenya by teaching the people of her country the importance of trees to their lives and their land, and by teaching them to plant trees themselves. She taught this to women, children, soldiers, and even prisoners. She was able to solve her problem because of her great determination. She didn't give up.

> (This response would receive a full score because it correctly identifies the problem and the solution and clarifies *how* the problem was solved—both the actions and the attitudes of the problem-solver.)

Score = 1

In this story, Wangari Maathai solved her problem by teaching the people of Kenya to plant trees. This made the land more beautiful.

> (This response would receive partial credit because it is basically correct. However, the trees served a greater purpose than just making the land "more beautiful." Also, there is no elaboration here as to the specifics of how Wangari solved her problem.)

Score = 0

In this story, some people came and chopped down all of the trees in Kenya and the land looked awful and people had to buy food at the grocery store and they couldn't afford it and a lady was shocked when she came home from college and she could hardly believe her eyes.

> (Aside from the very disjointed nature of this response, it only addresses the problem, making no mention of the solution. This student may have understood the solution but got so sidetracked by the details of the problem that the intent of the response was lost.)

PLANNER FOR SHARED READING

Objective (strategy focus): <u>A2-c</u>: How did [   ] solve his/her problem?

◎ <u>In this story, how did Wangari Maathai solve her problem?</u>
How will student learning be measured at the end of the lesson? (What will count as "success?")

Text: _Planting the Trees of Kenya: The Story of Wangari Maathai_   **Pages:** <u>Whole book</u>

BEFORE READING	**Establish prior knowledge, purpose, and predictions**	**Prior knowledge:** Where is Kenya? (Find this on a map; discuss a few basic facts about this country which you can access via an Internet site). Think of people you know (or know about) who have made a difference to our world by helping to solve a problem. (Students might mention Martin Luther King, Jr.). What character traits are useful for solving problems? **Predictions:** Look at the title and cover of this book. What problem do you predict will need to be solved? **Purpose for reading:** This is a story about a woman named Wangari Maathai. As we read it, let's see what she did to solve the problem she faced.
	Introduce/ review vocabulary	sacred native landscape export topsoil urged
	Introduce the objective (How to find and use the evidence)	**Making the <u>reading</u> strategic** Look for the problem toward the beginning of the story. However, sometimes a story begins with a description of the way things were before the problem occurred. Once you've noticed the problem, find evidence that shows _why_ this problem is serious. Then notice how the problem gets solved. Who solves it? What actions help to resolve the problem? What personal traits of the character contributed to the problem's solution?

DURING READING	**Model and practice finding evidence for the objective**	**The best evidence:** **Model:** **pp. 1-6:** Evidence of the way things were before the problem: the beauty of Kenya with so many trees **pp. 7-8:** THE PROBLEM: Trees had been cut down, which ruined the land and led to sickness and poverty **p. 9:** The land without trees was as barren as a desert **p. 12:** No shade, no topsoil, dirty streams and rivers **p. 13:** Wangari helps people recognize that they are part of the problem—and could be part of the solution **Practice:** **p. 16:** Begins to plant trees and teaches others to plant trees **p. 18:** The difficulties Wangari encountered—but she didn't give up **pp. 19-20:** More problems—and perseverance **p. 21:** "Everyday people" making a difference **p. 24:** Gave seedlings to schools **p. 25:** Gave seedlings to inmates and soldiers **pp. 27-28:** The results—30 years later
	Model and practice other strategies	**Connecting?** Connect to a problem you helped to solve that made a real difference to yourself or someone else. **Visualizing/Picturing?** What do you picture in your mind that gives you a sense of the problem in this story? **Wondering?** Wonder about the personal qualities that made it possible for one little person to make such a big difference. **Predicting/Guessing?** At what point in this story were you able to predict how Wangari would solve her problem? **Noticing?** Notice the evidence of the severity of this problem. (What were some of the results of having fewer trees?) **Figuring out?** Figure out what is important to Wangari. Figure out why the author wrote this book.

	Discussion questions	**Question related to the objective** **A2-c:** How did Wangari Maatthai solve the problem in this story? **Other questions** **C1-a:** You may not have been to Kenya, but that is not important to making a meaningful connection to this story. What do you think the author wants you to connect to? Make a connection to something that you consider important to this story. **C2-b:** Which part of this story was the most interesting or surprising to you? **D1-d:** The author uses personification as she describes Kenya at the beginning and end of this story. Find the personification, and explain why the author personifies the land in this way. What is she trying to show?
	Written response to text	**Making the <u>writing</u> strategic** • See *That's a Great Answer*, p. 67, for a template matched to this objective. • Model the response using the template. • Remove your response and ask students to write the response themselves using the template—choosing their own evidence if possible.
	Other follow-up activities	**Oral language, fluency, vocabulary, comprehension, reading extensions, writing extensions** **Oral language/fluency:** Write and give a speech that Wangari Maathai might have delivered to the people of Kenya about the devastating effects of cutting down the trees—and what they could all do to help to solve the problem. **Vocabulary:** See *Vocabulary Connections* activity on the CD. **Comprehension:** *Constructing Meaning*: One Word, p. 160; What's in a Picture, p. 165; A Message from the Author, p. 186. Good Question to Ask, p. 195. **Reading extensions:** These books all feature people who made a difference: • *Martin's Big Words: The Life of Dr. Martin Luther King, Jr.* by Doreen Rappaport • *Mandela: From the Life of the South African Statesman* by Floyd Cooper • *Harvesting Hope: The Story of Cesar Chavez* by Kathleen Krull **Writing extensions:** This is a quote from Wangari Maathai: "We need to promote development that does not destroy our environment." Make a list of at least five ways that we can develop our world in a "green way" that does not destroy our natural resources. Turn your list into a poster and illustrate it.
	Reflect on reading and writing strategy	• When you look for the solution to a problem in a story, what should you try to identify (actions that resolved the problem, relevant character traits)? • Is there always a solution to a problem in a story? Why does an author sometimes not make the solution clear?

OBJECTIVE

A2-d: How did _____ change from the beginning to the end of the story?

BOOK

The Raft by Jim LaMarche

INTRODUCTION TO THE BOOK

In this story, Nicky goes to visit his grandma for the summer, and he is *not* looking forward to the experience: Grandma lives deep in the woods and is a self-proclaimed "river rat" who doesn't even own a TV! What will Nicky do with himself day after day? At first he regards this fate as tortuous, but ever so slowly, his feelings change—toward both Grandma and life in the woods. And he discovers some things about himself along the way. Beautiful watercolor illustrations add a magical element to this beautiful story of the joy that can be found in the simple things in life.

WHY THIS IS A GOOD BOOK FOR TEACHING THIS OBJECTIVE

I like this book for teaching about how a character changes because the change does not happen all at once with a spectacular event that jolts the character into a state of hyper-awareness about the error of his former ways. Instead, the change is gradual, gently nudging the character toward a more complete sense of self—the way real change more typically happens for a person. While most children won't be able to relate directly to Nick's newfound life as a child of the river, they will have fun imagining themselves in this virtual Huck Finn role.

OTHER OBJECTIVES THAT MAY BE ADDRESSED BY RE-READING THIS BOOK

- **A1-d:** What would be another good title for this story?
- **B2-a:** Why did the author include the paragraph on p. 5 about the appearance of the living room? What did he want the reader to know and understand?
- **C1d:** Using information from the story, explain whether or not you would have wanted to be Nicky spending the summer with Grandma.
- **D2-c:** Write a paragraph that Nicky might have written in his journal a) the night he arrived at Grandma's, or b) the night before he returned home from Grandma's.

OTHER BOOKS MATCHED TO THIS OBJECTIVE TO LEAD STUDENTS TOWARD INDEPENDENCE (Remember to chart the evidence when you use a picture book so that students may provide specific details from the text)

- *A Picnic in October* by Eve Bunting
  This is the story of a family that expresses its patriotism by picnicking at the base of the Statue of Liberty once each year. At first, the children in the family think this is strange, indeed, but grow to respect the tradition as they reflect on what America means to them.

- *Something Beautiful* by Sharon Dennis Wyeth
  This powerful story describes a young girl's search for "something beautiful" in her urban neighborhood where "beauty" is difficult to find amid homeless people asleep in cardboard boxes, graffiti scrawled on doorways, and alleys laden with trash. But this girl looks more deeply and does find the beauty she seeks—in such traditions as a game of double-dutch, and in the smile of her baby cousin. By the story's end, a sense of empowerment has replaced powerlessness.

- *Owen & Mzee* by Isabella Hatkoff, Craig Hatkoff, and Dr. Paula Kahumbu
  This is the true story of a growing friendship between a baby hippo named Owen and a giant tortoise named Mzee. When a tsunami separated the little hippo from his mother, he was initially very angry and hard to manage. But once Owen arrived at the animal shelter in Kenya and met the old turtle, things began to change. Over time, the two animals became inseparable. Although this is a story about animals, its message about how friendship develops extends well beyond the animal world.

SCORING STUDENTS' RESPONSES

 A2-d: Explain how Nicky changed from the beginning to the end of the story.

Score = 2

At the beginning of the story, Nicky was grumpy about spending the whole summer at his grandmother's house by the river. He didn't think there would be anything fun to do. Then he discovered an old raft and with it, he explored the river, learned to fish, found out about animals of the forest, and he even carved some sketches of animals into the wood of the raft. By the end of the story, he had become a river rat like his grandma. He now thought his grandma was cool, and he loved living near the river.

> (This answer would receive a score of 2 because it is very specific about the details in the text that caused Nicky to change. It shows how the character's feelings change over time.)

Score = 1

At the beginning of the story, Nicky didn't like the river or his grandmother. By the end of the story, he changed his mind. He didn't want to leave the river to go home, and he thought his grandmother was nice.

> (This score would receive a score of 1 because it basically identifies the character's changed thinking. But it doesn't elaborate on why the character changed or give examples from the text that show the change.)

Score = 0

Nicky was a boy who went to his grandmother's house at the river. He learned to fish and he drew some animals on the raft.

> (This answer would receive a score of 0 because it just very generally summarizes the story. There is no attempt at describing how the character changed.)

PLANNER FOR SHARED READING

Objective (strategy focus): <u>A2-d:</u> <u>How did the character change from the beginning to the end of the story?</u>

 <u>Explain how Nicky changed from the beginning to the end of the story.</u>
How will student learning be measured at the end of the lesson? (What will count as "success?")

Text: <u>*The Raft* by Jim LaMarche</u>   **Pages:** <u>Whole book*</u>

*It might take more than one day to read this book.

<table>
<tr>
<td rowspan="3" style="writing-mode:vertical">BEFORE READING</td>
<td>Establish prior knowledge, purpose, and predictions</td>
<td>Prior knowledge: What is a raft? Have you ever been to a river? Tell what it was like. Did you ever meet someone who you didn't like at first, but then you figured out the person was really nice?
Predictions: Based on the title and the cover illustration, what do you think this story might be about?
Purpose for reading: As we read this story, think about how Nicky changes.</td>
</tr>
<tr>
<td>Introduce/ review vocabulary</td>
<td>chuckled   scattered   cluttered   sketches   hovering   drifted   chores</td>
</tr>
<tr>
<td>Introduce the objective (How to find and use the evidence)</td>
<td>Making the <u>reading</u> strategic
Pay special attention to the way this character is acting at the beginning of the story. Find places where the author *shows* what this character thinks at first. Read carefully to notice where the character's thinking begins to change. Keep looking for small signs of change. How does the character act at the end of the story? Look for the *most* change close to the end of the book.</td>
</tr>
</table>

DURING READING	**Model and practice the focus strategy**	**The best evidence:** **Model:** (Negative feelings) **p. 1:** Nicky complained about going to Grandma's—no TV; tears started again; no kids there **p. 4:** Sad expression on Nicky's face **p. 5:** Comment about grandma having eyes in the back of her head **p. 7:** No fish in this stupid river (Beginning to change) **p. 10:** Interested in the raft he found **Practice:** **p. 11:** Spent all evening with the raft (more interest) **p. 14:** Nicky and Grandma spent the day on the raft (also look at facial expressions). **p. 15:** Interested in all of the river animals **p. 17:** Slept on the raft; wanted to draw pictures of the animals **p. 19:** Showed sketches to Grandma—respected her opinion **p. 23:** Nicky and Grandma went swimming together (enjoyed each other). **p. 28:** Saved a fawn **p. 31:** Painted fawn on raft—to leave his mark on the river; said, "Just like you, Grandma…a river rat." (changed mind about river *and* Grandma)
	Model and practice other strategies	**Connecting?** Any personal experiences that were similar to Nicky's? How were your feelings like his? **Visualizing/Picturing?** What words does the author use that really help you picture Grandma? The river? The raft? **Wondering?** How did the raft magically appear? How did those drawings get on the raft? **Predicting/Guessing?** Do you think Nicky will return to Grandma's next year? Explain. **Noticing?** Notice how Grandma helped Nicky have fun—without really saying anything to him. **Figuring out?** What was responsible for Nicky's changed feelings?

AFTER READING	**Discussion questions**	**Question related to the objective:** **A2-d:** Explain how Nicky changed from the beginning to the end of the story. **Other questions** **A1-d:** What would be another good title for this story? **C2-a:** Which part of this story do you think was most important? Why? **D3-a:** How can you tell that the river was important to Grandma?
	Written response to text	**Making the <u>writing</u> strategic** • See *That's a Great Answer*, p. 69, or *Teaching Written Response*, pp. 90-91, for a template matched to this objective. • Model the response using the template. • Remove your response and ask students to write the response themselves using the template—choosing their own evidence if possible.
	Other follow-up activities	**Oral language, fluency, vocabulary, comprehension, word work, reading extensions, writing extensions** **Fluency:** Select a page where Nicky and/or Grandma speaks. Practice reading that page until you have just the right tone of voice so that you show the meaning of the passage not just by *what* you say, but by *how* you say it. **Vocabulary:** See *Vocabulary Connections* activity for this book on the CD. **Comprehension:** These follow-up activities may be found in *Constructing Meaning through Kid-Friendly Strategy Instruction*: I Have a Connection, p. 158; Picture This, p. 164; Prove It!, p. 174; Character Study, p. 185. **Reading extensions:** These books focus on a character's connection with a river: • *River Boy: The Story of Mark Twain* by William Anderson • *Minn of the Mississippi* by Holling C. Holling • *Letting Swift River Go* by Jane Yolen • *A River Ran Wild: An Environmental History* by Lynne Cherry **Writing extensions:** Pretend you are Nicky. Write a letter to Grandma after you return home, telling her how much you enjoyed your visit. Be specific!
	Reflect on reading and writing strategy	• When you are looking for how a character changes, what do you do? • Why is it important to understand how a character changes throughout a story? • By thinking about how a character changes, how might that help you as a person?

A2-e: What is the setting of this story?

BOOK

Momma, Where Are You From? By Marie Bradby

INTRODUCTION TO THE BOOK

This book describes not just a place in time, but a place within the heart. As her daughter asks, "Momma, where are you from?" the mother replies with a series of poetic reminiscences that describe images from her childhood: "I'm from Monday mornings, washing loads of clothes in the wringer washer…." "It's where the school bus took my older brothers and sisters way across town past school. . . . after school. . . . until it came to a school where all the children were brown. . . . ." Although the exact time is not specified, the story appears to unfold in the pre-Civil Rights South as evidenced by examples such as that above, of segregation and discrimination. More important to the message of this book, however, is that this setting among family and community is one of abiding love.

WHY THIS IS A GOOD BOOK FOR TEACHING THIS OBJECTIVE

I'm not sure which I love more in this book: the simple, poetic text that evokes so many inspiring images—or Chris Soentpiet's magnificent paintings on each page, that for me, depict perfectly the tone that the author intended. This book is a perfect example from both author and illustrator of how the right words and pictures create for the reader not just the time and place of a setting, but also its mood. That's why this book is a good one for teaching readers about setting—and a good book for teaching writers how to develop a setting in their own writing.

OTHER OBJECTIVES THAT MAY BE ADDRESSED BY RE-READING THIS BOOK

- **A1-b:** What is the theme of this story?
- **C1-d:** Would you want to "come from" where Momma came from? Why or why not?
- **D3-b:** How are your customs different from the customs described in this story?

OTHER BOOKS MATCHED TO THIS OBJECTIVE TO LEAD STUDENTS TOWARD INDEPENDENCE (Remember to chart the evidence when you use a picture book so that students may provide specific details from the text)

Like the "Momma" book, the texts below describe experiences that characters endured because of the time and place where the story occurred. The goal is not just to have students recognize elements of the setting, but to understand that the events they describe probably would not have happened, or would have happened differently, if the story had been set somewhere else, or at another time.

- *Henry's Freedom Box* by Ellen Levine
  This is a true story of a slave who mailed himself to freedom.

- *The Cats in Krasinski Square* by Karen Hesse
  This Holocaust story features a young girl who hatches a plan to foil the Gestapo by setting free dozens of wild cats in Krasinski Square just as the Gestapo are attempting to stop a group of children from smuggling food and other supplies into the Warsaw Ghetto.

- *Baseball Saved Us* by Ken Mochizuki
  A group of Japanese-American children learn to survive the perils of their internment camp following World War II by involving themselves with the game of baseball.

SCORING STUDENTS' RESPONSES

 A2-e: Tell about the setting of *Momma, Where Are You From?*

Score = 2

This story is set a long time ago in the South, probably before Martin Luther King. You can tell that because black and white children are not allowed to go to school together. In this setting a long time ago, life was different. For example, a fish man used to drive by in his wagon to sell fish. There was an ice man, too. The most important thing about this setting is that there was a lot of love. Families got together and had big parties with food and dancing. You could tell by the looks on their faces, that everyone was having fun.

> (This answer would receive a score of two because it shows an understanding of both time and place with specific examples of each. It also includes the tone or mood created by the setting.)

Score = 1

This story takes place a long time ago when people had old fashioned furniture and they wore old fashioned clothes. But the people still had fun.

> (This answer is generally correct, but lacks the specifics that would have made it eligible for full credit.)

Score = 0

This story is about a girl and her mom and the girl asks her mom where she comes from and the mom tells her.

> (This response would receive a 0 because it doesn't describe the setting at all. You get the sense that this student might *know* something about the setting, but no information is provided.)

PLANNER FOR SHARED READING

Objective (strategy focus): <u>A2-e:</u> <u>What is the setting of this story?</u>

 <u>Tell about the setting of *Momma, Where Are You From?*</u>

How will student learning be measured at the end of the lesson? (What will count as "success?")

Text: <u>*Momma, Where Are You From* by Marie Bradby</u>   **Pages:** <u>Whole book</u>

<table>
<tr>
<td rowspan="3" style="vertical-align:middle">BEFORE READING</td>
<td>Establish prior knowledge, purpose, and predictions</td>
<td>Prior knowledge: Where is your family from? (Students may give you the name of a country, or possibly a town or city in your state.) Do your parents ever talk about where they were from? Did they like living there? How can you tell?

Predictions: By looking at the cover and a few pages in the book, do you have any predictions about when this story takes place? Do you think it is happening now, or something that happened a while ago? Why? By looking at expressions on people's faces, would you say the people look happy or sad?

Purpose for reading: As we read, we will think about the setting of this story. We'll look for specific details that show this setting and we'll try to figure out how the characters in the story feel about this setting.</td>
</tr>
<tr>
<td>Introduce/ review vocabulary</td>
<td>bleaching   wring   simmer   stash   sprinkled</td>
</tr>
<tr>
<td>Introduce the objective (How to find and use the evidence)</td>
<td>Making the <u>reading</u> strategic:
Where and when a story takes place is called its setting. In most stories, the author gives you information about the setting right at the beginning of the story, so be sure to look there for details that show something about where and when the story is taking place. Also try to figure out how the characters feel about the setting. You can tell that by the things they say, and even by the illustrations. (Look at the expressions on their faces.) In some stories the setting is very important and really helps you understand the story. In other stories, the setting isn't a big deal; the story really could take place anywhere. Think about stories that you know: What is the setting? Think of a story where the setting is important. Think of a story where the setting isn't too important.</td>
</tr>
</table>

		The best evidence:
DURING READING	**Model and practice the focus strategy**	**Model:** **pp. 3-4:** clothes on clothes line; wringer washer; peach basket full of laundry; wash board **pp. 5-6:** shelled beans; old fashioned stove; clothing **pp. 7-12:** peddlers with horse-drawn wagon selling fish, rags, ice **Practice:** **pp. 15-16:** being neighborly **pp. 17-18:** old fashioned school with pot-belly stove; segregation **pp. 19-20:** simple outdoor games; signs of discrimination—cleaning houses, no sidewalks, different schools **pp. 21-22:** chores—starching/ironing clothes **pp. 23-26:** family parties with lots of food and dancing **pp. 27-28:** black and white collage of happy memories; sounded so good, daughter wanted to "go there," too.
	Model and practice other strategies	**Connecting?** If someone asked you where you were "from," how would you answer in a manner similar to the little girl in this story? **Visualizing/Picturing?** The illustrator creates such vivid pictures you can practically picture yourself in this setting. What other senses help you to feel like you are part of this scene: What do you hear? Taste? Smell? **Wondering?** Did you ever wonder what it would be like to live in a different setting? Where? What do you think it might be like? **Predicting/Guessing?** If you asked your parent where they were from, how do you predict they would respond? **Noticing?** What details do you notice in this book that give you a really good idea of this setting? **Figuring out?** What can you figure out about this setting beyond what the author specifically tells you or shows you?

AFTER READING	**Discussion questions**	**Questions related to the objective** **A2-e:** What is the setting of this story? **Other questions:** **B1-d:** Find two parts of this story that could be considered a *description*. What makes these parts a *description*? **B2-a:** Why does the author include the black and white collage at the end of the book? **C2-b:** Which part of this story was the most interesting or surprising to you? **D1-b:** On p. 16, the author says, "Where families grew into a neighborhood as close as a knit sweater." Why does the author use this simile? What does she mean?
	Written response to text	**Making the <u>writing</u> strategic** • See *That's a Great Answer*, p. 72, or *Teaching Written Response*, pp. 47-48, for a template matched to this objective. • Model the response using the template. • Remove your response and ask students to write the response themselves using the template—choosing their own evidence if possible.
	Other follow-up activities	**Oral language, fluency, vocabulary, comprehension, reading extensions, writing extensions** **Oral language:** Interview someone older than you. It could be a grandparent, parent, aunt, uncle, or friend. Ask where the person is from. Be sure to ask for details so you can picture the setting in your mind. Take some notes and tell your classmates about this setting. **Vocabulary:** See *Vocabulary Connections* activity for this book on the CD. **Comprehension:** These follow-up activities may be found in *Constructing Meaning through Kid-Friendly Strategy Instruction*: Connecting to Time and Place, p. 161; What's in a Picture, p. 165. **Reading extension:** The setting of the stories below is very important to the story. Identify significant aspects of the setting in each case: • *Appalachia* by Cynthia Rylant • *Mama Panya's Pancakes* by Mary and Rich Chamberlin • *Sitti's Secrets* by Naomi Shibab Nye **Writing extension:** See the *Where are you from?* Template on the CD. Create a personal narrative using the same style as *Momma, Where Are You From?*
	Reflect on reading and writing strategy	• What kinds of stories are likely to have settings that are really important to the story itself? (stories set in a different time or place) • How do you identify elements of a setting? • How can the setting help you to understand the characters in a story? (You can tell how they feel about their life experiences.)

▶ OBJECTIVE

A3-a: Briefly summarize this story

BOOK

The Princess and the Pizza by Mary Jane

INTRODUCTION TO THE BOOK

This is a not-so-typical fairytale about a princess named Paulina who has lost her princess role due to her father's decision to step down from the throne. She desperately wants to get back to princessing and is elated when a queen from a neighboring kingdom is seeking potential brides for her son, the prince. But there are a few hurdles she must overcome first. Her final test is to produce a feast fit for royalty. Despite a few mishaps along the way, she creates a delicious new dish: pizza—and wins the right to the prince's hand. But alas, she decides to forgo the prince and open a pizza parlor.

WHY THIS IS A GOOD BOOK FOR TEACHING THIS OBJECTIVE

Fairytales are perfect for summarizing because they follow a traditional narrative (problem/solution) structure and contain a reasonable number of complications before the problem gets solved—which keeps the written summary appropriately brief. I love using this text for shared lessons because it entertains the teachers as much as it engages the students. It's funny and clever, with numerous references to other fairytales and a writing style that is spunky and sharp.

OTHER OBJECTIVES THAT MAY BE ADDRESSED BY RE-READING THIS BOOK

- **A2-d**: How did _____ change from the beginning to the end of the story?
- **A4-b**: If the author added another paragraph to the end of the story, it would <u>most likely</u> tell about _____. Use information from the story to support your answer.
- **C1-c**: Would you like _____ for a friend? Why or why not?

OTHER BOOKS MATCHED TO THIS OBJECTIVE TO LEAD STUDENTS TOWARD INDEPENDENCE (Remember to chart the evidence when you use a picture book so that students may provide specific details from the text)

The books below have a traditional problem/solution plot structure and would be good for summarizing:

- *For the Love of Autumn* by Patricia Polacco
Most of Patricia Polacco's books are problem/solution stories and this one also follows that pattern. In this story, a teacher's beloved kitty disappears for weeks at a time, and as it turns out, has been befriended by a gentleman in the neighborhood who thought the cat was a stray. Eventually, the cat comes back and the teacher meets the man who has been caring for it. The happy ending in this case is that the teacher and the cat-sitter get married and live happily ever after with their special kitty. How's that for a modern-day fairytale!

- *Probuditi!* By Chris Van Allsburg
Chris Van Allsburg is known for his surprise endings, which makes summarizing this story interesting; you have to really pay attention to the very last page, or you miss the big surprise! In this story a mischievous little boy turns his sister into a dog one afternoon—and spends the rest of the day trying to return her to her former "sister" state before his mom returns from her hair appointment. After many false attempts he finally succeeds. Or had he actually turned her into a dog after all? Good mix of fantasy and typical kid behavior.

- *Hewitt Anderson's Great Big Life* by Jerdine Nolen
A tiny boy is born to two gigantic parents who truly do believe that "bigger is better." Hewitt proves them wrong on numerous occasions, helping his family out of scrapes. But Mom and Dad are not convinced until the very end when they finally concede, "Big or small, either is best of all."

SCORING STUDENTS' RESPONSES

 A3-a: Briefly summarize *The Princess and the Pizza*

Score = 2

In this story a princess named Paulina wants to get back to princessing. She enters a contest to marry a prince in a faraway kingdom and has to pass some tests. First there's the essay. Next there's a glass slipper to wear. Finally she has to make a feast. She doesn't think she stands a chance, but ends up inventing pizza. She wins, but decides she'd rather open a pizza restaurant than marry the prince.

> (This response would receive full score because it accounts for all of the story elements and provides a *brief* summary of the story's plot that shows a clear relationship between the problem and the solution. The reader doesn't really need to specify the three tests, but including these is fine if the basic idea of each test is just mentioned without adding all the story details.)

Score = 1

In this story a princess wants to marry a prince. She has to pass some tests, but first she has to sleep on a bed with a pea. She can't sleep because she is a real princess. In order to win, she makes a feast. She makes pizza and wins.

> (This response contains some of the basic story elements, but focuses too much on a small detail—sleeping on the bed with a pea. It also fails to account for the ending of the story—rejecting the prince—which is the real point of this text.)

Score = 0

In this story a princess is always getting in trouble because she doesn't like the queen. She makes pizza. She wins the contest.

> (This is not really a summary of the story. There is no context that explains why the princess was making pizza, or what the contest was about. This student got sidetracked by the dialogue in the text which is definitely engaging, but is not a substitute for the plot.)

PLANNER FOR SHARED READING

Objective (strategy focus): A3-a: Briefly summarize this story

◎ Briefly summarize *The Princess and the Pizza*

How will student learning be measured at the end of the lesson? (What will count as "success?")

Text: *The Princess and the Pizza* by May Jane and Herm Auch   **Pages:** Whole book

BEFORE READING	**Establish prior knowledge, purpose, and predictions**	**Prior knowledge:** This story is a fairy tale. What do you know about fairytales? (Elicit insights such as "the power of three," "good triumphs over evil, the characters are sometimes princes and princesses, there is often magic involved, the prince is often "big and strong," and the princess is typically lovely, but weak, etc.) **Predictions:** Based on the title and the cover, what do you expect this story to be about? **Purpose for reading:** Let's read to summarize this story.
	Introduce/ review vocabulary	humble (shack) competition escorted muttered bolt upright paced scrumptious generous (piece) stomped
	Introduce the objective (How to find and use the evidence)	**Making the <u>reading</u> strategic** • Review story elements using the *Story Part Cards* found on the CD. • At the beginning of the story: look for the characters, setting, and problem. • In the middle of the story: look for (three) events. • At the end of the story: look for the solution and the ending.

DURING READING	**Model and practice finding evidence for the objective**	**The best evidence:** **Model:** **p. 1:** Character—Princess Paulina; setting: a kingdom; problem: Paulina missed princessing **p. 4:** Problem—Paulina decided to enter a contest to marry Prince Drupert **Practice:** Events— **p. 9:** first test-write an essay—Paulina made the cut **p. 11:** wear glass slipper—Paulina made the cut **p.13:** cook a royal feast—Paulina, by accident, invented pizza Solution **p. 24:** Paulina wins the contest, but refuses to marry the prince **p. 27:** Paulina opens a pizza restaurant—and is worried that her father might marry Queen Zelda
	Model and practice other strategies	**Connecting?** Connect to other fairytales that this story references **Visualizing/Picturing?** Picture the conversation between Paulina and Queen Zelda **Wondering?** How did the authors make this story so funny? Why is it funny? **Predicting/Guessing?** Could you predict the ending? Why or why not? **Noticing?** What details did you notice about this story that made it different from most fairytales? **Figuring out?** What is the author's message here? What are the authors trying to show?

AFTER READING	**Discussion questions**	**Question related to the objective** **A3-a:** Briefly summarize this story. **Other questions** **A1-a:** What is the theme of this story? **B3-b:** Which details show that Paulina was not your "typical" princess? **D1-c:** How did the authors create humor in this book? **D2-c:** Using information in this story, write a paragraph that could have appeared in Paulina's journal after she won the cooking contest.
	Written response to text	**Making the <u>writing</u> strategic** • Discuss all components of the summary by holding up individual *Story Part Cards* and asking students to identify each story component (characters, setting, etc.) • Practice giving an oral summary. (Ask individual students for each part in sequence.) • Explain the written response template, but do not model the writing unless necessary. • Provide students with "Alternate Summary Template" found on the CD (not the frame from *That's a Great Answer* or *Teaching Written Response*).
	Other follow-up activities	**Oral language, fluency, vocabulary, comprehension, reading extensions, writing extensions** **Oral language/fluency:** Practice reading a page of this story that includes dialogue between Princess Paulina and Queen Zelda. How do you think each person would talk? **Vocabulary:** Complete the *Vocabulary Connections* activity for this story. **Comprehension:** from *Constructing Meaning:* Character study, p. 185; Reading with all of my Senses, p. 168; Friends I Might have Known, p. 162. **Reading extensions:** Read some other "fractured fairytales." What makes these stories different from more traditional fairytales? • *The Paper Bag Princess* by Robert N. Munsch • *The True Story of the Three Little Pigs* by Jon Scieszka • *The Principal's New Clothes* by Stephanie Calmenson • *Cinder Edna* by Ellen Jackson • *Prince Cinders* by Babette Cole **Writing extensions:** Write the essay that you think Paulina might have written for the contest: "Why I Want to Have the Gracious and Exquisitely Beautiful Queen Zelda for My Mother-in-Law."
	Reflect on reading and writing strategy	• How do you go about summarizing a story? What do you look for? • Why is summarizing important? Give some "real life" examples of things you might need to summarize.

A3-b: Summarize the important things that happened in this [book] in order.

BOOK

A River Ran Wild: An Environmental History by Lynne Cherry

INTRODUCTION TO THE BOOK

This book chronicles the history of the Nashua River from its pristine beginnings as a Native American settlement, through the coming of English settlers, to the period of industrialization and subsequent pollution, to its eventual re-beautification. It is a true account with vivid illustrations that tell the story as eloquently as the words, themselves. The text is surrounded by smaller pictures around the margins of each page with detailed illustrations that add depth to the story's content.

WHY THIS IS A GOOD BOOK FOR TEACHING THIS OBJECTIVE

This is a good book for this objective for although there is technically a "story" with a problem and a solution, making it possible for students to summarize using the traditional narrative summary format (characters, problem, setting, events, solution), it is more clearly a time line depicted through a sequence of events. Students need to understand that not all texts should be summarized using the narrative elements. This book makes that point quite well.

OTHER OBJECTIVES THAT MAY BE ADDRESSED BY RE-READING THIS BOOK

- **A2-e:** What is the setting of this story? Give details from the story to support your answer.
- **B1-d:** Can this part of the [story/text] be described as: a description, an explanation, a conversation, an opinion, an argument, or a comparison? How do you know?
- **C2-a:** Which part of the story/article do you think was *most* important? Use information from the story to explain why you chose that part.
- **D3-a:** How does the author/character show that _____ is important to him/her?

OTHER BOOKS MATCHED TO THIS OBJECTIVE TO LEAD STUDENTS TOWARD INDEPENDENCE (Remember to chart the evidence when you use a picture book so that students may provide specific details from the text)

The books described below would be more appropriate for summarizing a sequence of events rather than using narrative elements because the format is not problem/solution. Books that typically work for this "sequential summary" are texts such as biographies that depict the major event's in a person's life from birth to death (or a particular portion of a person's life), "how-to" books that take the reader through the steps of a process from start to finish (such as building a house), life-cycle books (from tadpole to frog), and timelines of historical events (such as *A River Ran Wild*).

- ***A Caribou Journey* by Debbie S. Miller**
  This book describes the life of a caribou in its Arctic habitat. It's perfect for a sequential summary because the text is relatively brief with clearly identified events in a caribou's journey from birth through adulthood.

- ***Minty: A Story of Young Harriet Tubman* by Alan Schroeder**
  This text works well for a sequential summary because it is a *partial* biography, describing only Harriet Tubman's early life. Significant events of her childhood are vividly portrayed through both the words and detailed illustrations.

- ***Show Way* by Jacqueline Woodson**
  It's not easy to find a book that is simply a timeline, but this one fits the bill perfectly. In this autobiographical account, Woodson briefly describes stories of bravery from the lives of many past generations in her family—from the earliest days of slavery to the birth of her own daughter.

SCORING STUDENTS' RESPONSES

 A3-b: Summarize the important events in the life of the Nashua River in order.

Score = 2

A long time ago when the Indians lived there, the Nashua River was beautiful and clean. Then settlers came and took over the land. After that they started to build factories and that polluted the river. Eventually, people got concerned and decided to get rid of all the pollution. Finally the river is back to being beautiful.

> (This response would receive full score because it provides an accurate sequence of the most important events in the life of the Nashua River without including unnecessary details.)

Score = 1

Before people lived near the Nashua River there were lots of animals like turtles and beavers. The water was beautiful and clean. The Indians came and they took really good care of the land and the river got its name because of the pebbles on the bottom. They built a village and they planted corn. When settlers came they traded furs and got knives. Then the river got polluted and everyone was sad, but now it is clean.

> (This response would receive partial credit. Although this answer is long, it omits some key events—the way the river got polluted, and was then cleaned up. It also focuses too much on details such as the animals that lived by the river and the way the river go its name.)

Score = 0

The Nashua River got really polluted. It was disgusting. The fish died and you couldn't even see the bottom. It also smelled really bad.

> (No credit for this response. It is not a summary. It describes the polluted river in some detail, but there is no context for this: what it was like initially, how the pollution occurred, or what happened to make the river clean and beautiful once again.)

PLANNER FOR SHARED READING

Objective (strategy focus): <u>A3-b:</u> <u>Summarize the important things that happened in this</u> <u>[book] in order.</u>

 <u>Summarize the important events in the life of the Nashua River in order.</u>
How will student learning be measured at the end of the lesson? (What will count as "success?")

Text: <u>*A River Ran Wild* by Lynne Cherry</u>   **Pages:** <u>It may take more than one day</u>
<u>to read this book</u>

BEFORE READING	**Establish prior knowledge, purpose, and predictions**	**Prior knowledge:** Give some examples of rivers that you have seen. Are these rivers clean or polluted? How can you tell? What might cause a river to be polluted? **Predictions:** Based on the title and cover of this book, what do you think it might be about? **Purpose for reading:** As we read this book. Let's think about the sequence of events so we can summarize it when we have finished reading.
	Introduce/ review vocabulary	generations trespass disrupted murk mourned vision fragrant
	Introduce the objective (How to find and use the evidence)	**Making the <u>reading</u> strategic** When you summarize text you need to decide if it's a story with a problem and a solution (which you can summarize in the usual way—characters, problem, setting, events, solution), or if the text is just *part* of a story, or if the story is more a sequence of events without a real problem and a solution. If the story doesn't have a clear problem and solution, you need to write a different kind of summary. One kind of summary is a list of important events in the sequence that they happened: First, next, then, after that, finally… (Introduce the *Sequence of Events* cards included on the CD if these would be helpful to students as they identify the important events in the text.) *A River Ran Wild* is an example of a text that is best summarized by listing the sequence of events. As you read, keep track of the important events that happened, in the order that they occurred. You should look for about four or five important events in all.

	Model and practice finding evidence for the objective	**The best evidence:** **Model:** **p. 5-7:** Native people settled on the banks of this river which they named Nash-a-way-River with the Pebbled Bottom, and took good care of it, killing only what they needed for food and clothing. **pp. 9-13:** Greedy settlers arrived and did not consider the effect on the environment as they built sawmills, cut down trees, and killed more animals than they needed. This caused wars between the native people and the settlers. **Practice:** **pp. 15-19:** New machines brought "progress" to the Nashua River, but destroyed the river with pollution from plastics, chemicals, etc. The river was smelly and dirty. **pp. 21-23:** People recognized that something must be done to clean up the river **pp. 25-28:** The Nashua River is clean once again.
	Model and practice other strategies	**Connecting?** What current environmental issues are you familiar with that have tried to stop pollution and take better care of our environment? **Visualizing/Picturing?** Which scene described in this book can you see vividly in your mind? What words help you picture this? Can you add some details of your own? **Wondering?** Did this book make you wonder about ways that you could help to protect our environment? How could you get involved? **Predicting/Guessing?** What do you predict might have become of the Nashua River and its surroundings if people had not stepped in to save it from further destruction? (Think of how one bad thing leads to something else…and something else….) **Noticing?** The border illustrations give you even more details about this story. Look closely at the border illustrations on one page. What additional information do these pictures provide? **Figuring out?** Why do you think the author wrote this book? What did she want us to think about and understand?

AFTER READING	**Discussion questions**	**Question related to the objective** **A3-b:** Summarize the important events in the life of the Nashua River in order. **Other questions** **B1-b:** What caused the Nashua River to change initially? What were the effects? What caused the Nashua River to change again at the end of the book? **B2-b:** Why did the author write a "story" about this river? (Why not just a news article telling the history of the Nashua River?) **C2-b:** Which part of this story was most interesting or surprising to you? Why? **D2-b:** Imagine you are going to give a talk to your class about the Nashua River. What two points would you be sure to include in your speech?
	Written response to text	**Making the <u>writing</u> strategic** • **A3-b:** Summarize the main events that occurred in the life of the Nashua River. • Chart the main events in the life of the Nashua River (use the sequence indicated in *Modeling/Practicing* section.) • See *That's a Great Answer*, p. 76, for template as a place to begin, or create a template of your own. (You might want five events here: *first, next, then, after that, finally.*) • Model the beginning of the response with the first two events in the life of the Nashua River (arrival of the native people and arrival of the settlers). • Ask students to complete the response by adding the remaining important events.
	Other follow-up activities	**Oral language, fluency, vocabulary, comprehension, reading extensions, writing extensions** **Oral language/fluency:** After completing the writing extension activity below, practice reading your dialogue until you can read it fluently with expression. Read both parts yourself, or invite a friend to read one of the parts. **Vocabulary:** See *Vocabulary Connections* activity on the CD. **Comprehension:** These follow-up activities may be found in *Constructing Meaning through Kid-Friendly Strategy Instruction*: Visualize Vocabulary, p. 166; Picture This, p. 164; True or False, p. 171; The Question Is. . . , p. 172 **Reading extensions:** These books relate to protecting our environment: • *Just a Dream* by Chris Van Allsburg • *The Great Kapok Tree: A Tale of the Amazon Rain Forest* by Lynne Cherry • *The Sea, The Storm, and the Mangrove Tangle* by Lynne Cherry **Writing extensions:** Imagine that you are conducting an interview with a factory owner along the Nashua River who is contributing to the pollution of the river in order to make a living. How could you convince him or her that this pollution needs to stop? Remember that this person's income is at stake, so she or he will be hard to convince. Write the dialogue that you would have with this man or woman: What will she say? What will you say?
	Reflect on reading and writing strategy	• How can you tell if a story should be summarized using characters, setting, problem, etc.—or if you should just tell events in order? • When you want to summarize a story by telling events in order, how do you make sure you get the most important events?

◤ OBJECTIVE

A3-c: Briefly summarize this article or informational text

BOOK

Extra! Extra! Fairy-Tale News from Hidden Forest by Alma Flor Ada

INTRODUCTION TO THE BOOK

This book is written and laid out in newspaper format with articles that feature favorite fairytale characters such as Jack (*Jack and the Beanstalk*), Geppetto (*Pinocchio*), the Tortoise (*Tortoise and the Hare*), and many others. Local news, international news, op-ed pieces, sports, and even advertisements synthesize various fairy tales into stories, that like real news, are continued from day to day. One central story that ultimately incorporates several characters involves the disappearance of young Jack up a tall beanstalk where it is rumored he has encountered a very large and unfriendly giant. The format of this text is its strongest feature—though the storyline does hang together reasonably well.

WHY THIS IS A GOOD BOOK FOR TEACHING THIS OBJECTIVE

This book is perfect for this objective because it presents several short selections (the different types of stories included in a newspaper), so students can locate the *who, what, when, where. . .* in many short pieces—with more independence each time. Students will enjoy the clever references to the fairytales they enjoyed as young children—if, in fact, they know these stories. Even if students are not familiar with the fairytales themselves, this book will still make sense to them as a story told in newspaper format. It just won't seem quite as humorous! Because there are several distinct articles here, you can model with one or two, and then gradually lead students to more independence as you apply this objective to subsequent articles.

OTHER OBJECTIVES THAT MAY BE ADDRESSED BY RE-READING THIS BOOK

- **B1-d:** There are several Editorials throughout this book. Can these be considered a conversation, opinion, description, or explanation? (The same question can be asked for Local News and International News.)
- **B2-b:** Why did the author write this story as a series of news paper articles?
- **C2-c:** Did you like this book? Why or why not?

OTHER BOOKS MATCHED TO THIS OBJECTIVE TO LEAD STUDENTS TOWARD INDEPENDENCE (Remember to chart the evidence when you use a picture book so that students may provide specific details from the text)

These books also contain short segments that can be summarized as "news articles," answering the "5 *w* and *h*" questions. Model with the first one or two segments, and then gradually lead students to greater independence using a "news summary" format.

- *The Secret Knowledge of Grown-Ups* by David Wisniewski
This book is really funny, but it requires a fairly sophisticated sense of humor. Formatted as a "file," it contains eight adult rules such as "Eat your vegetables" and "Drink plenty of milk." For each rule there is the "official reason:" Eat your vegetables because they're good for you; and the "truth": You eat your vegetables to keep them under control. Then there are a couple of pages describing what life would be like if you didn't know "the truth: If your veggies were "out of control," for example, meat-eating vegetables such as giant celery would stalk the plains looking for unsuspecting children to consume. Details abound supported by rollicking cartoon-like illustrations.

- *Oh, Freedom!: Kids Talk About the Civil Rights Movement With the People Who Made It Happen* by Casey King and Linda Barrett Osborne
This book is a series of interviews between different children and various individuals (mostly regular, not-so-famous folks) who experienced segregation before and during the Civil Rights movement. Kids will be engaged because the questions come from children of about their age pictured with the adults they're interviewing. Each interview is well-suited to summarizing using the traditional "5 *w* and *h* questions."

- *Fairytale News* by Colin Hawkins and Jacqui Hawkins
This book is a prequel of sorts to *Extra! Extra!. . .* with more "fracture fairytale" episodes to summarize using a "news summary" format.

SCORING STUDENTS' RESPONSES

 Briefly summarize the *Hidden Forest News* from March 3

Score = 2

An oversized vine mysteriously grew up overnight in Hidden Forest and some of the residents like Mrs. Bear and Mr. McGregor were really alarmed because they thought it was dangerous.

> (This response would receive full credit because it answers the essential *who, what, when, where,* and *why* questions that are important to summarizing a news article.)

Score = 1

This story has lots of fairytale characters in it like Mr. McGregor from *Peter Rabbit* and Mrs. Bear from *The Three Bears*. It is a story but it is also a newspaper article. There is a vine growing like in *Jack and the Beanstalk*.

> (This response includes some of the essential news article ingredients, but it is missing a key element: the problem. Without that, there is no real sense of the story that is being summarized.)

Score = 0

This is the story of Jack climbing up the beanstalk. He will meet a giant. He will trick the giant and he will get a golden egg. Then he and his mother will be rich.

> (This isn't a summary at all. This student is basing her response entirely on background knowledge, which is somewhat common with struggling readers. They think they can skip the actual reading and respond based on prior knowledge that appears to be relevant. Just as in this case, it almost never works out: no fake reading!)

PLANNER FOR SHARED READING

Objective (strategy focus): <u>A3-c:</u> <u>Briefly summarize this article or informational text</u>

 <u>Briefly summarize the *Hidden Forest News* from March 3</u>
How will student learning be measured at the end of the lesson? (What will count as "success?")

Text: <u>*Extra! Extra! Fairy-Tale News from Hidden Forest*</u>   **Pages:** <u>1-2*</u>

*This lesson focuses on the first article, (Hidden Forest News: March 3. This same lesson format could apply to all other articles in this book as well.

BEFORE READING	**Establish prior knowledge, purpose, and predictions**	**Prior knowledge:** What are some different kinds of articles you find in a newspaper? (Children might mention news, sports, letters-to-the editor, etc.) What are some of the fairytales you remember from when you were younger? (Fairytales that are referenced in this book include *Jack-and-the-Beanstalk, Peter Rabbit, Pinocchio, The Little Red Hen, The Tortoise and the Hare,* and others. **Predictions:** Based on the title, what kind of book do you expect this to be? (Look at a couple of the pages to show the newspaper formatting, and the kinds of articles News, International, Sports, Op-Ed) **Purpose for reading:** Based on today's reading, we will try to briefly summarize one of these news articles.
	Introduce/ review vocabulary	**Newspaper terms useful for students to know for this entire book:** Local News Opinion Editorial International News **Words useful for students related to this article:** mysterious resembling alarming oversized residence residents determined
	Introduce the objective (How to find and use the evidence)	**Making the <u>reading</u> strategic** When you read to summarize a news article, an easy way to do this is to look for answers to the "5 w and h" questions. These are: *who, what, when, where, why,* and *how.* Usually, the author answers these questions right at the beginning of an article. The rest of the article gives you the details related to the topic, but you shouldn't include many details in your summary. In a newspaper, articles that can be summarized this way could be *local* news, *international* news, *sports,* or *feature stories. Letters-to-the-editor* might be better summarized by looking for the main idea and supporting details since they express a point of view and you want to find the writer's evidence for his or her opinion.

DURING READING	**Model and practice finding evidence for the objective**	**The best evidence for p. 1: Hidden Forest News** __Model:__ **First paragraph:** Answers *what*: A huge vine resembling an oversized beanstalk; Answers *when*: grew overnight; Answers *where*: in Hidden Forest __Practice:__ **Second paragraph:** Answers *who*: Mr. McGregor is upset about this **Third paragraph:** Answers *why*: It's a danger to everyone—people could get killed; Answers *who*: Mrs. Bear
	Model and practice other strategies	**Connecting?** Any text-to-text connections? **Visualizing/Picturing?** Can you picture the beanstalk looking like a "stairway?" **Wondering?** How will the author use the newspaper format to tell her story? **Predicting/Guessing?** At the end or the article, the author mentions "Mrs. Blake and her won, Jack not being home." Do you have any predictions about *why* Jack might not have been home? **Noticing?** What nonfiction "newspaper" features do you notice on this page? **Figuring out?** Why did the author choose these particular fairytale characters to feature here: Mr. McGregor, Mama Bear, Jack?

Discussion questions	**Question related to the objective** **A3-c:** Briefly summarize *Hidden Forest News* from March 3 **Other questions** **A2-b:** What is the main problem in this story? **A4-b:** If the author added other articles to this book, what might he or she include? **B1-d:** Can paragraph 3 of this article (Hidden Forest News, March 3) be considered a description, an explanation, an opinion, or a conversation?	
Written response to text	**Making the <u>writing</u> strategic** • See *That's a Great Answer*, p. 78, for a template matched to this objective. • Model the response using the template. • Read another article in this book such as *Hidden Forest News* from March 5 and ask students to look for answers to the "5 *W* and *H* questions" more independently and then to complete the Answer Frame for this question.	
Other follow-up activities	**Oral language, fluency, vocabulary, comprehension, reading extensions, writing extensions** The activities below apply to this entire book, not just this first article: **Oral language/fluency:** The information in this book has been presented as a series of newspaper articles. However, you could convert this information to a newscast format, instead. Write and present one of the articles as a news report (*Hidden Forest News* or *International*) or as an interview (*Opinion-Editorial*). Try to sound like a news reporter as you deliver your story orally to your classmates. **Vocabulary:** See *Vocabulary Connections* activity on the CD. **Comprehension:** These follow-up activities may be found in *Constructing Meaning through Kid-Friendly Strategy Instruction*: Info-Gram, p. 193; Good Questions to Ask, p. 195; I'm a Word Watcher; p. 195. **Reading extensions:** These fractured fairytales also by Alma Flor Ada are well-written and would be useful for the teaching of letter-writing in the same way that *Extra! Extra!* is useful for teaching about the structure of a newspaper. **Writing extensions:** Add another article to this book. It could be an *Editorial*-Opinion, *a Sports* article, or a *Local* or *International* news story. Feature some fairytale characters in your article and make sure that the characters you choose are well matched to the story you are telling.	
Reflect on reading and writing strategy	• How do you find the information you need to summarize a news article? • Where, in an article, do you find this information? • How might your summary be different if you summarize a *Letter-to-the Editor* rather than a news story?	

A4-a: Predict what will happen next in this story.

BOOK

Silver Packages by Cynthia Rylant

INTRODUCTION TO THE BOOK

This story begins as a wealthy man is saved from a terrible accident by people from the local community—in the hills of rural Appalachia. To show his appreciation, he gives back to the community by returning to the town each year at Christmas time on the back of a train, from which he throws beautifully wrapped silver packages to the children who eagerly wait by the tracks. One little boy hopes every year that inside his silver gift will be a doctor's kit. That dream never comes true. But the boy grows up and another of his dreams is realized, and he, too, gives back. The ending is obvious enough that many children will be able to predict the final page.

WHY THIS IS A GOOD BOOK FOR TEACHING THIS OBJECTIVE

I tried not to select texts with a holiday or seasonal theme for this book because I didn't want to limit the appropriateness of lessons to a particular time of year. But *Silver Packages* transcends its "Christmas" setting, and is more about the spirit of "giving back" than it is about the Christmas spirit of giving. This is a good book for making predictions because the child in the story wishes every year for a particular gift: Will this be the year he receives it? Students can predict several times as the story unfolds—and may see the pattern that emerges. Can they predict the ending? They might—if they recognize the author's intent and the real message she wishes to convey.

OTHER OBJECTIVES THAT MAY BE ADDRESSED BY RE-READING THIS BOOK

- **A1-b:** What is the theme of this story?
- **C1-a:** Make a personal connection to an experience.
- **C2-a:** Which part of the story/article do you think was *most* important? Use information from the story to explain why you chose that part.
- **D2-c:** Using information in the text, write a paragraph that could have appeared in _____'s journal after _____ occurred.

OTHER BOOKS MATCHED TO THIS OBJECTIVE TO LEAD STUDENTS TOWARD INDEPENDENCE (Remember to chart the evidence when you use a picture book so that students may provide specific details from the text)

These books build suspense and encourage intermediate grade readers to predict as they read in order to figure out how the story will end.

- *The Stranger* by Chris Van Allsburg

  The identity of "the stranger" in this book is never really revealed, even at the end of the story. But readers will begin to put the pieces together as they read in order to make an educated guess.

- *Goin' Someplace Special* by Patricia C. McKissack

  The author keeps readers guessing about this "someplace special" as they story develops. While the events of the story become somewhat predictable, the final page is always a surprise to students when the author at last reveals the identify of this most special place.

- *Jin Woo* by Eve Bunting

  This story addresses the age-old issue of sibling rivalry, in this story viewed through the arrival of an adopted baby from Korea. David, the big brother and narrator of the story, announces that "he could wait longer," as his parents express their joy about their new son. A letter to David from Baby Brother (with a little help from Mom) puts things in perspective. Will children be able to predict the transformation of David's feelings toward his new brother? Probably…but the focus here on adoption adds an interesting dimension for students to consider.

SCORING STUDENTS' RESPONSES

◎ **A4-b:** Predict the gift that Frankie will receive from the rich man the year after he gets the socks and cowboy holster.

Score = 2

I predict that Frankie will get mittens this year. I think he will get mittens because in the story it says that his fingers are cold and they hurt. I think he might get a toy, too, because last year he got something to wear and something to play with. I think that will happen again.

> (This is a very plausible prediction and the reader has noticed the details in the text that lead to this prediction: reference to cold hands and a pattern of receiving a toy, as well.)

Score = 1

I think Frankie will get a doctor's kit this year. He still wants one and the rich man gives toys and clothes. So maybe Frankie will finally get the kit.

> (This response would receive partial credit because the author's reference to the doctor's kit is repeated, showing that it is important to the story. Still, the reader has missed the clue that the rich man is giving warm items of clothing because these people are poor. It is also unlikely that the problem in the story would be solved so soon. What would happen in the rest of the book?)

Score = 0

I think Frankie might get a football this year. Or maybe he will get a basketball. He probably likes sports.

> (This is not a good prediction based on text evidence. The reader has made a guess based on background knowledge and a couple of activities that boys this age typically enjoy—but there is nothing in the story that supports this.)

PLANNER FOR SHARED READING

Objective (strategy focus): <u>What do you predict will happen next in the story?</u>

 <u>A4-a:</u> Predict what will happen next in *Silver Packages*
How will student learning be measured at the end of the lesson? (What will count as "success?")

Text: <u>*Silver Packages* by Cynthia Rylant</u>   **Pages:** <u>Whole book</u>

<table>
<tr>
<td rowspan="3" style="writing-mode: vertical-rl">BEFORE READING</td>
<td>Establish prior knowledge, purpose, and predictions</td>
<td>Prior knowledge: What do you know about the author, Cynthia Rylant? What is the setting of many of her stories? Where is Appalachia? What do you know about life in Appalachia?
Predictions: Based on the title and the cover of this book, and what you know about Cynthia Rylant, what do you think this book might be about?
Purpose for reading: As we read this book, let's try to predict what will happen next. Let's also try to predict how the story will end.</td>
</tr>
<tr>
<td>Introduce/ review vocabulary</td>
<td>delight   debt   repaying   particular</td>
</tr>
<tr>
<td>Introduce the objective (How to find and use the evidence)</td>
<td>Making the <u>reading</u> strategic
In order to make a good prediction, you need to think about what the author has told you about the character and the problem so far: What does the character care about? How has he or she behaved so far? The author gives you clues that help you predict what will happen, but you have to read carefully to notice them. They won't jump right out at you; you need to look closely. When you predict what will happen next, you should also be able to tell why based on a clue you noticed in the text.</td>
</tr>
</table>

Model and practice finding evidence for the objective	**The best evidence:** **Model:** **p. 2:** I predict that somehow the children will get gifts from the train since it said "it might as well be Santa Claus." **p. 4:** I'm wondering why the author told this part about the rich man who had the car accident. Maybe he has something to do with the gifts. **p. 5:** I'm noticing I was right that the rich man had something to do with the gifts. I predict we might find out what is in the "sparkling silver packages" the man brings. **p. 8:** Predict what the man will give Frankie. **Practice:** **p. 9:** Did you change your prediction? Why or why not? **p. 11:** Predict what is in the box that the man is holding. **p. 14:** Predict what Frankie will want next year. **p. 15:** Predict what the man will give the boy this Christmas. (What are the clues?) **p. 17:** What do you predict might happen next? How do you think the story might end? Why? **p. 19:** What do you think Frankie might do now that he's an adult? Why do you make this prediction? **p. 22:** Is this the end of the story? What else could happen? **p. 24:** What do you predict will happen now? Why? **p. 26:** Why is the man running to the little girl? **p. 27:** What do you think Frankie is going to say to the little girl? **p. 28:** Could you predict this ending? What were the clues?
Model and practice other strategies	**Connecting?** Connect to a time when you were really generous to someone. **Visualizing/Picturing?** What were some of the feelings that Frankie experienced in this story? Picture the expression on his face for each of these feelings. **Wondering?** What did you wonder about as we read this story? **Predicting/Guessing?** Could you predict the ending? What were the best clues? **Noticing?** What did you notice about Frankie right from the beginning that helped you predict the ending? **Figuring out?** What was the author's intent in writing this story?

Discussion questions	**Question related to the objective** **A4-a:** Predict what will happen next in *Silver Packages*. **Other questions** **A1-b**: What is the theme of this story? **B2-a**: Why does the author repeat Frankie's wish for a doctor's kit on so many pages? **C1-a:** Connect to a time when you wished for a special gift and didn't receive it. How were your feelings the same or different from Frankie's feelings? **D2-a:** Write a paragraph that Frankie might have included in his journal one of those Christmases when he wished for a doctor's kit but didn't receive it.
Written response to text	**Making the <u>writing</u> strategic** • See *That's a Great Answer*, p. 81, for a template matched to this objective. • Model the response by stopping on p. 8 and writing about what you predict the rich many will give to Frankie. • Stop after a few more pages and ask students to complete the template for what *they* predict the rich man will give Frankie now. • You can also stop right before the ending and ask children to complete the template predicting what Frankie will say to the little girl.
Other follow-up activities	**Oral language, fluency, vocabulary, comprehension, reading extensions, writing extensions** **Oral language/fluency:** The first page of this story sets the tone by raising suspense about the Christmas Train. Practice reading this page until your voice sounds mysterious enough to make readers curious about what will happen next. **Vocabulary:** See *Vocabulary Connections* activity on the CD. **Comprehension:** These follow-up activities may be found in *Constructing Meaning through Kid-Friendly Strategy Instruction*: I'm Connected, p. 159; Picture This, p. 164; True or False, p. 171; Character Study, p. 185. **Reading extensions:** These stories also celebrate the spirit of giving back: • *Planting the Trees of Kenya: The Story of Wangari Maathai* by Claire Nivola • *The Summer My Father Was Ten* by Pat Brisson • *My Rows and Piles of Coins* by Tololwa Mollel **Writing extensions:** Make a list of ten random acts of kindness that you could "give" to someone. What would you give? Who would you give it to? Why?
Reflect on reading and writing strategy	• What do you need to consider in order to make a good prediction? • What kinds of clues can you look for to help you predict? • Why are some stories harder to predict than others?

A4-b: If the author added another paragraph to the end of the story, it would most likely tell about _____. Use information from the story to support your answer.

BOOK

The Empty Pot by Demi

INTRODUCTION TO THE BOOK

This simple Asian folktale with rich, whimsical illustrations and sparse text begins with the Emperor announcing an unusual test to select an heir to his throne: The child of the kingdom who raises the most beautiful flowers from a seed given by the Emperor will be his successor. Ping, known for his green thumb, cannot get his seed to grow at all, and is humiliated to bring his empty pot to the king—especially because all of the other children present the king with pots of flowers that are lush and colorful. But the king is not the least bit disappointed by Ping's empty pot. He then confesses that all of the seeds he gave to the children had been cooked, and thus would not grow. Ping had the courage (and the integrity) to remain honest even when he had much to gain by cheating as the other children had done. He is declared the new Emperor of all the land.

WHY THIS IS A GOOD BOOK FOR TEACHING THIS OBJECTIVE

This is a good book for adding an epilogue of sorts because it ends just with the resolution: Ping has won the contest and has been declared the new emperor. But what kind of an emperor will Ping be? He has demonstrated both courage and honesty. If the author added another paragraph, would it show him engaged in acts of courage as the emperor? Would there be another test of his honesty, or would he test the honesty of his subjects? Students should be able to infer the probable content of an extension to this story based on what they have learned about Ping's character.

OTHER OBJECTIVES THAT MAY BE ADDRESSED BY RE-READING THIS BOOK

- **A1-a:** What lesson does _____ learn in this story?
- **A3-a:** Briefly summarize this story.
- **C1-c:** Would you like _____ for a friend? Why or why not?
- **D3-a:** What was important to [the king]?

OTHER BOOKS MATCHED TO THIS OBJECTIVE TO LEAD STUDENTS TOWARD INDEPENDENCE (Remember to chart the evidence when you use a picture book so that students may provide specific details from the text)

Students could also extend the endings of these texts:

- ***The True Story of the Three Little Pigs* by Jon Scieszka**

  In this story the Wolf tells his side of the story, explaining how two little piglets ended up dead after he accidentally knocked their houses down when he was trying to borrow a cup of sugar. Do the cops believe him? Is his story believable? Will he be sent to jail? Will he go free? You decide and write a paragraph about what happens to the wolf next.

- ***Dear Mrs. LaRue: Letters from Obedience School* by Mark Teague**

  At the end of this story Ike the dog is back home with Mrs. LaRue having broken out of the Brotweiler Canine Academy, and miraculously saving Mrs. LaRue from being hit by an oncoming truck. But is he truly reformed? Will he now be a "good dog" or will he resume his former mischievous ways? You write the next paragraph and decide what will become of Ike.

- ***Just a Dream* by Chris Van Allsburg**

  Books by Chris Van Allsburg always leaving you thinking about what could happen next, and this one is no exception. Right now, it's just a dream for Walter: Will the future be full of trash and pollution? Or will we have a cleaner, greener environment? You decide. In a paragraph that could follow the last page in this book, tell about the future you see for our world. What will that future look like?

SCORING STUDENTS' RESPONSES

A4-b: If the author added another paragraph to the end of *The Empty Pot*, it would most likely tell about Ping when he became an emperor. What kind of emperor would Ping be? Would he still show the same character traits? What did Ping do as an emperor?

Score = 2

If the author had added another paragraph to this story, it would most likely have told about Ping being a great and truthful Emperor. For example, if he found a pot of gold but knew that it wasn't his, he would have asked his knights to ride around the kingdom looking for the real owner. This could happen next because Ping has shown himself to be truthful before when his seed didn't grow, and he would probably be truthful during his whole life.

> (This response would receive full score because it provides a plausible extension to the story. There is an example from the book, and even an example that *shows* what kind of an Emperor Ping would be. The reader also indicates how his next paragraph would be consistent with what he already understands about Ping.)

Score = 1

If the author had added another paragraph it would most likely tell about Ping being an Emperor. I think he would be a good Emperor and always be fair and honest.

> (This response would receive partial score. The reader indicates that Ping would probably be honest, but doesn't indicate why this extension aligns with traits demonstrated by the character. There is no evidence from the text, and no example from the proposed next paragraph.)

Score = 0

If the author had added another paragraph it would most likely tell about Ping being an Emperor who ruled a big kingdom. His kingdom would be so big that he would take one month to ride around it on his horse.

> (This response would receive no credit because there is nothing in the text that connects to this extension. It is not a logical inference. The story did not mention anything about the size of the kingdom or about Ping's horse.)

PLANNER FOR SHARED READING

Objective (strategy focus): <u>A4-b</u>: <u>If the author added another paragraph to the end of the story, it would most likely tell about [   ]. Use information from the story to support your answer.</u>

🎯 <u>If the author added another paragraph to the end of *The Empty Pot*, it would most likely tell about Ping when he became an emperor. What kind of emperor would Ping be? Would he still be honest and brave? What did Ping do as an emperor?</u>

How will student learning be measured at the end of the lesson? (What will count as "success?")

Text: <u>*The Empty Pot* by Demi</u>   **Pages:** <u>Whole book</u>

BEFORE READING	**Establish prior knowledge, purpose, and predictions**	**Prior knowledge:** This story is a folktale. What is a folktale? Folktales were told by people all over the world even before stories were written down. They were often told to teach a particular lesson. As we read, think about the lesson that this tale teaches. **Predictions:** By looking at the picture on the cover, where do you think this story might take place? What could the title mean? **Purpose for reading:** Today as we read we will think about what might happen if the author continued the story for one more page. You will get to decide what *you* think would happen next. You will need to think about what happened *during* the story in order to decide what might happen *next*.
	Introduce/ review vocabulary	swarmed rich (soil) transferred overheard tended worthy courage admire
	Introduce the objective (How to find and use the evidence)	**Making the <u>reading</u> strategic** In order to decide what could happen *next*, you will need to think about what happened *during* the story. What kind of person did Ping (the character) show himself to be? How will those traits be useful to him in the future? Don't just *tell* what happens next, try to *show* what happens by thinking up an adventure for Ping.

DURING READING	**Model and practice finding evidence for the objective**	**The best evidence:** **Model:** **p. 1:** Ping was excellent at getting flowers to grow. **p. 7:** Flowers were going to be very important because they would decide who would become the next emperor. **p. 10:** Ping was the happiest of all. **p. 11:** Ping planted his seed carefully. **Practice:** **p. 13:** Nothing grew in his pot. **pp. 14-15:** Ping planted his seed in a bigger pot and got new soil. **pp. 16-17:** Nothing grew for the whole year. **p. 19:** All of the other children had beautiful flowers. **p. 20:** Ping was ashamed of his empty pot. **p. 22:** Ping's father said is was ok; he had done his best. **p. 25:** The Emperor frowned when he saw the other flowers. **p. 28:** Ping cried when he spoke to the emperor about his empty pot. **p. 29:** The Emperor smiled and said he'd found someone worthy of being Emperor; the other beans had been cooked and could not grow. **p. 30:** The Emperor said he admired Ping for telling the truth and would reward him with his entire kingdom.
	Model and practice other strategies	**Connecting?** Connect to a time when you needed to have courage. **Visualizing/Picturing?** Picture the look on Ping's face when his seed wouldn't grow; when he approached the Emperor; when he was declared the new Emperor. **Wondering?** Wonder how else the Emperor could have determined the heir to his throne. **Predicting/Guessing?** At what points in this story did you predict what would happen next? **Noticing?** What details in the story showed what kind of a person Ping really was? **Figuring out?** Figure out the lesson that this story teaches.

AFTER READING	**Discussion questions**	**Question related to the objective** **A4-b:** If the author added another paragraph to the end of *The Empty Pot*, it would most likely tell about Ping when he became an emperor. What kind of emperor would Ping be? Would he still be honest and brave? What did Ping do as an emperor? **Other questions** **A1-a:** What lesson does _____ learn in this story? **A3-a:** Briefly summarize this story. **B2-a:** Why did the author include these sentences: "How beautiful all the flowers were! But the Emperor was frowning and did not say a word." **C1-a:** Make a connection to a time when you needed to have courage to do the right thing.
	Written response to text	**Making the <u>writing</u> strategic** • See *That's a Great Answer*, p. 83, or *Teaching Written Response*, pp. 188-189, for a template matched to this objective. • Model the response using the template. • Remove your response and ask students to write the response themselves using the template—choosing a different story outcome if possible.
	Other follow-up activities	**Oral language, fluency, vocabulary, comprehension, reading extensions, writing extensions** **Oral language/fluency:** See the excerpts from this text (*Quotes spoken by Characters in* The Empty Pot) on the CD. Practice reading these quotes until you can read them fluently and sound like the character saying each line. **Vocabulary:** See *Vocabulary Connections* activity on the CD. **Comprehension:** These follow-up activities may be found in *Constructing Meaning through Kid-Friendly Strategy Instruction*: One Word, p. 160; Friends I Might Have Known, p. 162; A Message from the Author, p. 186; Summary Frame for Story Text, p. 188. **Reading extensions:** The stories below are Asian folktales. Students can identify the message of each and compare them to *The Empty Pot*. • *How Tiger Got His Stripes: a Folktale from Vietnam* by Rob Cleveland • *The Stonecutter: A Japanese Folktale* by Gerald McDermott • *The Girl Who Drew a Phoenix* by Demi **Writing extensions:** Write a thank-you note that Ping may have written to the Emperor after he was named the new Emperor of the kingdom: What would Ping say to the Emperor? What would he tell him about the kind of Emperor he would be when he ruled the land?
	Reflect on reading and writing strategy	• How do you decide what might happen next if the author added another paragraph or page to the end of the story? • How can you make your new paragraph interesting to readers (show don't tell. . .).

Chapter Nine

STRAND B LESSONS

Developing an
Interpretation

OBJECTIVE

B1-a: What caused _____ to happen in the story? What were some of the effects?

BOOK

Beatrice's Goat by Page McBrier

INTRODUCTION TO THE BOOK

There are so many books to share with children where the *cause* produces a negative *effect*. (the results of war, discrimination, joblessness, etc.) I wanted instead to find an uplifting story that demonstrated the capacity of the human spirit to succeed in spite of the odds. I found such a story in *Beatrice's Goat*. Set in Eastern Africa, this is a true story of the enormous impact of the gift of a small goat to the life of a family. Because they received this goat, the children of the family were able to drink goat's milk—which made them healthier. The young daughter sold the extra milk each morning—and saved enough money to achieve her life-long dream: going to school. The family looks forward to the day that kids will be born to their goat; they will sell the babies to pay for the new house they want to build. They look forward to the day that many families in their village will have goats; surely this will raise the standard of living for them all.

WHY THIS IS A GOOD BOOK FOR TEACHING THIS OBJECTIVE

In addition to the positive nature of this story, it also celebrates individual resourcefulness, and a culture of need rather than greed. The book provides so many examples of the goat's benefits to the lucky family that receives it. Students will easily see how one very small kindness can reap many rewards. This is a story simple enough for younger students will understand, but with enough meaning for older students to appreciate.

OTHER OBJECTIVES THAT MAY BE ADDRESSED BY RE-READING THIS BOOK

*   **A2-e:** What is the setting of this story? Give details from the story to support your answer.
*   **A3-a:** Briefly summarize this story.
*   **A4-b:** If the author added another paragraph to the end of the story (or article), it would <u>most</u> <u>likely</u> tell about _____.
*   **C2-b:** Which part of this [story/article] was most interesting or surprising to you? Why?
*   **D3-a:** How does the author/character show that _____ is important to him/her?

OTHER BOOKS MATCHED TO THIS OBJECTIVE TO LEAD STUDENTS TOWARD INDEPENDENCE (Remember to chart the evidence when you use a picture book so that students may provide specific details from the text)

The following books reinforce "cause and effect" by demonstrating the impact of determination, perseverance, and personal actions on the achievement of one's dreams:

- *My Rows and Piles of Coins* **by Tololwa Mollel**
  This book, set in Tanzania, tells the story of Saruni, who wants more than anything to own a bicycle so he can help his mother carry heavy goods to market. His generosity and determination reap unexpected rewards—and a very happy ending for Sarun.

- *My Freedom Trip* **by Frances Park and Ginger Park**
  This is the story of how a little girl's courage and faith helped her to escape enemy soldiers, traveling in the dark of night from North Korea to "the land of freedom" (South Korea). Note to teachers: the little girl leaves her mother behind and never sees her again, which may be too intense for some children.

- *Silver Packages* **by Cynthia Rylant**
  This story shows *cause* and *effect* from a variety of perspectives. First, a rich gentleman is saved from a terrible accident in the mountains of Appalachia and repays the good deed by distributing presents to the children of the town, throwing silver packages from a train as it passes through the area each Christmas. Then, one of the recipients of those packages, wishing each year for a present he never receives, repays the kindness in his own way. This is a heartwarming story that is more about giving than it is about Christmas.

SCORING STUDENTS' RESPONSES

 B1-a: What caused Beatrice's life to change? Identify at least two of the changes.

Score = 2

Beatrice's life changed because her family received a goat. Because of the goat, everyone in Beatrice's family could be healthier since they now had milk to drink. Also, Beatrice sold the extra milk and saved the money she raised. After a while, she had enough money to buy a uniform and books so she could go to school. Going to school was her biggest dream. Because of the goat, Beatrice's life got much better!

> (This response would receive full credit because it identifies the *cause* of the changes in Beatrice's life. It also explains the *effects* of having the goat—two specific ways thatBeatrice's life changed for the better.)

Score = 1

Beatrice's life changed because she got a goat and everyone in her family was very happy because now they had a good life and other people in their town will get a goat, too.

> (This response would receive partial credit. It identifies the *cause* correctly, but is too general in the *effects* brought about by having a goat.)

Score = 0

Beatrice got a goat so she could have a nice pet. She took good care of her goat.

> (This student would not receive any credit for this response. The purpose of having a goat was not to "have a nice pet." Beatrice did take care of the goat. But the purpose of the goat was to provide more income and better nutrition to raise the family's standard of living.)

PLANNER FOR SHARED READING

Objective (strategy focus): <u>B1-a:</u> <u>What caused [   ] to happen in the story?</u>

◎ <u>Think about *cause* and *effect* in the story *Beatrice's Goat*. How did life in Beatrice's</u>
<u>family life change because of the goat?</u>
      How will student learning be measured at the end of the lesson? (What will count as "success?")

Text: <u>*Beatrice's Goat* by Page McBrier</u>   **Pages:** <u>Whole book</u>

<table>
<tr>
<td rowspan="3">BEFORE READING</td>
<td>Establish prior knowledge, purpose, and predictions</td>
<td>Prior knowledge: [Locate Uganda on a map of Africa.] What do you think it would be like to live in a village in Uganda? (Look at the front cover of the book for some hints.)
Predictions: Why do you think a goat was important to Beatrice?
Purpose for reading: As we read, let's think about cause and effect. What kind of effect did the goat have on Beatrice's life, and her family's life?</td>
</tr>
<tr>
<td>Introduce/ review vocabulary</td>
<td>sturdy   coarse   yearned   sleek   disbelief   rustle</td>
</tr>
<tr>
<td>Introduce the objective (How to find and use the evidence)</td>
<td>Making the <u>reading</u> strategic
When you are looking for cause and effect, sometimes it is easier if you notice the effects first. As you read, look for ways that the characters' or people's lives have changed. Then work backward to identify what caused that change. The cause will probably be close to the beginning of the text. Sometimes the cause is not stated in the text at all; you have to figure it out from events in the book and your background knowledge about the topic. Sometimes the author describes what life was like before the event that caused the change.</td>
</tr>
</table>

DURING READING	**Model and practice finding evidence for the objective**	**The best evidence:** **Model:** **p. 1:** Many things are new to Beatrice and her family (an effect… don't know cause yet). **p. 3:** It's all because of a goat named Mugisa (the cause) **pp. 6-8:** What life was like *before* Mugisa **p. 9:** Beatrice doesn't understand how a goat could have *any* effect. **Practice:** (the remaining evidence shows the *effect*) **p. 13:** Mugisa gave birth to two kids (three goats would be better than one for extra income). **p. 16:** Goat's milk would make Beatrice and her family healthier. **p. 18:** Beatrice sold the extra milk to earn money. **p. 22:** Because she sold the goat's milk, Beatrice would have the money to go to school—her lifelong dream. **p. 21:** One of the kids would be sold for much money; family would be able to build new house. **p. 22:** More families will receive goats, which will bring about good things for other families, too.
	Model and practice other strategies	**Connecting?** Connect to something that caused a positive change in your life: What was the *cause*? What was the *effect*? **Visualizing/Picturing?** What words help you picture the village where Beatrice lived? **Wondering?** Did you wonder about other effects that a goat could have on a family or a community? **Predicting/Guessing?** Predict what might happen next in Beatrice's life because of Mugisa **Noticing?** Notice details about life in this village in Uganda. Would you want to live here? Explain. **Figuring out?** Think about what *you* can do to support families across the world to improve their way of life.

AFTER READING	**Discussion questions**	**Question related to the objective** **B1-a:** What caused Beatrice's life to change? Identify at least two of the changes. **Other questions** **A2-e:** What is the setting of this story? Give details from the story to support your answer. **A4-b:** If the author added another paragraph to the end of the story (or article), it would <u>most likely</u> tell about _____. **C2-b:** Which part of this [story/article] was most interesting or surprising to you? Why? **D1-b:** The author uses lots of similes in this story. Choose one of the similes and explain why the author chose it.
	Written response to text	**Making the <u>writing</u> strategic** • **B1-a:** In the book *Beatrice's Goat*, explain what caused Beatrice's life to change. Identify at least two of the changes that took place. • See *That's a Great Answer*, p. 87, for a template matched to this objective as a place to begin, or create a template of your own. • Model the response using two *effects*. • Remove the template and ask students to write their own answer—choosing other relevant details from the text if possible.
	Other follow-up activities	**Oral language, fluency, vocabulary, comprehension, reading extensions, writing extensions** **Oral language/fluency:** Practice reading aloud the page where Mama tells Beatrice that their family will receive a goat. How did Beatrice feel at first about receiving this goat? Make your voice sound like you think Beatrice felt at the time. **Vocabulary:** Complete the *Vocabulary Connections* activity for this book (on the CD). **Comprehension:** These follow-up activities may be found in *Constructing Meaning through Kid-Friendly Comprehension Strategy Instruction*: One Word, p. 160; Connecting to Time and Place, p. 161; Reading with all of my Senses, p. 168; Character Study, p. 185. **Reading extensions:** These books all demonstrate how livestock can change lives: • *Faith the Cow* by Susan Bame Hoover • *Give a Goat* by Jan West Schrock • *One Hen—How One Small Loan Made a Big Difference* by Katie Smith Milway **Writing extensions:** Heifer Project International is responsible for many people (including Beatrice) receiving goats and other livestock that improve their standard of living by reducing hunger. Check the website for Heifer International: www.heifer.org. Consider sponsoring a fundraiser to raise money for Heifer. Write a letter. Make a poster. Get your message out to your classmates, your school, or your community.
	Reflect on reading and writing strategy	• How do you identify *cause* and *effect* in a text? • Why is it important to understand the *causes* that led to particular *effects*?

B1-b: What happened at the beginning, in the middle, and at the end of this text?

BOOK

This is the Dream by Diane Z. Shore and Jessica Alexander

INTRODUCTION TO THE BOOK

This simple but evocative text chronicles events before, during, and after the Civil Rights movement. Page borders of photographs from poignant moments in history accompany paintings of large, clear images on each double-page spread. The text itself is sparse and lyrical in a "House-that Jack-Built" sort of way, but the powerful message comes through nonetheless. Each historic moment is depicted *before*: "These are the buses—a dime buys a ride, but the people are sorted by color inside"; *during*: "These are the passengers, on weary feet, walking until they can choose their own seat"; *after*: "This is the bus that roars through the streets, and all of the passengers choose their own seats." Decades of American race relations are thoughtfully represented here in a mere 32 pages.

WHY THIS IS A GOOD BOOK FOR TEACHING THIS OBJECTIVE

I typically reserve this objective for the primary grades as a first step in preparing students to retell or summarize text. But this book lends itself perfectly to addressing *beginning, middle,* and *end* in a more sophisticated manner as it examines a belief system (and laws) that changed over time. The text itself is brief and leaves lots of time for discussing the message and the details revealed in the illustrations and page borders.

OTHER OBJECTIVES THAT MAY BE ADDRESSED BY RE-READING THIS BOOK

- **A1-d:** What would be another good title for this text?
- **B1-a:** What caused _____ to happen?
- **C2-a:** Which part of this text do you think is the *most* important? Why?
- **D2-b:** Imagine that you were going to give a talk to your class about [Civil Rights] what two points from this text would you be sure to include? Why?

OTHER BOOKS MATCHED TO THIS OBJECTIVE TO LEAD STUDENTS TOWARD INDEPENDENCE (Remember to chart the evidence when you use a picture book so that students may provide specific details from the text)

The following books reinforce the concept of *beginning, middle,* and *end* as a progression through stages to achieve a goal:

- *Sweet Clara and the Freedom Quilt* **by Deborah Hopkinson**
  This book chronicles Clara's life journey from a slave designing a "freedom quilt," to running away, to attaining her freedom.

- *The Royal Bee* **by Ginger Park and Frances Park**
  This book follows the life of a young boy in Korea in the nineteenth century. At first his family is so poor that he is not even allowed to go to school. Despite the odds he finds a way to get an education. In the end he represents his school at the "Royal Bee," an opportunity to win a scholarship to a prestigious secondary school.

- *Iditarod Dream: Dusty and His Sled Dogs Compete in Alaska's Jr. Iditarod* **by Ted Wood**
  This photo-journal is longer than most picture books and would take several days to read. It is an engaging account of a young teen in Alaska who prepares for the Jr. Iditarod race, races with his dogs across the snow-covered Alaskan wilderness, and reaps the rewards of a hard-won competition.

SCORING STUDENTS' RESPONSES

B1-b: In the book *This is the Dream*, identify at least one event from the *beginning* of the book, one event from *the middle* of the book, and one event from *the end* of the book.

Score = 2

At the beginning of this book, black children and white children were not allowed to go to the same schools. Then a few black children started to go to white schools even though they were not welcome and had to be protected from violence. At the end, the laws were changed and now all races of children go to school together.

> (This response would receive full score because it references specific incidents from *before* Civil Rights, *during* Civil Rights, and *after* Civil Rights. These incidents represent the *beginning, middle,* and *end* of the book. Additionally, all three examples relate to "going to school" although this would not be necessary to obtain full score.)

Score = 1

At the beginning of this book black people and white people were not nice to each other. In the middle, people like Martin Luther King tried to change laws so everyone would be equal. At the end, everyone was equal and the laws were fair.

> (This answer would receive partial credit. The student clearly understood the sequence of events in this text that led to integration, but neglected to reference specific examples.)

Score = 0

This book is about laws that were unfair to black people, like they couldn't drink from the same fountains or go to the same schools or eat at the same restaurants. People were mean.

> (This answer would not receive any credit because the student missed the point of *beginning, middle,* and *end.* Although the references from the beginning of the text were accurate, there is no indication that the situation changed.)

PLANNER FOR SHARED READING

Objective (strategy focus): <u>**B1-b:**</u> <u>What happened at the beginning, in the middle, and at the end of the story?</u>

◎ <u>In the book *This is the Dream*, identify at least one event from the *beginning* of the book, one event from *the middle* of the book, and one event from *the end* of the book.</u>
How will student learning be measured at the end of the lesson? (What will count as "success?")

Text: <u>*This is the Dream* by Diane Shore and Jessica Alexander</u> **Pages:** <u>Whole book</u>

<table>
<tr>
<td rowspan="3">BEFORE READING</td>
<td>Establish prior knowledge, purpose, and predictions</td>
<td>Prior knowledge: Did you ever hear the term Civil Rights before? When was the Civil Rights era? What was it about? What does this term mean? Do you know of anyone who fought for Civil Rights? (Students might mention Martin Luther King, Jr. or other Civil Rights leaders.)
Predictions: (Look at the title and the cover.) What clues do they provide about this text? What do you think "the dream" might be?
Purpose for reading: This text has a very clear beginning, middle, and end. Let's read carefully to see if we can identify the events that occurred during each of these parts.</td>
</tr>
<tr>
<td>Introduce/ review vocabulary</td>
<td>Words in the book: separate-but-equal   harsh   denying   justice   violence   triumphs   rallied
Words/term not in the book, but might be important for students to understand this text: segregation   prejudice   equality   integration   desegregation   Freedom March   boycott   sit-in   discrimination</td>
</tr>
<tr>
<td>Introduce the objective (How to find and use the evidence)</td>
<td>Making the <u>reading</u> strategic
<ul>
<li>In order to correctly identify the beginning, middle, and end of a text, notice where the situation changes. One simple way of thinking about this would be:</li>
<li>Beginning: What life was like at first (In a story, this is usually where the characters, setting, and problem are introduced.)</li>
<li>Middle: What life was like as people or characters are trying to change something (In a story, this is usually where the characters or people are trying to solve the problem.)</li>
<li>End: What life was like after the changes were made (In a story, this is where the problem gets solved and the author shows how everything ends.)</li>
</ul></td>
</tr>
</table>

	Model and practice the focus strategy	**The best evidence:** **Model:** <u>Beginning</u>: **p. 2:** separate drinking fountains **pp. 3-4:** sitting in the back of the bus **pp. 5-6:** "whites only" restaurants **pp. 7-8:** separate libraries **Practice:** **pp. 9-10:** separate schools, hospitals, etc. <u>Middle</u>: **pp. 11-12:** integrating the schools **pp. 13-14:** bus boycotts **pp. 15-16:** restaurant sit-ins **pp. 17-18:** Freedom Marches **pp. 19-20:** Civil Rights leaders <u>End</u>: **pp. 21-22:** drinking from the same fountain **pp. 23-24:** no more back-of-the-bus **pp. 25-26:** restaurants open to all **pp. 27-28:** libraries open to all **pp. 29-30:** integrated schools
	Model and practice other strategies	**Connecting?** Connect to any form of discrimination that you might have experienced **Visualizing/Picturing?** Which illustration (or border picture) do you think you will remember for the longest time? Why? **Wondering?** What did you wonder about as we read this text that the author did *not* answer? **Predicting/Guessing?** Do you think the children who lived *before* the Civil Rights era would have predicted that an African American president would be elected in 2008? Why or why not? **Noticing?** What details did you notice in the "border pictures" that added to your understanding of this text? **Figuring out?** Do you think that the election of President Obama adds a "new chapter" to the history of race relations in the United States? Why or why not?

AFTER READING	**Discussion questions**	**Question related to the objective** **B1-b:** What happened at the beginning, in the middle, and at the end of *This is the Dream*? **Other questions** **B1-a:** What caused the Civil Rights movement to come about? **C2-d:** What was your first reaction to this text? Explain. **D2-b:** Imagine you are going to give a talk to your class about Civil Rights. What two points would you be sure to include in your speech?
	Written response to text	**Making the <u>writing</u> strategic** • **B1-b:** In the book *This is the Dream*, identify at least one event from the *beginning* of the book, one event from the *middle* of the book, and one event from the *end* of the book. • See *That's a Great Answer*, p. 91, for a template matched to this objective. • Model the response using one or two details from each part of the text (*beginning, middle, end*) • Remove the template and ask students to write their own answer—choosing other relevant details from the text if possible.
	Other follow-up activities	**Oral language, fluency, vocabulary, comprehension, reading extensions, writing extensions** **Oral language/writing:** Pretend that you are a Civil Right leader. Write and deliver a speech that you might have given in the 1960s, pleading for justice and equality. **Vocabulary:** Complete the *Vocabulary Connections* activity for this book (on the CD). **Comprehension:** These follow-up strategy activities may be found in *Constructing Meaning through Kid-Friendly Strategy Instruction*: Active Reader Report, p. 155; Visualize Vocabulary, p. 166; The Question Is…, p. 172 **Reading extensions:** These books all demonstrate a sequence of events (*beginning, middle,* and *end*) in a personal struggle for respect and acceptance: • *Dad, Jackie, and Me* by Myron Uhlberg • *Rosa* by Nikki Giovanni • *From Miss Ida's Porch* by Sandra Belton **Writing extension:** Select one situation described in this book (drinking from different water fountains, going to different schools, boycotting busses, etc.) Write a skit that shows a child about your age involved in this situation.
	Reflect on reading and writing strategy	• How do you decide whether a portion of text is *the beginning, the middle,* or *the end*?

B1-c: Compare these two characters

BOOK:

As Good as Anybody by Richard Michelson

INTRODUCTION TO THE BOOK

Martin Luther King Jr. grew up in the American South at a time when African Americans did not enjoy the same rights as other Americans. Abraham Joshua Heschel grew up in Europe when Jews were not welcome in Germany. Martin Luther King Jr. became a preacher. Abraham Heschel became a rabbi. This is the story of the friendship forged by these two men, and how together they turned their personal struggles with discrimination into a passionate effort to attain justice for all.

WHY THIS IS A GOOD BOOK FOR TEACHING THIS OBJECTIVE

While most students will be familiar with Martin Luther King Jr. and his pursuit of equal rights for all Americans, fewer children will know about Abraham Heschel. Unlike many "compare/contrast" texts where there are more differences than similarities, this story contains many commonalities between these two individuals. While the content is significant, the author presents the information in a manner that is easily accessible to intermediate grade students.

OTHER OBJECTIVES THAT MAY BE ADDRESSED BY RE-READING THIS BOOK

- **A1-d**: What would be another good title for this story?
- **A2-c:** How did Martin Luther King and Abraham Heschel attempt to solve the problem of discrimination? Give details from the story to support your answer.
- **B2-b:** Why did the author write a picture book about these two people?
- **C1-c:** Which person in this book would you like to know and why?

OTHER BOOKS MATCHED TO THIS OBJECTIVE TO LEAD STUDENTS TOWARD INDEPENDENCE (Remember to chart the evidence when you use a picture book so that students may provide specific details from the text)

Each of the books below features two individuals whose lives intersected in a meaningful way.

- *Pink and Say* by Patricia Polacco
  Sheldon (Say) Curtis, a white fifteen year old, and Pinkus Aylee, an African American of about the same age, find each other on a Civil War battlefield where say has been injured. What they have in common transcends their differences as they confront the cruelties of war.

- *Teammates* by Peter Golenbock

   This is the story of the friendship that evolved between Jackie Robinson and Peewee Reese when they became Brooklyn Dodgers teammates in the early 1940s. Racism was very much alive not just in baseball, but in American society in general when Reese decided it was more important to follow his heart than to follow the discriminatory practices of other members of his team. Students can decide: Which are more important—the similarities that Reece and Robinson share, or the differences perceived by the rest of the world?

- *The Other Side* by Jacqueline Woodson

   You can use this book to meet almost any objective! The pre-Civil Rights South is the scene of this story that depicts the friendship that gradually develops between Clover, a young African American girl, and Annie, a white child. Although their mothers have told them not to step over the fence that divides their yards because "it's dangerous over there," they begin to understand that the racial differences that separate them are not as important the values they have in common. Sparse text, major message with *lots* of symbolism.

SCORING STUDENTS' RESPONSES

◎ **Compare Martin Luther King Jr. and Abraham Heschel. How are they similar? How are they different?**

Score = 2

Abraham Heschel and Martin Luther King Jr. were similar and different. They were different because Abraham was Jewish, born in Europe, and grew up to be a rabbi. Martin was African American, born in the American South, and was a Christian minister. They were alike because they both cared about equal rights and they marched together for justice.

   (This response would receive full score because it includes specific examples of these men's similarities and differences and focuses on *important* points.)

Score = 1

Abraham Heschel and Martin Luther King Jr. both believed in freedom. They came from different places, but they had a lot in common and they became friends.

   (This response would receive partial credit because it answers the question generally, but needs more specific details.)

Score = 0

Abraham Heschel and Martin Luther King Jr. were friends. They were in a march together. They liked each other. One was black and one was white.

   (This response would receive no credit because it misses the point of the story. It is repetitive [friends/liked each other], and it focuses on a difference [black/white] that is not elaborated.)

PLANNER FOR SHARED READING

Objective (strategy focus): <u>B1-c:</u> <u>Compare these two people</u>

🎯 <u>Compare Martin Luther King Jr. and Abraham Heschel. How are they similar? How are</u> <u>they different?</u>

How will student learning be measured at the end of the lesson? (What will count as "success?")

Text: *As Good as Anybody* by Richard Michelson   **Pages:** <u>Whole book*</u>

*More than one day may be needed to read this book
**In this book, African Americans are frequently referred to as "colored people." Remind students that while this term is not used or accepted today, it was very common during the time when Martin Luther King was fighting for equal rights.

<table>
<tr>
<td rowspan="3">BEFORE READING</td>
<td>Establish prior knowledge, purpose, and predictions</td>
<td>Prior knowledge: What do you know about Martin Luther King? What was life like for African Americans, especially in the South, during the time that Martin Luther King was growing up?
Predictions: Based on the title and the picture on the cover, what do you think this book might be about?
Purpose for reading: This book is about Martin Luther King and someone you may not have heard of named Abraham Heschel. They become friends. As we read, we will try to find similarities and differences between their lives.</td>
</tr>
<tr>
<td>Introduce/ review vocabulary</td>
<td>stomped   rejoiced   injustice   deeds   respect   ignorant
jeered   poverty</td>
</tr>
<tr>
<td>Introduce the objective (How to find and use the evidence)</td>
<td>Making the <u>reading</u> strategic
When you compare two people or characters, look for important things about their lives that may have been similar or different: Where and when did they live? What was their childhood like? Did they have a similar problem? Did they solve problems the same way? What was important to them? What did they accomplish in their life? Why are they remembered today? Be sure you can explain these similarities and differences with specific evidence from the text.</td>
</tr>
</table>

DURING READING	**Model and practice finding evidence for the objective**	**The best evidence:** **Model:** **p. 3:** MLK: Many signs that said WHITES ONLY **p. 4:** MLK: Angry about injustice; father told him he should be "looking up" **p. 6:** MLK: Wanted to get rid of injustice *now* **p. 8:** MLK: Mother told him he was "just as good as anybody" **Practice:** **p. 10:** MLK: Became a minister like his dad; fought for equality—stay off the buses **p. 14:** MLK: Participated in many freedom marches **p. 18:** AJH: Born in Poland Father told him he "was as good as anybody." **p. 19:** AJH: cared about others (gave money to the poor) **p. 23:** AJH: Became a rabbi like his father; When Hitler came to power, much discrimination against Jews (ordered out of Germany) **p. 25:** AJH: Angry at injustices **p. 26:** AJH: Couldn't sit down in crowded train **p. 30:** AJH: Marched all over America for freedom **p. 32:** AJH: Answered MLK's call for protest march in Alabama **p. 33:** MLK and AJH: Joined hands to march for peace
	Model and practice other strategies	**Connecting?** Standing up for something you believe is important **Visualizing/Picturing?** Picturing various scenes in the book **Wondering?** Wondering why people discriminate against people who are different from themselves **Predicting/Guessing?** Predicting what MLK and AJH might have talked about as they marched together in Alabama **Noticing?** All of the similarities between Martin and Abraham **Figuring out?** Why were Martin and Abraham such good friends?

AFTER READING	**Discussion questions**	**Question related to the objective** **B1-c:** Compare Martin Luther King Jr. and Abraham Heschel. How are they similar? How are they different? **Other questions** **A1-d:** What would be another good title for this story? **B2-a:** Martin's mom, Abraham's dad, and Martin, himself at different times in the story say, "Don't ever forget that you are just as good as anybody!" Why do you think the author repeats this line three times said by three different people? **C1-c:** Which person in this book would you like to know and why? **D2-c:** Using information in the text, write a paragraph that could have appeared in Martin Luther King's \ journal after he got a call from Abraham Heshel saying he wanted to march with him in Alabama.
	Written response to text	**Making the <u>writing</u> strategic** • **B1-c:** Compare Martin Luther King Jr. and Abraham Heschel. How are they similar? How are they different? • See *That's a Great Answer*, p. 96, for a template matched to this objective*. • Model the response using two details about each person. • Remove the template and ask students to write their own answer—choosing other relevant details from the text if possible. • *This template may need to be modified slightly for this response. The CD included with *That's a Great Answer* provides answer frames in Word Format which can be easily modified.
	Other follow-up activities	**Oral language, fluency, vocabulary, comprehension, reading extensions, writing extensions** **Oral language/fluency:** Some quotes spoken by different people in this book are provided in a document with other materials from this lesson on the CD. Practice reading each one until you think you sound like the person saying these words. **Vocabulary:** Complete the *Vocabulary Connections* activity for this book (on the CD). **Comprehension:** These follow-up strategy activities may be found in *Constructing Meaning through Kid-Friendly Strategy Instruction*: **Reading extensions:** The following books are about fighting for "rights" of various kinds: • *Harvesting Hope: The Story of Cesar Chavez* by Kathleen Krull • *Rosa* by Nikki Giovanni • *Who Cares about Animal Rights?* By Michael Twinn **Writing extensions:** Write the dialogue that you think Abraham and Martin might have had as they marched together in Selma, Alabama in 1965: Did they discuss their life as children? Did they talk about the injustice in the world? Did they talk about how they could make the world a better place? They probably had a really meaningful conversation. Try to capture their thinking in your dialogue. Perform your dialogue for your class.
	Reflect on reading and writing strategy	• How do you go about comparing two different people or characters? • What are some of the things you could compare about two lives?

B1-d: Can this part of the [story/text] be described as: a definition, a description, an explanation, a conversation, an opinion, an argument, or a comparison? How do you know?

BOOK

Dear Mrs. LaRue by Mark Teague

INTRODUCTION TO THE BOOK

This is a charming book and a real kid-pleaser. Ike, a rambunctious (not to mention precocious) pup finds himself at Brotweiler Canine Academy where he's been sent by his owner, Mrs. LaRue, to improve his doggie manners and repent for a few misdemeanors such as tormenting the neighbor's cats and helping himself to one too many pies from the kitchen counter. He begs. He pleads. He invents a plethora of excuses which he hopes will convince Mrs. LaRue to rescue him from his unhappy and quite undignified obedience school experience. Full-color illustrations depict the "reality" of Brotweiler Academy, while black and white thought bubbles show how Ike is interpreting his current state of affairs.

WHY THIS IS A GOOD BOOK FOR TEACHING THIS OBJECTIVE

Ike's voice is heard loud and clear as he argues, explains, describes and willingly shares his opinions about Brotweiler Academy and the injustice of being "sentenced" to such an undeserved fate. It's not so easy to find multiple modes of self expression between the covers of a single book—but *Dear Mrs. LaRue* fits the bill nicely. Typically, many of these means of expression are present one at a time, in different types of text: Lots of poems and some narrative texts contain abundant *description*. Letters-to-the-Editor feature *opinions* and *arguments*. Plays and stories use *conversation* to move their plots forward. Expository texts are full of *explanations* and *definitions*. Once teachers begin to notice these features as they read with children, it is easy to point them out to students on-the-go: "Oh, look, right here the author is giving us her *opinion* about...."

OTHER OBJECTIVES THAT MAY BE ADDRESSED BY RE-READING THIS BOOK

- **A1-d:** What would be another good title for this story?
- **A2-e:** What is the setting of this story? Give details from the story to support your answer.
- **D1-c:** How did the author create humor in this book?
- **D3-a:** What was important to Ike? What was important to Mrs. LaRue?
-

OTHER BOOKS MATCHED TO THIS OBJECTIVE TO LEAD STUDENTS TOWARD INDEPENDENCE (Remember to chart the evidence when you use a picture book so that students may provide specific details from the text)

These books all contain varied modes of expression for students to ponder:

- *A Picnic in October* **by Eve Bunting**
  Opinions, explanations, arguments, conversations, and descriptions abound in this story about a family's annual pilgrimage to Liberty Island to celebrate the Statue of Liberty's birthday. Young Mike has had about enough of this foolishness. But as he talks with his grandma and some of the new Americans who have also come out to celebrate, he realizes that this isn't so foolish after all—and offers a ginger-ale toast to "Brava, Bella."

- *Something Beautiful* **by Sharon Denis Wyeth**
  As she searches for "something beautiful" in her not-so-beautiful world, the main character in this story hears a lot of opinions and explanations, engages in a few conversations, and recognizes the details of her life—some of which she ultimately feels empowered to change.

- *She's Wearing a Dead Bird on her Head!* **Bt Kathryn Lasky**
  This book about the early days of the Massachusetts Audubon Society is full of the opinions and arguments of women for and against the practice of wearing fancy hats that featured the plumes of exotic birds. Of course there are some conversations, too, descriptions of the bizarre hats themselves, and a few factual explanations, too.

SCORING STUDENTS' RESPONSES

◎ **B1-d: In the story *Dear Mrs. LaRue* find some examples of descriptions, explanations, opinions, conversations, and arguments.**

Sample scoring is provided for the following excerpt to show the criteria to keep in mind:

> Dear Mrs. LaRue,
>
> … This is a PRISON, not a school! You should see the other dogs. They are BAD DOGS, Mrs. LaRue! I do not fit in. Even the journey here was a horror.

Score = 2

This part of the text is an opinion. I know this is an opinion because Ike just *thinks* his school is a prison. It isn't a real prison. And he can't prove the dogs are bad. He probably can't prove the trip was a horror either. He just wants Mrs. LaRue to think he is being treated unfairly.

(This response would receive full score because it correctly identifies Ike's *opinion*. It also offers plenty of evidence as support.)

Score = 1

This part of the text is an opinion. I know this is an opinion because it tells how Ike feels.

(The reader is correct that this is an *opinion*. However, no evidence is provided.)

Score = 0

This part of the text is a conversation because Ike is talking to Mrs. LaRue. He is telling her that the other dogs are bad. He doesn't fit in. He had a bad journey.

(No points for this response. Ike is not having a conversation with Mrs. LaRue. Also, this reader just repeats the wording from the text with no explanation.)

PLANNER FOR SHARED READING

Objective (strategy focus): B1-d: Can this part of the story be described as: a definition, a description, an explanation, a conversation, an opinion, an argument, or a comparison?

◎ In the story _Dear Mrs. LaRue_ find some examples of descriptions, explanations, opinions, conversations, and arguments.

      How will student learning be measured at the end of the lesson? (What will count as "success?")

Text: _Dear Mrs. LaRue_ by Mark Teague   **Pages:** Whole book

<table>
<tr>
<td rowspan="3">BEFORE READING</td>
<td>Establish prior knowledge, purpose, and predictions</td>
<td>Prior knowledge: Did you ever wish your dog (or any pet) could talk, so you could know what it was thinking? What thoughts might go through a dog's mind when it gets left home alone when you go out? What thoughts might a dog have when he watches you eating a delicious piece of cake?

Predictions: In this story, the author shows us the thoughts that are going through Ike's mind based on letters he writes to his owner. Based on the cover, what kind of thoughts do you think Ike has?

Purpose for reading: As we read this story, let's find examples of the different ways that Ike expresses himself to make his thoughts seem real.</td>
</tr>
<tr>
<td>Introduce/ review vocabulary</td>
<td>obedience   howl   mistreated   misconceptions
severely   queasy   bluffing   endured</td>
</tr>
<tr>
<td>Introduce the objective (How to find and use the evidence)</td>
<td>Making the <u>reading</u> strategic
A person (or in this case, a dog) can express himself/herself in lots of different ways—for example: arguing, explaining, describing, or giving an opinion. (Review the meaning of each of these terms. See the Target page or p. 99, of That's a Great Answer for a definition of each: conversation, argument, etc.) As we read, let's try to find examples of each of these. You can also consider: Is there one main way that Ike expresses himself throughout this book.</td>
</tr>
</table>

DURING READING	**Model and practice finding evidence for the objective**	**The best evidence:** **Model:** **p. 2:** explanation of why Ike is in Obedience School **p. 3:** opinion—bad dogs **p. 6:** argument—"Ike, don't eat the chicken pie...." **p. 7:** explanation—about the cats **p. 9:** description—of life in Obedience School **Practice:** **p. 13:** argument—life is a nightmare **p. 15:** description—of how Ike feels **p. 18:** description—fun in the park **p. 19:** explanation—of how Ike plans to run away **p. 24:** argument—lots of reasons why Mrs. LaRue should take Ike back
	Model and practice other strategies	**Connecting?** In your own life, when is it most useful to: describe, explain, argue, give an opinion? **Visualizing/Picturing?** How did the illustrator in this book show what was "real" and what Ike just imagined? **Wondering?** Why do you think the author wrote this story? **Predicting/Guessing?** What other adventures might Ike have based on the kind of dog he seems to be? **Noticing?** What did you notice about Ike's personality? Do you know any dogs like Ike? **Figuring out?** What makes this book so much fun? Why is it funny?

AFTER READING	

Discussion questions	**Question related to the objective:** **B1-d:** Find some examples in this book of explanations, descriptions, opinions, and arguments. **Other questions** **A2-e:** What is the setting of this story? Give details about this setting. **C1-c:** Would you like to have a dog like Ike? Why or why not? **D1-e:** How did the author create humor in this book?
Written response to text	**Making the <u>writing</u> strategic** • Provide students with excerpts from this story. • Students can work alone or with a partner to determine whether each excerpt could be described as a description, argument, opinion, or explanation. • Complete answer frame for two excerpts based on the template in *That's a Great Answer*, p. 100 (also included on the CD with activities for this book).
Other follow-up activities	**Oral language, fluency, vocabulary, comprehension, reading extensions, writing extensions** **Oral language/fluency:** Select a page from *Dear Mrs. LaRue* and practice reading it until you sound just as you think Ike would have sounded. Is your tone angry? Desperate? Whiny? **Vocabulary:** Complete the *Vocabulary Connections* activity for this book (on the CD). **Comprehension:** These follow-up activities may be found in *Constructing Meaning through Kid-Friendly Comprehension Strategy Instruction*: Choose One Word that Best Describes Allie, p. 160; Picture This, p. 164; Summary Frame for Story Text, p. 188. **Reading extensions:** Mark Teague has written other books about Ike that students might also enjoy: • *Letters from the Campaign Trail: LaRue for Mayor* • *Detective LaRue: Letters from the Investigation* **Writing extensions:** In this story, Ike writes lots of letters to Mrs. LaRue hoping he can convince her that his point of view is right. Do you think Ike is right or wrong? Write a letter to Ike in which you either agree with him or with Mrs. LaRue. Give lots of reasons for your point of view.
Reflect on reading and writing strategy	• What are some different ways that a character or person can express himself or herself? (explain, describe, argue, give an opinion, etc.) • Define each of these means of self-expression. • What kind of text would be likely to include description? Explanations? Opinions? Arguments?

OBJECTIVE

B2-a: Why did the author include this paragraph?

BOOK

The Wretched Stone by Chris Van Allsburg

INTRODUCTION TO THE BOOK

This story develops as a series of journal entries by the captain of the ship, *The Rita Anne*. He tells of an adventure at sea with his crew who have discovered a strange glowing rock on a tropical island, and brought it aboard the ship. This mysterious object has a dreadful affect on the sailors who were once energetic and creative individuals and enthusiastic readers. Now they sit endlessly in front "the rock." They no longer show any interest in music, dancing, or books. And worst of all, they are ultimately transformed into apes, barely able to stand upright. Their lack of attention to anything other than "the rock" nearly causes a disaster at sea. They survive, though "the rock" goes dark! In the end, they return to their former, more fully human selves and the captain disposes of "the rock."

WHY THIS IS A GOOD BOOK FOR TEACHING THIS OBJECTIVE

This book is perfect for this objective because each journal entry provides clues about what the mystery object is, though the author never comes right out and answers the question directly. The reader must continually wonder: Why did the author include *this* bit of information? Or: Why did the author tell me *that*? Even the pictures hint at the mystery object's identity. Looking more deeply into the details of this story will lead the reader past the surface level adventure-at-sea to a more insightful understanding of the author's message. While no definitive answer is provided, could all of these clues be telling us that the "wretched stone" might be something like a TV—and that too much TV can lead to some pretty nasty outcomes? (Sh! Don't tell the kids…. See if they can figure this out for themselves as they decide why the author included particular observations in each journal entry.)

OTHER OBJECTIVES THAT MAY BE ADDRESSED BY RE-READING THIS BOOK

- **A1-b:** What is the theme of this story?
- **A3-a:** Briefly summarize the story.
- **B2-b:** Why did the author write this story as a series of journal entries?
- **C1-a:** Make a personal connection to the "big idea" of this story.
- **C2-c:** Did you like this story? Why or why not?

OTHER BOOKS MATCHED TO THIS OBJECTIVE TO LEAD STUDENTS TOWARD INDEPENDENCE (Remember to chart the evidence when you use a picture book so that students may provide specific details from the text)

Chris Van Allsburg is a master of telling stories that go deeper than the words on the page. Books by Van Allsburg that would be well-suited to this objective are:

- ***The Stranger***
  Who is the stranger that has come to stay with Farmer Bailey? While the stranger is there, summer continues on the Bailey's farm. Then one day the stranger blows on a leaf and it mysteriously changes from green to red. The author provides clues about the stranger's identify, but also leaves room for varying interpretations—great material for a thoughtful class discussion.

- ***Just a Dream***
  Is this a dream or a nightmare? Where does reality end and fantasy begin? Van Allsburg urges readers to consider what their future will look like based on their concern for the environment? This story is told through the illustrations as well as the words, and will lead readers to insights about the theme as well as generate important personal connections.

- ***The Witch's Broom***
  Minna Shaw finds a "pre-owned" witch's broom in her garden and is delighted at its ability to help her perform tasks around the house (sweeping, etc.) The neighbors, however, have a different opinion of this wicked contraption, and do everything they can to get rid of it. Who is right? Is the broom really "evil" as its former witch-owner? How will the story end? This tale gives readers the opportunity to rethink their views on forces of good and evil: Can we draw easy conclusions about such things?

SCORING STUDENTS' RESPONSES

 B2-a: Why did the author include the journal entry from June 6 (second part)?

Score = 2

This journal entry is about what the rock looked like. I think the author included the description of "the rock" because he wanted readers to be able to visualize it. He says it is about two feet across, roughly textured, gray, and some of it is flat and smooth as glass. There is a light coming from it. Also, it is heavy. I think the author wanted me to understand that this thing is not really a "rock" because a real rock couldn't be described in this way. He wants me to begin to think about what this rock might be.

> (This response would receive full score because it references the text specifically, and although the reader has not figured out "the rock's" identity, the response clearly indicates that this information provides a useful clue to solving the puzzle eventually.)

Score = 1

This journal entry is about finding the rock. I think the author included the description so I would know what the rock looks like. It is gray and rough and about two feet wide. It is definitely a funny rock because there is a light coming from it.

> (This response would receive a partial score. Although it notes specific features of the rock, this student has missed the point—at least for now—that this "rock" is most likely not a rock at all. There is no suggestion that the reader is looking for a meaning beyond surface level understanding although she does note that the rock is "funny looking.")

Score = 0

This journal entry is about finding a rock. The men lifted it into the ship. Then they set sail and sailed away.

> (This response would not receive any points. It merely paraphrases the content of the journal entry with no indication of what the rock looks like, and no hint that "the rock" might not really be a rock at all, or have any special significance to the story.)

PLANNER FOR SHARED READING

Objective (strategy focus): B2-a: <u>Why did the author include this [paragraph]?</u>

 <u>Explain why the author included particular information in each journal entry</u>
How will student learning be measured at the end of the lesson? (What will count as "success?")

Text: <u>*The Wretched Stone* by Chris Van Allsburg</u>   **Pages:** <u>Whole book</u>

<table>
<tr><td rowspan="3" style="writing-mode: vertical-rl">BEFORE READING</td><td>Establish prior knowledge, purpose, and predictions</td><td>Prior knowledge: Have you read any other books by Chris Van Allsburg? What do you expect to find in books by this author? (elements of fantasy, mystery, a message that you have to figure out for yourself)
Predictions: Based on the title and the picture on the cover, what do you expect this story might be about?
Purpose for reading: The title is The Wretched Stone. As we read, let's try to figure out what the "wretched stone" is, and what the author wants us to know based on each entry in his journal.</td></tr>
<tr><td>Introduce/ review vocabulary</td><td>wretched   omen   accomplished   consulted
overpowering   gaze   grave   alert   abandon</td></tr>
<tr><td>Introduce the objective (How to find and use the evidence)</td><td>Making the <u>reading</u> strategic
Go back and reread the journal entry you are wondering about. What is it about? Remember that the author is giving you this information because he wanted you to understand something beyond just the words on the page. What did the author want you to figure out? Each journal entry is like a piece of a puzzle. When you put the pieces together you will see that the "big idea" of the story.</td></tr>
</table>

DURING READING	**Model and practice finding evidence for the objective**	**The best evidence:** <u>**Model:**</u> **May 9:** The men are accomplished; many read; some play musical instruments, good storytellers. (The author is letting us know the character traits of the crew.) **May 17:** Members of the crew keep busy by singing and dancing and amusing each other with stories (The author is telling us how creative the sailors are.) **June 6:** The island looks nice, but has an "overpowering stink;" no life on it; water too bitter to drink. (The author is telling us that while something may *look* good at first glance, it may be an illusion.) <u>**Practice:**</u> **June 6 (cont'd):** The "rock" is two feet across, roughly textured, gray, with a portion that is flat and smooth as glass; has a glowing light; heavy. (The author wants us to think about what this object looks like: Can you picture this in your mind? Is there anything in "real life" that resembles this?) **June 10:** The crew is fascinated by the rock; they gaze at silence at it; no more music and storytelling; sailors are content. (The author wants us to see the effect the "rock" is having on the crew; no more creativity; happy to passively watch.) **June 13:** The sailors rarely speak; they are stopped over; shriek at the rock. (The author is letting us know more about the negative effect of "the rock.") **June 14:** The sailors locked themselves in the hold with the rock; they don't help to sail the ship. (The author wants us to see that nothing else matters to the sailors except "the rock.") **June 15:** The sailors have turned into apes; they grin at the terrible rock—also look at picture that accompanies this entry. (The author wants us to see that "the rock" has transformed the sailors into a lower life form.) **June 16:** "The rock" has gone dark due to a lightning storm; the sailors seem lost. (The author wants us to see that "the rock" was powered by electricity; the sailors can't seem to function without it.) **June 19:** The captain is playing the violin and reading to the crew; the crew seems more alert. (The author wants us to see that creativity can inspire the sailors to become more fully alive.) **June 28:** The sailors have returned to normal; those who read recovered most quickly. (The author wants us to see that READING can help you reach your potential.) **July 12:** The sailors have an unusual appetite for the fruit on the island. (The author wants us to see that the sailors now value what is created by nature.)
	Model and practice other strategies	**Connecting?** Once you have figured out the "big idea" of this story, can you make any connections? Have you ever been in a situation where "the rock" controlled too much of your life? **Visualizing/Picturing?** Did picturing help you to figure out the real identify of "the rock?" What did you picture that helped you reach this conclusion? **Wondering?** Did you wonder why the author wrote this story? Was he trying to tell a story about a sea voyage? **Predicting/Guessing?** What did you predict "the rock" would be at various points throughout this story? Did you abandon any of your predictions? Why? **Noticing?** What details were the most helpful in helping you determine the identity of "the rock." **Figuring out?** At what point did you finally figure out the rock's identity. If you didn't figure it out during the first reading, go back and look again at various journal entries once the identity has been revealed to you. What did you miss the first time?

AFTER READING	**Discussion questions**	Question related to the objective **B2-a:** Why did the author include the journal entry from June 6 (second part)? * *A similar question could be asked for *any* journal entry. **Other questions** **A1-a:** What lesson do the sailors learn in this story? How can you tell that they have learned this lesson? **A3-a:** Briefly summarize this story. **B1-d:** Read the second part of the journal entry for June 6. Can it be described as a definition, a conversation, a description, or an opinion? Why? **C1-a:** Make a personal connection to the "big idea" of this story. (Remember, this is not really about an adventure in a boat!)
	Written response to text	**Making the <u>writing</u> strategic** • See *That's a Great Answer*, p. 103, or *Teaching Written Response*, pp. 95-96, for a template matched to this objective. • Model the response using the journal entry from June 6. • Ask students to respond to the journal entry from June 15 or June 28, using the template if needed.
	Other follow-up activities	**Oral language, fluency, vocabulary, comprehension, reading extensions, writing extensions** **Oral language/fluency:** Should the captain have given his crew a lecture about spending too much time with "the rock." Write and present a speech that the captain could have written that might have solved "the rock" problem before it turned into a disaster. **Vocabulary:** Complete the *Vocabulary Connections* activity for this book (on the CD). **Comprehension:** These follow-up activities may be found in *Constructing Meaning through Kid-Friendly Comprehension Strategy Instruction*: Active Reader Report, p. 115; Best Quote, p. 175; S.O.L.V.E., p. 182; A Message from the Author, p. 186. **Reading extensions:** Read these (or other) books by Chris Van Allsburg. Is there a "big idea" that is deeper than the story itself? What is it: • *The Stranger* • *The Widow's Broom* • *The Polar Express* • *Just a Dream* **Writing extensions:** Write a journal entry that one of the sailors might have written on June 10? (First reread the journal entry that the captain wrote on that date.) How would the sailor's entry be different?
	Reflect on reading and writing strategy	• Why is it important to look for a deeper meaning to a story? • How do you go about figuring out why the author included particular information in a text?

B2-b: Why did the author write a [poem/story/nonfiction book, etc.] about this?

BOOK

Remember: The Journey to School Integration by Toni Morrison

INTRODUCTION TO THE BOOK

This is not your garden-variety picture book. It's a photo-journal with more than fifty sepia-tone photographs depicting life in the South during the years of school desegregation. Some pictures are not captioned, leaving the reader to imagine the context. Most, however, have been labeled by Morrison with bits of internal dialogue based on what the photo suggests. I prefer to let students imagine the thinking behind the pictures for themselves. These are powerful photographs and do not need to be narrated in order to convey their message. Among the scenes depicted here: The exterior of "Daneel Colored Public School," as well as the interior which clearly demonstrates that "separate is not equal;" teenage boys carrying placards that announce "We won't go to school with Negroes;" a classroom that is empty except for a few black students with the caption: "When they let us in the school, none of the white students came…." The final photo in the book shows the faces of four young girls with the words, "Things are better now. Much, much better. But remember why and please remember us." The rest of this caption identifies these girls as the four who were killed in the Birmingham church bombing in 1963.

WHY THIS IS A GOOD BOOK FOR TEACHING THIS OBJECTIVE

This is a good book for this objective because its format is so different from typical story texts that it's relatively easy for students to discern its distinctive features: Mostly pictures (black and white photographs), and just a few words that describe the pictures. Why did the author choose this format? These images "tell the story" more dramatically than any book on this topic ever could. All those words that surface repeatedly in texts about the Civil Rights era spring to life from these pages: in the pained expressions on children's faces, the Jim Crow signs that scream discrimination, the deplorable conditions of "colored" schools—and the awful derogatory language used to distinguish between the races. I often pair this text with the poem "The Battle of Birmingham" (Dudley Randall).

OTHER OBJECTIVES THAT MAY BE ADDRESSED BY RE-READING THIS BOOK

- **A4-b:** If the author added another paragraph to the end of the story (or article), it would <u>most likely</u> tell about _____.
- **B3-b:** Which facts (details) show that _____?
- **C1-b:** Make a personal connection to a feeling.
- **D2-b:** Imagine you are going to give a talk to your class about _____. What two points would you be sure to include in your speech?
- **D3-a:** What is important to the author?

OTHER BOOKS MATCHED TO THIS OBJECTIVE TO LEAD STUDENTS TOWARD INDEPENDENCE (Remember to chart the evidence when you use a picture book so that students may provide specific details from the text)

These books all represent organizational patterns that are not strictly "story narrative." Students can consider how the format of the text contributes to its meaning.

- *Nettie's Trip South* by Ann Turner
  This story is written as a letter to her cousin back home in the North by a little girl who travels south prior to the Civil War. She is distressed by what she sees, particularly a slave auction which makes her physically ill. Guide students to recognize that the letter format adds voice to the writing; the little girl is able to express herself more passionately because she is "talking to" an audience with whom she has a strong connection.

- *The Wretched Stone* by Chris Van Allsburg
  This book is written as a series of short journal entries chronically a voyage a sea where a "wretched stone" is nearly responsible for the demise of a ship. As with the book above, the journal format lends itself to a completely honest voice as the intended audience of a journal is actually oneself.

- *The Red Book* by Barbara Lehman
  This book is about two children who independently discover a little red book and because of it, eventually find each other—showing the power of a good book to magically transport you to faraway places, and form connections with the outside world. The thing about this book is that there are no words. Why not? Why did this author create a story with only pictures? This book generates wonderful discussion, but is best used with a small group because the book itself is tiny and kids need to be up close to take in all the details.

SCORING STUDENTS' RESPONSES

 B2-b: Why did the author write a <u>photo journal</u> about this topic?

Score = 2

I think that a photo journal was just right for this book because it uses photographs to tell a story. Even if the author had written a long story with a lot of words, it wouldn't have shown as much about segregation as some of these pictures. I felt so sad inside when I looked at the picture with the black children in the classroom, but the white kids had all stayed home. And the school for the black kids was old and not as good as other schools. These pictures will stick in my mind.

> (This is a very thoughtful answer and shows that this reader understands the features of a photo journal as well as how using this format added to the impact of this information.)

Score = 1

The author wrote a photo journal because she wanted us to see what life was like when black children and white children went to different schools. It wasn't fair, and you could see that in the pictures.

> (Which pictures? This student needed specific evidence, and also more information about why the photo journal format enhanced the author's message.)

Score = 0

There were lots of pictures in this book. They showed prejudice and segregation. Segregation is bad and we shouldn't have it.

> (This reader understood some of the author's message here, but doesn't tie that to the photo journal genre.)

PLANNER FOR SHARED READING

Objective (strategy focus): <u>B2-b:</u> <u>Why did the author write a [poem/story/nonfiction book, etc.] about this?</u>

 <u>Why did the author write a *photo journal* about "the journey to school integration?"</u>
How will student learning be measured at the end of the lesson? (What will count as "success?")

Text: <u>*Remember: The Journey to School Integration* by Toni Morison</u>   **Pages:** <u>Selected pages*</u>

Special Instructions: * I usually select about twelve pictures when teaching this lesson. I base my choices on the grade level of the students and their background knowledge on this topic. I almost always include photos of Civil Rights figures they know: Rosa Parks, Martin Luther King, and Ruby Bridges (though lots of students do not recognize Ruby Bridges.)

<table>
<tr>
<td rowspan="3" style="writing-mode: vertical-rl">BEFORE READING</td>
<td>Establish prior knowledge, purpose, and predictions</td>
<td>Prior knowledge: (To activate prior knowledge for this lesson I use the word splash—included with materials for this lesson on the CD. Write the words on a white board, SmartBoard, or on an overhead transparency. Ask children to identify a word they recognize and discuss each term briefly. This gives you a good sense of students' understanding of this period in history.)
Predictions: This book is not a "typical" story or informational text. It is made up of mostly pictures, in this case, pictures related to school integration. There are some captions, too, but the captions just describe the thoughts in the author's mind; they are not really the words spoken by the people in the pictures. What do you expect we will learn in this book? What will we see on these pages?
Purpose for reading: As we look at the pictures in this book, let's try to figure out why the author chose to write a <u>photo journal</u> about this topic instead of another kind of a book.</td>
</tr>
<tr>
<td>Introduce/ review vocabulary</td>
<td>These names and terms are important to this book although they are not all mentioned in the text. They are also included on the Word Splash (on the CD):
prejudice   Martin Luther King, Jr.   equality   discrimination
integration   Rosa Parks   Civil Rights   Jim Crow laws
violence   segregation</td>
</tr>
<tr>
<td>Introduce the objective (How to find and use the evidence)</td>
<td>Making the <u>reading</u> strategic
Think about the genre or structure of the text. What are the features of this type of text? In this case, our book is a photo journal. What are the important features of a photo journal (made up of mostly photos with captions that describe the pictures)? Figure out why the author thought that a photo journal was the best way to convey meaning about this topic to readers. Look carefully at the pictures as we look through this book: Why would the author have chosen mostly pictures to tell about this topic?</td>
</tr>
</table>

DURING READING	**Model and practice finding evidence for the objective**	**The best evidence:** Other pages may be chosen instead of the ones I've selected—but these do work pretty well. **Model:** **pp. 10-11:** I'm noticing that this school is an example of segregation. I'm also noticing the name of the school. We would never refer to black people today as "colored." But back then, this language was pretty common—though never considered very respectful. I'm also thinking that the author wants me to see that this school probably isn't as nice as those attended by white children (p, 11). Would you want to go to a school like this? **p. 15:** (reinforces the kind of schools attended by black children) **p. 27:** The word that comes to my mind when I see this picture is *violence.* And these are *kids* behaving this way. It makes me wonder where their parents were. Why didn't they stop them? Did they actually *approve* of this kind of behavior? **p. 30:** This child is wearing the kind of outfit worn by the Ku Klux Klan. What does this show? **Practice:** **p. 31:** What do you think is happening in this picture? (I cover the caption, so students can figure this out themselves.) **p. 45:** Who is this little girl? What is happening here? **pp. 52-53:** What are these pictures examples of (segregation, Jim Crow laws)? **pp. 56, 58, 59:** What are these people doing? (Students may be unfamiliar with the concept of a Freedom March.) **p. 62:** Who is this person? Why is she so famous? **pp. 64-65:** Who is this person? What speech was he giving here? **p. 72:** (Cover up the captions except for the four lines below the girls' photos) Why do you think the author is ending her book with the pictures of these four girls? (I often end my lesson here, without revealing the identify of the girls or their circumstances. I follow up the next day with a lesson on the poem, "The Battle of Birmingham" and students immediately see the connection.)
	Model and practice other strategies	**Connecting?** Can you make a personal connection to any of these pictures? Explain your connection. **Visualizing/Picturing?** Which photo in this book do you consider the most powerful? Why? **Wondering?** Which photo in this book raised new questions in your mind? What did you wonder about? **Predicting/Guessing?** What could you predict as we continued to look through this book? **Noticing?** What details were the most disturbing to you? **Figuring out?** Why did the author choose to write a photo journal about this topic? Why not a typical story or a nonfiction article?

AFTER READING	**Discussion questions**	**Question related to the objective** **B2-b:** Why did the author choose to write a <u>photo journal</u> about this topic? **Other questions** **D2-b:** If you were going to give a talk about school integration, what two points would you be sure to include? **D2-b:** Find a picture in this book that really "speaks to you." Imagine that you are the person in this picture. What would you have included in your journal after this situation had taken place? **D3-a:** What was important to this author?
	Written response to text	**Making the <u>writing</u> strategic** • **B2-b:** Why did the author choose to write a <u>photo journal</u> about this topic? • See *That's a Great Answer*, p. 106, for a template as a place to begin, or create a template of your own. • Model the response using two photos from the book as evidence. • Remove the template and ask students to write their own answer—using different photos from the text.
	Other follow-up activities	**Oral language, fluency, vocabulary, comprehension, reading extensions, writing extensions** **Oral language/fluency:** Write a new caption for a picture, or write a caption for a picture that doesn't have a caption. Practice reading your caption until your voice expresses the emotion that the photo conveys. **Vocabulary:** Complete the *Vocabulary Connections* activity for this book (on the CD). **Comprehension:** These follow-up activities may be found in *Constructing Meaning through Kid-Friendly Comprehension Strategy Instruction*: The Question is…, p. 172; Mirror, Mirror on the Wall…, p. 176; I Predict that I'll Remember, p. 183; A Message from the Author, p. 186. **Reading extensions:** These photo journals would also extend students' understanding of this genre: • *A Negro League Scrapbook* by Carole Boston Weatherford • *Over the Top of the World: Explorer Will Steger's Trek Across the Arctic* by Will Steger • *Snapshots from the Wedding* by Gary Soto (This book is "photo-journal-ish"; the illustrations are made originally of Sculpy clay and found objects.) **Writing extensions:** Create a photo journal of your own with three or more pictures that all relate to the same theme. Provide captions or extended descriptions.
	Reflect on reading and writing strategy	• What do you need to think about when considering why an author chose a particular genre? • Why might an author choose to create a photo journal about a topic rather than writing another kind of text?

OBJECTIVE

B3-a: Prove that the character is very _____.

BOOK

Uncle Jed's Barbershop by Margaree King Mitchell

INTRODUCTION TO THE BOOK

In this Depression-era story, Uncle Jed dreams of opening his own barbershop. He is close to achieving his dream when his niece becomes desperately ill and needs an operation. Uncle Jed offers up the money and begins to save again-when the banks fail. Finally, at age 79, Uncle Jed opens his shop, and although he dies soon after, he has succeeded in achieving his long-awaited goal.

WHY THIS IS A GOOD BOOK FOR TEACHING THIS OBJECTIVE

This is a good book for this objective because Uncle Jed demonstrates two character traits that students can readily identify—determination and generosity (though these could be labeled differently.) There is much evidence for both. I have used this book numerous times to introduce this objective and I model with one trait and ask students to then write their response with the other. Uncle Jed is a character with heart, and children are always intrigued by such selflessness.

OTHER OBJECTIVES THAT MAY BE ADDRESSED BY RE-READING THIS BOOK

- **A3-a:** Briefly summarize this story.
- **C1-b:** Make a connection to a feeling in this story.
- **D1-e:** Do you think the author made this story believable? Why or why not?
- **D2-c:** Using information in the text, write a paragraph that could have appeared in Uncle Jed's journal the night he finally opened his barbershop.

OTHER BOOKS MATCHED TO THIS OBJECTIVE TO LEAD STUDENTS TOWARD INDEPENDENCE (Remember to chart the evidence when you use a picture book so that students may provide specific details from the text)

These books also demonstrate strong character traits:

- *Minty: A Story of Young Harriet Tubman* by Alan Shroeder
  This partial biography of Harriet Tubman's childhood illustrates her strength of character—even from a young age.

- ***Jump! From the Life of Micheal Jordan* by Floyd Cooper**
  This story describes the early life of Michael Jordan, Although Michael wasn't a basketball sensation at first, he wouldn't give up. In fact, he wasn't even chosen at first for his high school varsity team. But his healthy competition with his brother Larry, and his determination to succeed finally made him a star.

- ***Rosa* by Nikki Giovanni**
  This well-written book describes the events of Rosa's life from that fateful day when she refused to give up her bus seat, highlighting her courage—and the courage of so many others who participated in the bus boycott that followed.

SCORING STUDENTS' RESPONSES

 B3-a: Find evidence in the story that Uncle Jed was very determined.

Score = 2

Uncle Jed showed that he was very determined many times in his life. He always wanted his own barbershop and saved money from when he was young. But then his niece got sick and he donated the money for her operation. After that he lost all his money in the bank when the banks went broke. He was really old when he opened his barbershop but it meant a lot to him because he worked so hard all his life to reach his goal.

> (This response would receive full score because there are two specific examples and they both support the claim that Uncle Jed was "determined.")

Score = 1

Uncle Jed was determined to open a barbershop. His life wasn't easy and he was very poor, but he never gave up. Finally, he got his shop and he was happy, but then he died.

> (This response would receive only partial credit because it lacks specifics. Yes, Uncle Jed was poor—but what in the story showed this?)

Score = 0

Uncle Jed was very determined. He cut his friends' hair. He walked to their houses. In the end he opened his barbershop and cut his niece's hair.

> (This response would not receive any score because the examples provided do not demonstrate determination. Although it does mention opening his own shop, this is not linked to the quality of determination.)

PLANNER FOR SHARED READING

Objective (strategy focus): B3-a: Prove that the character is very [   ].

◎ Find evidence in the story that Uncle Jed is very [   ].

How will student learning be measured at the end of the lesson? (What will count as "success?")

Text: _Uncle Jed's Barbershop_ by Margaree Mitchell   **Pages:** Whole book

BEFORE READING	**Establish prior knowledge, purpose, and predictions**	**Prior knowledge:** What is segregation? What was life like for black people during the time of segregation? What was The Great Depression? What happened to people during The Great Depression? **Predictions:** Based on the title and the cover, what do you think this story will be about? **Purpose for reading:** As we read, let's think about Uncle Jed's character traits and the evidence in the story that proves these traits.
	Introduce/ review vocabulary	relative lathered customers lotion delayed sparkled in <u>exchange</u> for segregation
	Introduce the objective (How to find and use the evidence)	**Making the <u>reading</u> strategic** As you read, notice Uncle Jed's actions and words. What do these things show about him? Let's use sticky notes to mark the places in the book where Uncle Jed is showing the kind of person he was. When we finish reading, decide on the word (or words) that you think _best_ describe Uncle Jed. Find at least two examples in the story that _show_ this trait.

DURING READING	**Model and practice finding evidence for the objective**	**The best evidence:** **Model:** Caring/loving/giving/generous: **p. 1:** go to customers' houses to cut their hair) **p. 3:** put lotion on Sarah Jean's neck Determined: **p. 5:** wanted to own a barbershop **p. 8:** held onto his dream even when no one believed in him and he as very poor **Practice:** Caring/loving/giving/generous: **p. 16:** Gave his barbershop money to Sarah Jean for her operation **p. 18:** Came to see Sarah Jean while she was recovering **p. 22:** Continued to cut people's hair even when they couldn't pay Determined: **p. 19:** Held onto his dream even when he lost his money in The Great Depression **p. 23:** Finally got his barbershop when he was 79 years old. **p. 28:** Taught Sarah Jean to dream, too.
	Model and practice other strategies	**Connecting?** Do you have any dreams that you would fight for, even if they were hard to achieve? **Visualizing/Picturing?** Can you picture the barbershop that Uncle Jed dreams of owning? Think of something else that might be in this barbershop that the author didn't mention. **Wondering?** The author mentions segregation and gives examples of the way black people were treated during this time in our history. What questions do you have about this that you are wondering about? **Predicting/Guessing?** The last sentence of this story is, "He taught me to dream, too." Predict what you think this means: What do you think the narrator might have been dreaming about? **Noticing?** What details did you notice about the setting of this story (the South during segregation and the Great Depression)? **Figuring out?** What do you think was important to the author of this book? What was her message? Why do you think she wrote this book?

	Discussion questions	**Question related to the objective** **B3-a:** Find evidence in the story that shows Uncle Jed as very _____. **Other questions** **A1-b:** What is the theme of this story? **A2-e:** What is the setting of this story? How is the setting important to the events of the story? **C1-c:** Would you like to know Uncle Jed? Why or why not? **D2-c:** Using evidence from the text, write a paragraph that Uncle Jed might have written in his journal after he finally opened his barbershop.
	Written response to text	**Making the <u>writing</u> strategic** • See *That's a Great Answer*, p. 110, or *Teaching Written Response to Text*, pp. 56-57, for a template matched to this objective. • Model the response using one character trait. Ask students to respond to the same question—identifying a different trait and finding evidence to support their choice.
	Other follow-up activities	**Oral language, fluency, vocabulary, comprehension, reading extensions, writing extensions** **Oral language/fluency:** Practice reading one of the pages until you sound like you imagine the narrator would sound, telling about Uncle Jed. **Vocabulary:** See *Vocabulary Connections* activity that accompanies this story. **Comprehension:** These follow-up activities may be found in *Constructing Meaning through Kid-Friendly Strategy Instruction*: Choose One Word that Best Describes Uncle Jed, p. 160; The Question is…, p. 172; Summary Frame for Story Text, p. 188. **Reading extensions:** These stories focus on characters who face financial hardships: • *Gettin' Through Thursdays* by Melrose Cooper • *Tight Times* by Barbara Shook Hazen • *Fly Away Home* by Eve Bunting **Writing extensions:** Write a speech that you could give to honor Uncle Jed for his lifetime of good deeds. What award would you give Uncle Jed? What would you include in your speech?
	Reflect on reading and writing strategy	• How do you decide on a word that best describes a character? • Ho do you locate evidence for something you are trying to prove when you are reading?

OBJECTIVE

B3-b: What facts (details) show that _____?

BOOK

The Flag We Love by Pam Muñoz Ryan

INTRODUCTION TO THE BOOK

This book describes the history behind the American flag, and what it symbolizes to the American people: pride, individual rights, respect, honor, patriotism, and the right to a good education. The story is told in rhyme with text boxes at the bottom of each page containing more details about each concept. The illustrations are bold and vivid and contribute to the overall sense of pride that this book strives to generate.

WHY THIS IS A GOOD BOOK FOR TEACHING THIS OBJECTIVE

This book is well-matched to this objective because it addresses the most central skill of content area reading: finding evidence to support a conclusion. Whether the content is social studies (as in the case of this book), science, or some other academic discipline, students first need to construct basic meaning about the topic by recognizing related facts. Then they can think critically about the topic's deeper meaning. There are plenty of details in this book to build that factual foundation. It also provides information at two levels: the main text, intended to build basic understanding for all readers, and the text boxes for those who desire more elaboration on each concept.

OTHER OBJECTIVES THAT MAY BE ADDRESSED BY RE-READING THIS BOOK

- **A1-c:** What is the main idea of this text?
- **B2-a:** Why does the author include the text boxes on each page?
- **C1-a:** Make a personal connection to this book.
- **C2-d:** What was your first reaction to this text? Explain.

OTHER BOOKS MATCHED TO THIS OBJECTIVE TO LEAD STUDENTS TOWARD INDEPENDENCE (Remember to chart the evidence when you use a picture book so that students may provide specific details from the text)

These books contain content knowledge at two levels: the basic text which addresses the most essential points, and text boxes or sidebars that elaborate on the content.

- ***One Tiny Turtle* by Nicola Davies**

  This book is a great example of narrative nonfiction—information about the loggerhead turtle presented in story form. There are plenty of facts that support various main points: the appropriateness of its name, how the loggerhead changes throughout its life, etc. Another thing I love about this book is the language. Beautiful word images show that nonfiction text can be written with the same elegance that is often found in fiction and poetry. Another plus: There's the story—and in smaller font, details that dig deeper.

- ***A Platypus, Probably* by Sneed Collard**

  There's something inherently fascinating about the platypus. The "main text" here presents just enough information to students who want to find evidence of the uniqueness of this mammal. A sub-text adds details for more sophisticated thinkers.

- ***Alaska* by Shelley Gill**

  This book offers a seasonal tour of our 49th state—its history, culture, wildlife, and geography. Basic information is presented in short rhymes accompanied by magnificent photographs. Two or more paragraphs of additional information supply lots more details.

SCORING STUDENTS' RESPONSES

 B3-b: Which facts/details show that our flag is a symbol of American patriotism?

Score = 2

The American flag is a symbol of patriotism. One thing that shows this is that explorers plant a flag when they reach their goal to show they are proud that their country reached this place. They even planted an American flag on the moon. Something else that shows the flag is a patriotic symbol is that you always say the Pledge of Allegiance to the flag at a ceremony and you put your hand on your heart to show how much you care about our country.

> (This response would receive full score because it provides two examples with sufficient details that accurately depict the flag as a symbol of patriotism.)

Score = 1

The American flag is a symbol of patriotism because it welcomes people to America and soldiers fly the flag when they are in a battle.

> (I would give this response partial credit as it is basically correct. However, more elaboration would show deeper understanding of *why* the flag is a symbol in these circumstances.)

Score = 0

Betsy Ross made the first flag. It was red, white, and blue, and it still has those colors. But now it has more stars.

> (No score for this response. It states an accurate detail about the flag, but does not address the flag's symbolism or connection to patriotism.)

PLANNER FOR SHARED READING

Objective (strategy focus): <u>B3-b:</u> <u>Which facts (details) show that [   ] ?</u>

 <u>Which facts/details show that our flag is a symbol of American patriotism?</u>

How will student learning be measured at the end of the lesson? (What will count as "success?")

Text: _The Flag We Love_ by Pam Munoz Ryan   **Pages:** <u>Whole book</u>

<table>
<tr>
<td rowspan="3" style="writing-mode: vertical-rl">BEFORE READING</td>
<td>Establish prior knowledge, purpose, and predictions</td>
<td>Prior knowledge: What do you know about our American flag? What does it look like? Why is it important to our country?
Predictions: By looking at the cover and the title, what do you expect to learn in this book? (Look at a few of the illustrations; notice how the text is structured—main text and text boxes with more details.) Do you think this will be a story with characters and an adventure, or an informational book with main ideas and details? How can you tell?
Purpose for reading: As we read, let's notice details that explain all the ways that our flag is a symbol of American patriotism.</td>
</tr>
<tr>
<td>Introduce/ review vocabulary</td>
<td>The two most essential terms here are symbol and patriotism. The other words are used in the text to describe our flag's various symbolic roles. Introduce them according to your students' vocabulary needs.

symbol   patriotism   radiant   ceremony   diligent
solemn   weary   festive   welcoming   valiant
righteous   brilliant   citizen</td>
</tr>
<tr>
<td>Introduce the objective (How to find and use the evidence)</td>
<td>Making the <u>reading</u> strategic
When you are trying to prove something with evidence in a text, you first need to understand what you're proving. Look for key words in the question. In this case, we have to prove that our flag is a symbol, so we need to think about what the word symbol means. Next, find examples that show what you are looking for. You should look for at least two examples—three would be even better.</td>
</tr>
</table>

DURING READING	**Model and practice finding evidence for the objective**	**The best evidence:** **Model:** **p. 4:** A flag in front of a school symbolizes a chance to learn and grow **p. 6:** Pledging the flag before a ceremony symbolizes our allegiance (patriotism) **p. 8:** Waving the flag during a battle symbolizes soldiers' refusal to give up **Practice:** **p. 10:** A flag can also symbolize a fallen hero (flag at half-mast or draped over a casket) **p. 12:** Planting a flag someplace special like the moon or the North Pole symbolizes that you reached this destination **p. 14:** A flag at a parade can symbolize celebration **p. 16:** A flag at a sports event like the Olympics symbolizes victory for your country **p. 18:** The flag near the Statue of Liberty symbolizes welcome to the land of liberty. **p. 20:** The flag left by astronauts on the moon symbolized peace. **p. 24:** A flag in a freedom march symbolizes righteousness and justice for all **p. 26:** A flag displayed with fireworks on the Fourth of July symbolizes brilliance and light **p. 28:** A flag pin symbolizes that we are patriotic citizens
	Model and practice other strategies	**Connecting?** Connect to a time when our flag has been important to you. **Visualizing/Picturing?** Find a flag in a picture. What does it symbolize in that picture? **Wondering?** Wonder what else our flag might symbolize. **Predicting/Guessing?** Predict the way different people react to our flag: soldiers, new people coming to our country, people from other countries who disagree with our government **Noticing?** What details about our flag did you learn that you didn't know before? **Figuring out?** Figure out why our flag is so important to our country.

Discussion questions	**Question related to the objective** **B3-b:** Which facts/details show that our flag is a symbol of American patriotism? **Other questions** **A1-c:** What is the main idea of this book? **A4-b:** If the author added another paragraph to the end of this book, it would <u>most likely</u> tell about _____. Use information from the book to support your answer. **C1-a:** Make a personal connection to a time when our flag has been important to you.
Written response to text	**Making the <u>writing</u> strategic** • See *That's a Great Answer*, p. 112, or *Teaching Written Response*, pp. 100-101, for a template matched to this objective. • Model the response using the template. • Remove your response and ask students to write the response themselves using the template—choosing their own evidence if possible.
Other follow-up activities	**Oral language, fluency, vocabulary, comprehension, reading extensions, writing extensions** **Oral language/fluency:** Find a poem or song about our flag or something else special about America. Practice the lyrics or words until you can say them with expression and feeling. Recite the song or poem for other classmates. **Vocabulary:** See *Vocabulary Connections* activity on the CD. **Comprehension:** These follow-up activities may be found in *Constructing Meaning through Kid-Friendly Strategy Instruction*: What's in a Picture, p. 165; Reading with all of my Senses, p. 168; A Message from the Author, p. 186; I'm a Word Watcher, p. 197. **Reading extensions:** These books celebrate America: • *A Picnic in October* by Eve Bunting • *America's White Table* by Margot Theis Raven • *A Paper Hug* by Stephanie Skolmoski • *H is for Honor: A Military Family Alphabet* by Devin Scillian • *America the Beautiful* by Katharine Lee Bates, illustrated by Neil Waldman Another book about symbolism would be *The Lotus Seed* by Sherry Garland, which describes an important symbol in the Vietnamese culture. **Writing extensions:** Write a poem about what the flag means to you. Your poem could be in the form of a haiku, a cinquain, free verse, or some other form.
Reflect on reading and writing strategy	• How do we go about finding details or facts to prove something in a text? • Why is it important to support our thinking about something with evidence?

Chapter Ten

STRAND C LESSONS

Making Reader/ Text Connections

C1-a: Make a personal connection to an experience in a text.

BOOK

Something Beautiful by Sharon Dennis Wyeth

INTRODUCTION TO THE BOOK

The little girl in this story learns to look beyond the sad conditions in her run-down neighborhood to find "something beautiful." She decides that *beautiful* means, "something that when you have it, your heart is happy." Moreover, she learns that the things in life that are truly beautiful are the every-day experiences, memories, and, treasures that may not cost anything—but hold great personal meaning. This is a very simple story with limited text, but a powerful message. The wonderful illustrations by Chris Soenpiet add even more depth to a narrative that will give readers renewed reason to have a happy heart.

WHY THIS IS A GOOD BOOK FOR TEACHING THIS OBJECTIVE

This book is great for making personal connections because it has a meaningful "big idea" to which students can relate: finding "something beautiful" in their own lives. Furthermore, it reinforces the important message that "beauty" doesn't need to be big and expensive. The story can be read easily in one sitting and would be appropriate for students of various grades. A few schools I know have used this book for a "whole school read."

OTHER OBJECTIVES THAT MAY BE ADDRESSED BY RE-READING THIS BOOK

- **A1-b:** What is the theme of this story?
- **A2-a:** Using information in the story, write a brief description of how _____ felt when…….
- **C2-d:** What was your first reaction to this text? Explain.

OTHER BOOKS MATCHED TO THIS OBJECTIVE TO LEAD STUDENTS TOWARD INDEPENDENCE (Remember to chart the evidence when you use a picture book so that students may provide specific details from the text)

These books all describe typical "kid experiences" to which children could probably connect:

*   ***My Rotten Redheaded Older Brother* by Patricia Polacco**
    This story about sibling relationships is good for personal connections. It's the age-old theme of thinking your brother/sister is a complete pain. But then in your hour of need, the sibling comes through in the most thoughtful, loving way.

*   ***Down the Road* by Alice Schertle**
    In this story a little girl wants to feel "grown up." She is proud when her parents then send her to the store all by herself to buy eggs. However, on the way home, she gets careless and all of the eggs break when she tries to pick a few apples from an apple tree. She is panicked that her parents will be angry with her, but Mom and Dad handle the situation with love and understanding. Students can connect to the idea of wanting to be given responsibility, and to not living up to the promises they have made.

*   ***Dream* by Susan Bosak**
    This book follows a person's dreams from infancy through old age with thoughtful insights and amazing illustrations by many different illustrators. Quotes about dreams on each page add another layer of text for readers to consider. Students can reflect on their own dreams for the future as they peruse the pages of this beautiful book.

SCORING STUDENTS' RESPONSES

The little girl in this story found something beautiful in her life. Use what you learned in this book to make a connection to something beautiful in your own life

Score = 2

In this story the little girl discovered lots of beautiful things in her life such as the fish sandwich that the diner lady made, and her baby cousin's laugh. Beautiful things don't have to cost money! That is like my life because I have lots of beautiful things, too that don't cost money. I have a best friend named Keisha and we share everything. It is beautiful to have a best friend because then you never feel lonely.

> (This response would receive full score because it provides examples from the text, but then identifies a personal connection that is different from the text examples—and is personally meaningful to the student. This student even indicates *why* her example is beautiful to her.)

Score = 1

In this story the little girl finds beautiful things like a smooth stone and her baby cousin's laugh. That is like my life because I have a pretty rock that is my lucky rock, and my baby cousin's laugh is beautiful to me.

> (This student would receive partial credit. While the response includes good evidence from the text, the personal examples just mimic the story details. There is no real thinking evident here, and it is questionable whether this connection has led the reader to a deeper understanding of the story.)

I think the sunset is beautiful because it has lots of colors and sometimes the sun looks like an orange ball. When the sun goes down, the horizon looks purple and it is just beautiful!

> (This student provides a great example of something that is personally beautiful, but fails to go back and connect it to the text. Therefore, it could not receive full credit.)

Score = 0

In the story the girl looks for beautiful things. I never looked for beautiful things.

> (This student has missed the point entirely! First, the evidence from the text is general, not specific. More importantly, the "big idea" of the story was about the "every day" things of beauty that we have available to us—if only we would pause to appreciate them.)

PLANNER FOR SHARED READING

Objective (strategy focus): <u>C1-a:</u> <u>Make a personal connection to an experience in a text</u>

◎ <u>The little girl in this story found something beautiful in her life. Use what you learned</u>
<u>in this book to make a connection to something beautiful in your own life</u>

How will student learning be measured at the end of the lesson? (What will count as "success?")

Text: <u>*Something Beautiful* by Sharon Dennis Wyeth</u>   **Pages:** <u>Whole book</u>

<table>
<tr>
<td rowspan="3">BEFORE READING</td>
<td>Establish prior knowledge, purpose, and predictions</td>
<td>Prior knowledge: When you think about "something beautiful" what comes to mind? What makes something "beautiful?" Would people always agree about what is "beautiful?" Why or why not?
Predictions: By looking at the title and the cover, what do you think this story might be about?
Purpose for reading: As we read, let's think about the word "beautiful" and try to make a connection to our own lives.</td>
</tr>
<tr>
<td>Introduce/ review vocabulary</td>
<td>alley   sizzles   giggle   stoop   cautioned</td>
</tr>
<tr>
<td>Introduce the objective (How to find and use the evidence)</td>
<td>Making the <u>reading</u> strategic
When you are trying to make a connection to an experience in a text, first figure out the "big idea" (or what the author wanted you to think about when he/she wrote the story.) Make a connection to this big idea—not a little detail. Remember, you need to think of an example that is <u>different</u> from an example that the author used.</td>
</tr>
<tr>
<td rowspan="2">DURING READING</td>
<td>Model and practice finding evidence for the objective</td>
<td>The best evidence:
<u>Model:</u>
p. 10: Beautiful…means: something that when you have it, your heart is happy.
p. 11: Ms. Delphine's fish sandwich
<u>Practice:</u>
p. 13: jump rope, beads, new shoes
p. 15: fruit store
p. 18: moves and sounds
p. 20: smooth stone
p. 21: baby's laugh
p. 25: pick up trash, erase the word die, plant flowers
p. 27: you!</td>
</tr>
<tr>
<td>Model and practice other strategies</td>
<td>Connecting? Can you connect to a feeling as well as the experience in this book?
Visualizing/Picturing? Which illustration in this book seems the most important or powerful to you? Why?
Wondering? What did you wonder about as you read this story?
Predicting/Guessing? Did you predict that this little girl would find something beautiful? Why or why not?
Noticing? What did you notice about the "beautiful things" in this story?
Figuring out? What did you figure out about finding something "beautiful?"</td>
</tr>
</table>

AFTER READING	**Discussion questions**	**Question related to the objective** **C1-a:** In this story the little girl looked for something beautiful in her life. Make a connection to something beautiful in *your* life. **Other questions** **A1-a:** What is the theme of this book? **C2-c:** Did you like this story? Why or why not? **D2-c:** Using information in the story, write a paragraph that could have appeared in the little girl's journal after she had asked her friends and family about having something beautiful in their life.
	Written response to text	**Making the <u>writing</u> strategic** • See *That's a Great Answer*, p. 117, of *Teaching Written Response*, pp. 173-174, for a template matched to this objective • Model the response using the template. • Remove your response and ask students to write their own response based on their own connection.
	Other follow-up activities	**Oral language, fluency, vocabulary, comprehension, reading extensions, writing extensions** **Oral language/fluency:** Interview a friend or family member about "something beautiful" in their life. Think of some good questions to ask such as: Where did you get your "something beautiful?" Why is it special to you? What special memories does it have for you? **Vocabulary:** Complete the *Vocabulary Connections* activity for this book found on the CD. **Comprehension:** These follow-up strategy activities may be found in *Constructing Meaning through Kid-Friendly Strategy Instruction*: Friends I Might Have Known, p. 162; What's in a Picture, p. 165; Reading with all of my Senses, p. 168; Best Quote, p. 175. **Reading extensions:** These books are about special memories or objects that have particular significance: • *The Keeping Quilt* by Patricia Polacco • *Betty Doll* by Patricia Polacco • *The Memory String* by Eve Bunting • *Small Beauties: The Journey of Darcy Heart O'Hara* by Elvira Woodruff **Writing extensions:** Write a story from your imagination in which your "something beautiful" plays an important part. Who are the characters? (One might be you.) What is the problem? How does the problem get solved? What is the significance of your "something special?"
	Reflect on reading and writing strategy	• When you are trying to make a personal connection to a text, what do you need to do? • Give an example of a *strong* connection to this text. Why is this connection strong? • Give an example of a *weak* connection to this text. Why is this connection weak?

C1-b: Make a connection to an important feeling in the story.

BOOK

One Green Apple by Eve Bunting

INTRODUCTION TO THE BOOK

I am always looking for texts that provide a positive view of mid-Eastern children or culture, and this story by Eve Bunting fits the bill perfectly. With her usual compassion, Bunting describes the anxiety faced by young Farah as she arrives at her new American school, and is immediately whisked away on a field trip to an apple orchard to pick apples and make cider. She feels misunderstood and isolated, and for a while, her classmates contribute to her sense of isolation. She drops her green apple into the cider press alongside the red apples of the other students, and her peers initially do not think the green apple belongs. But it is hard to turn the handle of the press, and when someone makes room for Farah, the class discovers that they make more progress as a team. The ride home from the orchard is less stressful with overtures of friendship from a few classmates.

WHY THIS IS A GOOD BOOK FOR TEACHING THIS OBJECTIVE

Feelings abound in this book. While all's well that ends well, and the main character is ultimately accepted by her classmates, the predominant feelings here center on isolation, rejection, and loneliness due to cultural and language differences. Hopefully as children connect to their own feelings of loneliness through this story, they will be less inclined to make quick judgments about peers who may come from diverse backgrounds.

OTHER OBJECTIVES THAT MAY BE ADDRESSED BY RE-READING THIS BOOK

- **A3-a:** Briefly summarize this story.
- **A4-b:** If the author added another paragraph to the end of the story (or article), it would most likely tell about _____.
- **D1-e:** Do you think the author made this story believable? Why or why not?
- **D3-b:** How are your customs different from the customs described in this story?

OTHER BOOKS MATCHED TO THIS OBJECTIVE TO LEAD STUDENTS TOWARD INDEPENDENCE (Remember to chart the evidence when you use a picture book so that students may provide specific details from the text)

Students will be able to relate to the strong feelings expressed by the characters in these books:

- *My Rotten Redheaded Older Brother* by Patricia Polacco
Feeling: jealousy of sibling. In this story, Trisha wishes she could do something—anything—better than her older brother, Richie. Well, she finally does. She stays on the merry-go-round *much* longer—and then falls off because she's so dizzy. "Rotten" Richie saves the day, which somehow changes the siblings' relationship for good. Kids will certainly relate to the sense of competition between siblings.

- *The Summer My Father Was Ten* by Pat Brisson
Feeling: remorse. Things get out of hand when some ten-year-old boys start fooling around, one afternoon and end up destroying the vegetable garden of an elderly neighbor. Everyone flees the scene except for this one boy who stays to apologize and make amends. He spends his life making up for his foolishness that one afternoon, and in the process a meaningful friendship is formed. Students will be able to connect to the notion of regretting foolish behavior, and righting a wrong.

- *Coming on Home Soon* by Jacqueline Woodson
Feeling: Missing a parent. In this story, a little girl desperately misses her mom who moves to a different city to find work following World War II. The little girl stays with her grandma who tries to remain cheerful, but there is no cheer in the little girl's heart. Eventually Mom returns, and her daughter is overjoyed. The illustrations contribute to the intense feelings in this book. Note that this topic might be too sensitive for a child who has lost a parent or who fears losing a parent.

SCORING STUDENTS' RESPONSES

 C1-b: Make a connection to a feeling in this story.

Score = 2

In the story Farah felt lonely because she couldn't speak English and her customs were different and she didn't fit in. She wore a dupatta on her head and people sounded mean when they talked about her country. I never moved to a different country, but once I went to a birthday party where I didn't know anybody. Everyone was talking about stuff I didn't know and I felt lonely and I couldn't wait to go home. I bet that's how Farah felt too.

> (This answer names an important feeling in the story, provides specific examples from the text, and makes a meaningful connection to a similar feeling in the reader's own life without relying on the same details mentioned in the text.)

Score = 1

In the story Farah felt like she wanted to go back to her old country. I would probably feel like that too if I was Farah.

> (This answer is accurate in describing how Farah felt, but fails to provide evidence from the text or a parallel example from the reader's own life: Explain a time when *you* were somewhere and felt like you wanted to go home.)

Score = 0

In the story Farah was happy because she got to go on a field trip and make cider. I wish we could go on a fieldtrip to make cider.

> (This response does not address a significant feeling in the story, and instead focuses on a detail—making cider.)

PLANNER FOR SHARED READING

Objective (strategy focus): <u>**C1-b:**</u> <u>Make a connection to a feeling in the story</u>

 <u>Make a connection to how Farah felt in this story.</u>
How will student learning be measured at the end of the lesson? (What will count as "success?")

Text: *One Green Apple* by Eve Bunting   **Pages:** <u>Whole book</u>

<table>
<tr>
<td rowspan="3">BEFORE READING</td>
<td>Establish prior knowledge, purpose, and predictions</td>
<td>Prior knowledge: Did you ever go somewhere and feel that you didn't fit in? Give an example. How did that make you feel?
Predictions: Look at the cover of this book. Can you make any predictions based on the girl you see here? What does it look like this story might be about?
Purpose for reading: This story is about a girl who is new to our country. Let's read to figure out how she felt, and try to make a connection. You will find several different feelings in this book, but decide which feeling the author probably wants us to think about the most.</td>
</tr>
<tr>
<td>Introduce/ review vocabulary</td>
<td>orchard   jolt   cruel   crooked   shrug</td>
</tr>
<tr>
<td>Introduce the objective (How to find and use the evidence)</td>
<td>Making the <u>reading</u> strategic
Think about how the character is feeling at different points in the story. Make sure you can name the feelings. Decide which feeling the author wants us to think about the very most. Think about a time when you have felt the same way. Make sure your example is different from the event in the story that created this feeling for the character in the story.</td>
</tr>
<tr>
<td rowspan="2">DURING READING</td>
<td>Model and practice finding evidence for the objective</td>
<td>The best evidence:
(Students may decide on other labels for these feelings—which is fine.)
<u>Model:</u>
p. 6: Homesick: wishes to go back home to her old country; sometimes classmates are cruel
p. 7: Different: thinks she doesn't fit in because she wears a dupatta
<u>Practice:</u>
p. 12: Lost: can't speak the language, afraid others will think she is stupid
p. 14: like an outsider: the little green apple was a lot like Farah
p. 21: like she has something to contribute: helping make cider
p. 22: accepted: when she starts to fit in
p. 27: capable: learning the language
p. 28: blending in: laughing in the same language</td>
</tr>
<tr>
<td>Model and practice other strategies</td>
<td>Connecting? Feeling awkward because you didn't feel like you fit in?
Visualizing/Picturing? What Farah would remember about her first days in America
Wondering? Wondering if Farah's classmates would make an effort to include her? Wondering why some students were cruel?
Predicting/Guessing? Predicting that Farah would probably do well in her new school eventually based on her attitude.
Noticing? All the ways life was hard for Farah because she was new to this country, and from a middle-eastern country
Figuring out? Why is life difficult for a newcomer to this country?</td>
</tr>
</table>

AFTER READING	**Discussion questions**	**Question related to the objective** **C1-b:** Connect to how Farah felt in this story. Think of a time when you have felt like Farah. **Other questions** **A1-:** What is the theme of this story? **A4-b:** If the author added another paragraph to the end of this story it would <u>most likely</u> tell about _____. Use information from the story (or article) to support your answer. **D2-c:** Using information in the story, write a paragraph that could have appeared in Farah's journal after she'd been to the apple orchard with her class.
	Written response to text	**Making the <u>writing</u> strategic** • See *That's a Great Answer*, p. 121, for a template matched to this objective. • Model the response using the template. • Remove your response and ask students to write their own response based on the evidence you chose, or other evidence in the story.
	Other follow-up activities	**Oral language, fluency, vocabulary, comprehension, reading extensions, writing extensions** **Oral language/fluency:** Find a place in the text where Farah is thinking thoughts inside her head. Practice reading one of these passages until you sound the way you imagine Farah would sound. **Vocabulary:** See the *Vocabulary Connections* activity on the CD related to this book. **Comprehension:** These follow-up activities may be found in *Constructing Meaning through Kid-Friendly Comprehension Strategy Instruction*: Friends I Might Have Known, p. 162; One Word, p. 160; What's in a Picture, p. 165 **Reading extensions:** Other books that describe the experiences of children who come to America: • *My Name is Jorge: On Both Sides of the River: Poems in English and Spanish* by Jane Medina • *Going Home* by Eve Bunting • *Upside Down Boy: El nino de cabeza* by Juan Felipe Herrera • *Marianthe's Story: Painted Words and Spoken Memories* by Aliki **Writing extension:** Imagine that you are Farah. Write a letter to a friend back home telling about your experiences in America so far. Do you like this country? Why or why not?
	Reflect on reading and writing strategy	• When you are connecting to a feeling, what do you need to do? • What makes a connection a *good* connection?

C1-c: Would you like _____ for a friend? Why or why not?

BOOK

Mercedes and the Chocolate Pilot by Margot Theis Raven

INTRODUCTION TO THE BOOK

This is a true story of the Berlin Airlift and candy that was dropped from the sky by pilot Gail Halvorsen. Young Mercedes wishes more than anything that the "Chocolate Pilot" as he has come to be known, will fly over her home in bombed out West Berlin and drop a few sweet treats for her to enjoy. Mercedes even sends Halvorsen a letter to aid her cause. And miraculously, the pilot responds, sending a letter in response—and a whole package of candy. But that's not the end of the tale. Twenty years later Halvorsen returns to Berlin and is invited to the home of a fellow pilot, who just happens to be the now-grown Mercedes. The friendship is rekindled and memories are relived. This is truly a touching story.

WHY THIS IS A GOOD BOOK FOR TEACHING THIS OBJECTIVE

This is a good book for this objective because it presents well-developed characters. While students could respond to this objective by considering either Mercedes or Colonel Halvorsen, focusing on Halvorsen would probably generate deeper thinking. Students who think more insightfully will think beyond the "chocolate" and recognize the humanitarianism that motivated Halvorsen to help children hope for a better world.

OTHER OBJECTIVES THAT MAY BE ADDRESSED BY RE-READING THIS BOOK

- **A2-e:** What is the setting of this story and how does it contribute to its message?
- **B2-b:** Why did the author write a picture book about this event that happened so long ago?
- **C2-b:** Which part of this [story/article] was most interesting or surprising to you? Why?
- **D3-a:** How does _____ show that _____ is important to him/her?

OTHER BOOKS MATCHED TO THIS OBJECTIVE TO LEAD STUDENTS TOWARD INDEPENDENCE (Remember to chart the evidence when you use a picture book so that students may provide specific details from the text)

These books contain characters with qualities that students might (or might not) desire in a friend:

- ***The Goat Lady* by Jane Bregoli**
  Her neighbors show little respect for Noelie Houle, an elderly lady who raises goats in her rundown barnyard, but some new children to the neighborhood come to love her as they see how she cares for her goats. For many years she has provided goats' milk to people who need it, and has sent her extra goats to poor people through Heifer International. Would you want this woman for a friend? Could you look past the dilapidated house and strange ways of this woman to recognize her generous heart?

- ***Odd Boy Out: Young Albert Einstein* by Don Brown**
  Albert is a little odd as a child. He's mean to his sister and frustrates his teachers because he seems to learn differently from other students. Sometimes he doesn't even try! However, he gets good grades. When someone gives him a geometry book, he works through the whole thing himself, and begins explaining mathematical principles that no one else understands. Eventually he becomes a scientist. He wins the Nobel Prize. He is, in fact, Albert Einstein. Do you think he'd be a good friend?

- ***Meet Danitra Brown* by Nikki Grimes**
  Danitra and her friend Zuri are typical middle-grade kids who live in an urban neighborhood. They each have their strengths and quirks. Danitra is "splendiferous" with a spunky attitude and a passion for the color purple. Zuri is a thinker and is the narrator of the twelve poems in this book that tell the story of a wonderful friendship. Which girl would you like for your friend? Or maybe you'd like both girls as friends!

SCORING STUDENTS' RESPONSES

 Would you like Lt. Halvorsen for a friend? Why or why not?

Score = 2

I would like Lt. Halvorsen for my friend. He is a really kind man and I like people who are kind. He made a lot of extra work for himself sending all of that candy down to the children of Berlin. He knew how it would cheer them to get a little treat after their city had been bombed. He took the time to send Mercedes a letter and a package of candy just for her. He was even her friend when she grew up. I would like a friend who cared about me for my whole life.

> (This response would receive full score because it connects to an important character trait that the reader admires in her own friends. It also provides specific evidence from the text that supports the trait.)

Score = 1

I would like Lt. Halvorsen for my friend because he is a nice man and always thinks about how he can help other people, especially children. He brought them candy.

> (This response would receive partial credit. It identifies a character trait—though "nice" is a bit vague. Other than the reference to bringing candy, there is no specific evidence.)

Score = 0

I would like to be Lt. Halvorsen's friend because he brings candy and candy is my favorite food. I know it isn't good for me, but I still like it. On Halloween I get a ton of candy and I hide it so my sister can't get it.

> (This response really shouldn't receive any points because it misses the message of the story. It also loses its focus, describing only how the reader feels about candy, not Lt. Halvorsen.

PLANNER FOR SHARED READING

Objective (strategy focus): <u>C1-c:</u> Would you like [   ] for a friend? Why or why not?

 <u>Would you like Lt. Halvorsen for a friend? Why or why not?</u>
How will student learning be measured at the end of the lesson? (What will count as "success?")

Text: <u>*Mercedes and the Chocolate Pilot* by Margot Theis Raven</u>   **Pages:** <u>Whole book*</u>

*You may need more than one day to read this book.

<table>
<tr>
<td rowspan="3">BEFORE READING</td>
<td>Establish prior knowledge, purpose, and predictions</td>
<td>Prior knowledge: This story takes place in Germany following World War II. What do you know about World War II and what happened in Germany during that war? (Students will probably have little background on this topic. However, there is a nice introduction to this topic, especially the Berlin Airlift, at the beginning of this book. Read this to students. Also show them the picture on the following page of Berlin 1948 to give them a sense of the devastation.)
Predictions: What do you think that a "chocolate pilot" might be? What do you anticipate that this story might be about?
Purpose for reading: As we read this story, we'll get to know this "chocolate pilot." Let's decide whether we would like this person for a friend, and why we feel this way.</td>
</tr>
<tr>
<td>Introduce/ review vocabulary</td>
<td>precious   cringed   heaved (a sigh of relief)   rubble   cot
lingered   fragile   epilogue</td>
</tr>
<tr>
<td>Introduce the objective (How to find and use the evidence)</td>
<td>Making the <u>reading</u> strategic
When you consider whether you'd like a character or person in a book for a friend, you first need to think about things you value in a friend. These might include generosity, loyalty, kindness, common interests, sense of humor, etc. Now look for evidence in the text where this character or person demonstrates these traits. Don't look only at what the person accomplished to decide if s/he would be a good friend. What makes someone a good friend is not what they *do*, but who they *are*. Also, keep an open mind. Be willing to look at personal qualities you may not have considered before.</td>
</tr>
</table>

DURING READING	**Model and practice finding evidence for the objective**	**The best evidence:** **Model:** **p. 5:** Lt. Halvorsen dropped candy from his plane as part of the Berlin Airlift. **pp. 7-8:** Lt Halorsen gave gum to a few lucky children at the airfield fence; he promised to drop candy when he wiggled his plane's wings. **p. 9:** Halvorsen made parachutes from handkerchiefs and attached candy. **Practice:** **pp. 15-16:** Halvorsen dropped more candy—but Mercedes didn't catch any. **p. 25:** Halvorsen read the letter from Mercedes with interest. **pp. 29-32:** Mercedes received a letter and a package of candy from Halvorsen. **p. 33:** The letter was very kind. **p. 35:** Halvorsen left Berlin, but had dropped candy for 7 months. **pp. 37-40: Epilogue:** Reunion with Mercedes and Halvorsen; Halvorsen continued to fly "candy missions" to refugee camps throughout his life.
	Model and practice other strategies	**Connecting?** Make a connection to a time when you were kind and generous to someone—or someone was kind and generous to you. **Visualizing/Picturing?** Try to picture Berlin after World War II. What do you see in your mind? **Wondering?** What else would you like to know about Lt. Halvorsen, the Berlin Airlift, or this time in history? **Predicting/Guessing?** At what points during this story were you able to predict what might happen next? **Noticing?** What details really stood out to you about Lt. Halvorsen? **Figuring out?** What was important to Lt. Halvorsen?

AFTER READING	**Discussion questions**	**Question related to the objective** **C1-c:** Would you like Lt. Halvorsen for a friend? Why or why not? **Other questions** **A2-e:** What is the setting of this story and how did it contribute to the events that occurred? **B1-d:** Can the Epilogue be considered an explanation, an opinion, a description, or a conversation? Explain your choice. **C2-b:** Which part of this story was most interesting or surprising to you? Why? **D1-b:** There are lots of similes in this text. Choose one and explain how it helps you picture what the author is describing.
	Written response to text	**Making the <u>writing</u> strategic** • See *That's a Great Answer*, p. 124, for a template matched to this objective. • Model the response using the template. • Remove your response and ask students to write the response themselves using the template if necessary—based on their own reason.
	Other follow-up activities	**Oral language, fluency, vocabulary, comprehension, reading extensions, writing extensions** **Oral language/fluency:** Practice reading Mercedes' letter to Lt. Halvorsen, or Lt. Halvorsen's letter to Mercedes. How do you think each person would sound? Would Mercedes sound anxious and hopeful? Would Lt. Halvorsen sound as kind as his actions showed him to be? **Vocabulary:** See *Vocabulary Connections* activity on the CD. **Comprehension:** These follow-up activities may be found in *Constructing Meaning through Kid-Friendly Strategy Instruction*: Active Reader Report, p. 155; I'm Connected, p. 159; Connecting to Time and Place, p. 161; Friends I Might Have Known, p. 162. **Reading extensions:** These stories all feature the devastation and poverty in Europe following World War II: • *One Thousand Tracings: Healing the Wounds of World War II* by Lita Judge • *Boxes for Katje* by Candace Fleming • *How I Learned Geography* by Uri Shulevitz **Writing extensions:** It is surprising that Mercedes did not write a thank you note to Lt. Halvorsen after he mailed the candy and letter to her. Write the letter that you think Mercedes should have written after she received that package. Be sure to give specific reasons why the candy and letter meant so much to you.
	Reflect on reading and writing strategy	• How do you go about considering whether you'd like a particular character or person in a book for a friend? • What are some of the things *you* look for in a friend to help you decide whether a character/person would be a good friend? • What kinds of surprises might you find in a book that would make you consider someone for a friend, even though at first you might have had a different opinion?

C1-d: Using evidence from the text, explain whether you would ever want to _____.

BOOK

Snowflake Bentley by Jacqueline Briggs Martin

INTRODUCTION TO THE BOOK

From the time he was a young child, Wilson Bentley thought snow was beautiful and he was determined to photograph it. His early photos of snowflakes revealed two important things: no two snowflakes are alike. And snowflakes are, in fact beautiful. Although he was often misunderstood, "Snowflake Bentley" followed his heart and achieved his lifelong goal, sending a worthy message to middle grade students who too often abandon their own goals to fit in with their peers.

WHY THIS IS A GOOD BOOK FOR TEACHING THIS OBJECTIVE

Snowflake Bentley is well matched to this objective because it describes in great detail something (a hobby) that students may or may not find intriguing. Would *you* want to study snowflakes for your entire life? The author's explanation of this passion may turn some children into believers: learning about snowflakes would be fascinating. Others may not be a bit convinced that these icy crystals are interesting at all. Either way, plenty of evidence is provided to respond to this question.

OTHER OBJECTIVES THAT MAY BE ADDRESSED BY RE-READING THIS BOOK

- **A1-b:** What is the theme of this story?
- **A3-b:** Summarize the main things that happened in this story.
- **B3-a:** Prove that [character/person] is very _____.
- **D2-b:** Imagine you are going to give a talk to your class about _____. What two points would you be sure to include in your speech?

OTHER BOOKS MATCHED TO THIS OBJECTIVE TO LEAD STUDENTS TOWARD INDEPENDENCE (Remember to chart the evidence when you use a picture book so that students may provide specific details from the text.)

The books below describe a way of life or an experience that may be different from the typical life experiences of many children today. It is easier for students to respond to this question about engaging in a particular experience if it is significantly different from what is very familiar to them.

- *Appalachia: The Voices of Sleeping Birds* **by Cynthia Rylant**
  This book is mostly a description of a place, the West Virginia community where Rylant grew up. The details of this setting may be very appealing to some students, and unattractive to others.

- *The Raft* **by Jim LaMarche**
  At first Nicky is dreading the thought of spending the summer with his rather unconventional grandma way off in the woods. But he discovers an old wooden raft, and that changes everything. Nicky paddles that raft up and down the river, getting to know both nature—and himself. Would *you* want to spend the summer on a raft? It's an interesting thought to ponder.

- *Momma, Where are you From?* **by Marie Bradby**
  This book is less about a *place* and more about a *time*—a time when despite being a little bit poor, and affected by the discrimination that plagued the pre-Civil Rights South, there was a strong sense of family and community. Would you have wanted to be a part of this community in this time?

SCORING STUDENTS' RESPONSES

C1-d: Using evidence from the text, explain whether you would ever want to study snowflakes like Snowflake Bentley.

Score = 2

I would love to study snowflakes like Snowflake Bentley. I never thought about this before, but I love art and I love looking at things under a microscope. I would like to see the tiny crystals and how delicate and intricate they are. I might put my pictures in a book and publish them, just like this man did.

> (This response would receive full score because the reader gave several specific reasons directly from the text for wanting to study snowflakes.)

Score = 1

I would not like to study snowflakes. I get cold when I go outside in the winter and this seems boring to me and I don't have a camera.

> (This student is relying mostly on background knowledge, but does make some general reference to the text—not having a camera, and being bored.)

Score = 0

I love the snow. I like to make snowmen, snow angels, and forts. I hope we have a blizzard next winter.

> (This response is just about snow, not snowflakes, and doesn't really address the question.)

PLANNER FOR SHARED READING

Objective (strategy focus): C1-d: <u>Using evidence from the text, explain whether you would</u> <u>ever want to: [   ].</u>

◎ <u>Using evidence from the text, explain whether you would ever want to study snowflakes</u> <u>like Snowflake Bentley.</u>

How will student learning be measured at the end of the lesson? (What will count as "success?")

Text: <u>*Snowflake Bentley*</u> by Jacqueline Briggs Martin   **Pages:** <u>Whole book</u>

<table>
<tr>
<td rowspan="3" style="writing-mode: vertical-rl;">BEFORE READING</td>
<td>Establish prior knowledge, purpose, and predictions</td>
<td>Prior knowledge: What do you know about snow? Have you ever really looked at a snowflake? What do you see?
Predictions: Look at the cover and title of this book. What do you predict that it will be about?
Purpose for reading: This is a true story about a man who loved snow—not playing in the snow, but studying snowflakes. As we read this story, think about whether you would ever want to study snowflakes, too.</td>
</tr>
<tr>
<td>Introduce/ review vocabulary</td>
<td>lantern   blades (of grass)   pelted   intricate   magnify jumbled   monument   delicate</td>
</tr>
<tr>
<td>Introduce the objective (How to find and use the evidence)</td>
<td>Making the <u>reading</u> strategic
When you are trying to decide whether or not you would want to experience something like a character or person in a book, or if you would want to live in a certain time or place, you need to keep an open mind—even if it's not something you initially thought you would like. What are the advantages? What are the disadvantages? Find lots of examples in the book to support your opinion. In this story, Snowflake Bentley spends his whole life studying snowflakes. You will find out what that was like for him. Then you need to decide if you would like this kind of life, too.</td>
</tr>
</table>

	Model and practice finding evidence for the objective	**The best evidence:** **Model:** **p. 2:** Willie's happiest days were snowstorm days. **p. 3:** He thought snowflakes were as beautiful as butterflies or apple blossoms. **p. 6:** He studied snowflakes under a microscope. **p. 8:** Tried saving snowflakes by drawing snow crystals, but they melted. **Practice:** **pp. 10-11:** Got a camera with its own microscope. **p. 14:** Didn't quit when first photos were a failure; figured out how to photograph snowflakes. **p. 16:** People made fun of Willie. **p. 17:** Studied snowstorms. **p. 19:** Never gave up—made hundreds of pictures. **p. 22:** Showed snow crystal slides to family and friends, gave photos as presents. **p. 24:** Published a book on snowflakes; never got rich. **p. 28:** There's a monument to Snowflake Bentley in the center of his town.
	Model and practice other strategies	**Connecting?** Is there something you love to do so much that it wouldn't bother you if no one understood how special it was to you? **Visualizing/Picturing?** What words would you use to describe a snowflake so you could picture it in your mind? **Wondering?** How do you think Willie Bentley became so interested in snowflakes? **Noticing?** Which details do you consider the most important in showing Willie Bentley's love of snowflakes? **Figuring out?** Willie Bentley really followed his heart. What does a person need to do in order to "follow his heart?"

AFTER READING	**Discussion questions**	**Question related to the objective** **C1-d:** Using evidence from the text, explain whether you would ever want to study snowflakes like Snowflake Bentley. **Other questions** **A3-b:** Summarize the main things that happened in this book. **B1-d:** On p. 16, Willie's neighbors said, "Snow in Vermont is as common as dirt. We don't need pictures." Is that an example of an explanation, a description, an opinion, or a conversation? Explain. **C2-b:** Which part of this story was most interesting or surprising to you? Why?
	Written response to text	**Making the <u>writing</u> strategic** • See *That's a Great Answer*, p. 126, for a template matched to this objective. • Model the response using the template. • Remove your response and ask students to write their own response—choosing their own evidence and reason if possible.
	Other follow-up activities	**Oral language, fluency, vocabulary, comprehension, reading extensions, writing extensions** **Oral language/fluency:** Work with a partner on this activity. Find a page that you like, and practice reading the basic text until your reading expresses the tone you think the author intended. Your partner will read the sidebar on the same page. That should be read as sort of a "news report" of the additional information. Can you sound like a real *authority* on the subject? **Vocabulary:** Complete the *Vocabulary Connections* activity for this book found on the (CD ??) **Comprehension:** These follow-up strategy activities may be found in *Constructing Meaning through Kid-Friendly Strategy Instruction*: Friends I Might Have Known, p. 162; What's in a Picture, p. 165; Questions … Questions … Questions, p. 170; Character Study, p. 185. **Reading extensions:** The following books feature snow in a significant way: • *The Three Snow Bears* by Jan Brett • *Snow* by Cynthia Rylant • *Owl Moon* by Jane Yolen **Writing extensions:** Imagine that you are giving Snowflake Bentley an award for his beautiful photographs of snowflakes. What would you say? Explain why you think he deserves this award and give lots of details about his many accomplishments. You might want to design the award, too.
	Reflect on reading and writing strategy	• How do you decide whether or not you would like to live in a particular place or time, or whether you would want to have the same kind of experiences as a character? • Why would good readers want to put themselves in the place of a character?

OBJECTIVE

C2-a: Which part of the story/article do you think was most important? Use information from the story to explain why you chose that part.

BOOK

The Other Side by Jacqueline Woodson

INTRODUCTION TO THE BOOK

This story appears to be set in the pre-Civil Rights era and is told by Clover, a black child. A fence separates the black side of town from the white side. Clover's mom has always told her "it's dangerous on the other side." But then one summer Annie, a white girl, moves in on other the other side of the fence, and the two girls begin to get curious about each other. Gradually, they become friends, first talking at the fence, and then sitting astride it. Eventually, Clover's friends join Clover and Annie on the fence. The final page of the story offers a glimpse into the future: "Someday somebody's going to come along and knock this old fence down," Annie said. Clover acknowledges, "Yeah, someday."

WHY THIS IS A GOOD BOOK FOR TEACHING THIS OBJECTIVE

My copy of this book has traveled with me all over the country. When I share books at workshops or during conference presentations, I often tell teachers that if they are only going to buy one book this year, please let this be the one! The text is sparse. The illustrations (by E. B. Lewis) are amazing. And the message is powerful. This book would be perfect for teaching many objectives, but I especially like it for determining *What is the most important part?* because in this case, that question is truly open-ended. Students could legitimately identify numerous critical moments in the story; it's all about defending one's opinion with evidence from the text and backing it up with critical thinking. I had planned to do this lesson once in a fifth grade classroom. However, when I arrived at the school, I was told that due to a scheduling problem, I'd need to work with a third grade instead. I gulped, wondering whether third graders could handle the depth of thinking that this book required. I shouldn't have worried; The insights were amazing and reminded me once again that young children's potential for rigor is boundless when they are challenged to stretch their minds—and given the tools to do so.

OTHER OBJECTIVES THAT MAY BE ADDRESSED BY RE-READING THIS BOOK

- **A4-b:** What might have happened next? If the author added another page to the end of the story, what might it have said? Use information from the story to support your answer.
- **B1-c:** Compare Annie and Clover. Are they more alike—or more different?
- **B2-a:** Why does the author include the words on the last page: "Someday somebody's going to come along and knock this old fence down," Annie said. And I nodded, "Yeah," I said. "Someday."
- **D3-a:** Why do you think the author wrote this book? (What is important to her?)

OTHER BOOKS MATCHED TO THIS OBJECTIVE TO LEAD STUDENTS TOWARD INDEPENDENCE (Remember to chart the evidence when you use a picture book so that students may provide specific details from the text)

Students can decide: for themselves: What is the most important part of each of these stories?

- *Melissa Parkington's Beautiful, Beautiful Hair* by Pat Brisson
  Students love this book and I do, too. Its message about the joy of giving cannot be repeated often enough in the classroom. I have used this book often with younger readers as there is a clear turning point, and it is frequently the turning point that readers perceive as most important in a story.

- *Thank You, Mr. Falker* by Patricia Polacco
  This is a wonderful book to address so many objectives. Students will easily recognize that Mr. Falker plays a key role in helping Trisha. But which moment, exactly, would you choose as the *most* important? This is an important question for all students to ponder: How do our teachers (and other role models) make a difference in our lives?

- *Henry's Freedom Box* by Ellen Levine
  Henry, born a slave, dreams of a world where he is free. But then he is sold away from his family to a new slave owner. He vows that one day he will achieve his dream of freedom and actually mails himself to Philadelphia. So, what is the key moment here? Students will have much to consider in this true story of determination and courage.

SCORING STUDENTS' RESPONSES

◎ **C2-a: Which part of *The Other Side* do you think was *most* important? Use information from the story to explain why you chose that part.**

Score = 2

I think the most important part of this story was when the girls introduced themselves to each other at the fence and Annie smiled at Clover. I think this because getting along with people begins by getting to know them. They started to give each other a chance. And also, Annie smiled at Clover. That shows that she welcomed her.

> (This answer would receive full credit because it cites a specific event in the text and then clearly explains why the event would be considered important. Note that there are many other incidents in the story that could be identified instead, with equally valid explanations.)

Score = 1

I think the most important part of this story was when the girls started to be friends. This is important because it shows that they were starting to accept each other and didn't think their race was so important.

> (This answer would receive partial credit because its reference to the text is vague: which part, specifically, demonstrated that "the girls started to be friends?" The end of the answer is valid and this student would have received full credit if a more specific example from the story had been provided.)

Score = 0

I liked the part when the girls were playing jump rope. It is fun to jump rope and the girls looked like they were having fun. I like to jump rope, too.

> (This response would receive no credit because the student doesn't really answer the question. Although the student may be implying that it was important for the girls to have fun together, that is not stated. The student may also have been confusing this with a question about making a text-to-self connection.)

PLANNER FOR SHARED READING

Objective (strategy focus): <u>C2-a:</u> <u>Which part of the story/article do you think was *most* important? Use information from the story to explain why you chose that part.</u>

◎ <u>Which part of *The Other Side* do you think was *most* important? Use information from the story to explain why you chose that part.</u>

How will student learning be measured at the end of the lesson? (What will count as "success?")

Text: <u>*The Other Side* by Jacqueline Woodson</u>   **Pages:** <u>Whole book</u>

BEFORE READING	**Establish prior knowledge, purpose, and predictions**	**Prior knowledge:** Write the following words on the board. They are not mentioned in the book, but are central to understanding this story. (I call this a Word Splash.): *Civil Rights, prejudice, segregation, integration, Martin Luther King, Jr.* Ask students what they know about these words. Tell them that they will want to think about these words as they listen to this story. **Predictions:** Look at the cover and title. What do you think is going on here? What might be happening in this story? **Purpose for reading:** As we read this story, let's think about what we would consider the most important part, and why that part is important.
	Introduce/ review vocabulary	**Words from the book:** stare brave **Other words related to Civil Rights:** prejudice segregation Integration equality
	Introduce the objective (How to find and use the evidence)	**Making the <u>reading</u> strategic** The turning point of a story is often considered the most important part. In some books, like this one, *lots* of parts could be considered the turning point—when something important changes. As we read this book, decide which part you think is really when things begin to change in the biggest way. Think about the evidence from the text *and* be able to explain *why* you think this is the most important part.

		The best evidence:
DURING READING	**Model and practice finding evidence for the objective**	**Model:** **p. 16:** Annie and Clover met at the fence, introduced themselves, and Annie smiled. **p. 17:** Clover smiled back at Annie; Annie talked about how nice it was up on the fence. **p. 20:** Annie helps Clover climb onto the fence. **Practice:** **p. 22:** Clover ignored her friends' disapproval of her friendship with Annie. **p. 24:** Clover's mom seemed to approve of her friendship with Annie. **p. 25:** All of the girls played jump rope together **p. 28:** The girls *all* sat on the fence and became friends **p. 29:** They talked about taking the fence down.
	Model and practice other strategies	**Connecting?** What is the "big idea" of this story? Do you know of any other stories that describe a similar situation? Can you connect this to any situations you know about currently in the world? **Visualizing/Picturing?** If you were to paint Annie or Clover, what feelings would their face show? Would this change from the beginning to the end of the story? Explain. **Wondering?** Why did the girls' mothers each think it was dangerous on the other side of the fence? **Predicting/Guessing?** Do you predict that the fence will come down soon after this story ends? Why or why not? **Noticing?** What details of this story seemed especially important to you? **Figuring out?** Figure out what the fence represents.

AFTER READING	**Discussion questions**	**Question related to the objective** **C2-a:** Which part of *The Other Side* do you think was *most* important? Use information from the story to explain why you chose that part. **Other questions** **A2-e:** What is the setting of this story? How would this story be different if it was happening today? **B1-c:** Compare Annie and Clover. Are they more similar or different? Explain. **B2-b:** Why does the author include the dialogue about the fence on the last page? **C2-d:** What was your first reaction to this story? Why? **D3-a:** What was important to this author? (Why do you think she wrote this story?)
	Written response to text	**Making the <u>writing</u> strategic** • See *That's a Great Answer*, p. 129, or *Teaching Written Response*, pp. 109-110, for a template matched to this objective. • Model the response using the template. • Remove your response and ask students to write their own response based on the incident you chose, or another incident in the story.
	Other follow-up activities	**Oral language, fluency, vocabulary, comprehension, reading extensions, writing extensions** **Oral language/fluency:** Pretend that you are a Civil Rights leader like Martin Luther King, Jr. Write a speech about the importance of equal rights for all people. Give the speech to your class, or to a group of students in your class. **Vocabulary:** Complete the *Vocabulary Connections* activity for this book found on the (CD ??) **Comprehension:** These follow-up strategy activities may be found in *Constructing Meaning through Kid-Friendly Strategy Instruction*: Connecting to Time and Place, p. 160; Friends I Might Have Known, p. 162; The Question Is…, p. 172; A Message from the Author, p. 186 **Reading extensions:** Read another book related to Civil Rights such as: • *Freedom Summer* by Deborah Wiles • *The Story of Ruby Bridges* by Robert Coles • *White Socks Only* by Evelyn Coleman • *This is the Dream* by Diane Shore and James Ransome **Writing extensions:** Pretend that you are Clover. Write a letter to Annie as if you are now old ladies. Talk about the summer you became friends and the thoughts that were going through your mind at the time. (If you would prefer, you could write the letter from Annie's point of view instead.)
	Reflect on reading and writing strategy	• How do you read to find the most important part of a story? • What kinds of information in a story might be important?

C2-b: Which part of this [story/article] was most interesting or surprising to you? Why?

BOOK

Goin' Someplace Special by Patricia C. McKissack

INTRODUCTION TO THE BOOK

Tricia Ann lives with her Grandma and begs to go to "someplace special" all by herself. Grandma isn't so sure that this is a good idea. But Tricia Ann prevails, and off she goes. Where is this "someplace special?" The author keeps readers in suspense. But along the way, Tricia experiences the hard realities of being a black child growing up in the pre-civil rights south: She must sit at the back of the bus. A "Whites Only" sign tells her to stay off the park bench where she wishes to sit. She accidentally ends up in the lobby of a fancy hotel and is rushed back out the door. When at last she reaches her destination she looks at the message chiseled across the front facing. You'll need to read the book yourself to learn the identity of this "someplace special." The author's note at the end of the book explains that this story is, in fact, autobiographical. And as she explains, her love of reading began here—and for such an important reason.

WHY THIS IS A GOOD BOOK FOR TEACHING THIS OBJECTIVE

This book works really well for this objective because the main character's destination is not revealed until the very last page; it is meant to be a surprise. I have found, though, that many students cite some of the evidence of segregation and prejudice as most surprising. While I had not anticipated this initially, it does make sense because Jim Crow laws are not part of their current reality. And aren't we glad about that!

OTHER OBJECTIVES THAT MAY BE ADDRESSED BY RE-READING THIS BOOK

- **A2-a:** Using information in the story, write a brief description of how _____ felt when….
- **A3-a:** Briefly summarize this story
- **B1-a:** What caused _____ to happen in the story?
- **C1-c:** Would you like _____ for a friend? Why or why not?
- **D2-c:** Using information in the text, write a paragraph that could have appeared in _____'s journal after _____ occurred.

OTHER BOOKS MATCHED TO THIS OBJECTIVE TO LEAD STUDENTS TOWARD INDEPENDENCE (Remember to chart the evidence when you use a picture book so that students may provide specific details from the text)

Chris Van Allsburg is the master of the surprise ending. Readers will enjoy piecing together the clues throughout these books to try to figure out the ending for themselves.

- *The Wretched Stone* **by Chris Van Allsburg**
  The "wretched stone" isn't a stone at all—but you don't know exactly what it is until the end of the story after the author has provided a few helpful hints. Even then, you need to be a discerning reader to put the puzzle pieces together.

- *The Stranger* **by Chris Van Allsburg**
  Who is this stranger who arrives mysteriously at the end of summer and leaves just as cold weather begins to set in? You can't be entirely sure, but could this be the fellow who causes leaves to change from summer green to autumn's red and orange?

- *Probuditi* **by Chris Van Allsburg**
  This story is for all the little boys who have ever wanted to transform their sister into a dog. The big brother in this story succeeds at this—or does he? The end of this story is not quite what you expect.

SCORING STUDENTS' RESPONSES

◎ **C2-b: What is the most interesting or surprising part of** *Goin' Someplace Special?* **Why?**

Score = 2

The most surprising part for me was when someplace special turned out to be the library because there was no segregation there. I didn't know that so many places were segregated like even the park bench and hotels. I can see why Tricia liked the library so much and wanted to go there.

> (This reader provided a thoughtful, detailed answer as to why this event was surprising and included specific evidence from the text.)

Score = 1

The most surprising part was when Tricia went to the library. I thought she might be going to visit a friend or maybe to the store. But I never guessed that the place would be the library.

> (This reader has answered *what*, but not *why*.)

Score = 0

I don't think this book was very interesting and I would never pick the library for a special place.

> (This reader has not answered the question. The question doesn't ask if the book was interesting; it asks about the most interesting or surprising *part*.)

PLANNER FOR SHARED READING

Objective (strategy focus): <u>C2-b: What is the most interesting or surprising part of the story?</u>

 <u>Decide what was the most surprising part for you in *Goin' Someplace Special.*</u>
How will student learning be measured at the end of the lesson? (What will count as "success?")

Text: *Goin' Someplace Special* by Patricia McKissack   **Pages:** <u>Whole book</u>

<table>
<tr>
<td rowspan="3">BEFORE READING</td>
<td>Establish prior knowledge, purpose, and predictions</td>
<td>Prior knowledge: What was life like for African Americans during the time of Martin Luther King Jr? (Share Word Splash—at end of this lesson). Ask students to share what they know about each term.)
Predictions: Based on the title, where do you think this "special place" might be?
Purpose for reading: Let's read this story to see if something surprises us.</td>
</tr>
<tr>
<td>Introduce/ review vocabulary</td>
<td>Word splash words/phrases related to the Civil Rights era: separate but equal   discrimination   segregation   Civil Rights   Rosa Parks   Jim Crow Laws   desegregation   prejudice   Freedom March   integration   equality
Words from the book: confident   bounded   inched   magnificent   strutted   spectacular   elderly   clenched</td>
</tr>
<tr>
<td>Introduce the objective (How to find and use the evidence)</td>
<td>Making the <u>reading</u> strategic
Think about the kinds of things that surprise you in a text. If it is a story, the <u>ending</u> might be surprising. It might be something that a character or person does or says that you didn't anticipate at other places in a text, too. In a nonfiction text, it might be something that you didn't already know that is hard to believe. Always think about *why* something is surprising to you.</td>
</tr>
</table>

DURING READING	**Model and practice finding evidence for the objective**	**The best evidence:** **Model:** **p. 2:** I can tell there's going to be a surprise somewhere because the author doesn't tell where this "Someplace Special" is. **p. 5:** Surprised to see that sign that says "Colored Section" **p. 14:** Surprised by the bench that said, "For Whites Only" **Practice:** **p. 15:** Surprised that black people couldn't eat at the restaurant **p. 21:** Surprised that the man was so mean to Tricia just because she walked into that hotel **p. 27:** Surprised that black people couldn't go into the theater through the front door **p. 31:** Surprised that "Someplace Special" was actually the library **Author's Note (p. 32):** Surprised that this story is *true*, that it is the author's own story of her childhood; surprised that this was how Patricia McKissack became a writer and a reader.
	Model and practice other strategies	**Connecting?** Connect to someplace that is very special for you. **Visualizing/Picturing?** Could you picture the scenes in this book clearly? Why or why not? **Wondering?** What questions did you have in your mind as you read? **Predicting/Guessing?** Why was it so hard to predict where Tricia Ann was going? **Noticing?** What evidence of discrimination did you notice in this book? **Figuring out?** Figure out what was important to Tricia Ann.

AFTER READING	**Discussion questions**	**Question related to the objective** **C2-b:** What was the most surprising to you in this story? **Other questions** **A2-e:** What is the setting of this story? **A3-a:** Briefly summarize this story **B2-a:** Why does the author include the author's note at the end of the book? **D3-a:** What was important to Tricia Ann?
	Written response to text	**Making the <u>writing</u> strategic** • See *That's a Great Answer*, p. 132, for a template matched to this objective. • Model the response using the template. • Remove your response and ask students to write their own response based on something else in the story that they considered surprising.
	Other follow-up activities	**Oral language, fluency, vocabulary, comprehension, reading extensions, writing extensions** **Oral language/fluency:** Practice reading one of the pages in this book that contains dialogue. Try to make your voice sound like both Tricia Ann and the person with whom she is speaking. **Vocabulary:** Complete the *Vocabulary Connections* activity for this book found on the (CD ??) **Comprehension:** *Constructing Meaning:* Connecting to Time and Place, p. 161; What's in a Picture?, p. 165; Best Quote, p. 175; S.O.L.V.E., p. 182 **Reading extensions:** Poet Jack Prelutsky is a master of the "surprise ending." Read some of his poems such as those listed below and try to predict the surprise at the end before it is revealed by the author: • *The New Kid on the Block* • *Louder than a Clap of Thunder* • *I'm Disgusted with my Brother* • *Belinda Blue* **Writing extensions:** This story takes place in the 1950's. That is at least 50 years ago. Tricia Ann would be old enough now to be a grandmother. Write a letter that Tricia might write now to her grandchildren telling them about what life was like when she was growing up in the south.
	Reflect on reading and writing strategy	• What makes something that you read surprising? • Where are you likely to find a surprise in a story? • What would make something surprising in a nonfiction text?

OBJECTIVE

C2-c: Did you like this [story/article]? Why or why not?

BOOK

Pebble: A Story About Belonging by Susan Milord

INTRODUCTION TO THE BOOK

In this story a pebble at the seashore yearns to fit in, to find its place in the world. Meanwhile, a little boy visiting the seashore looks for something special to bring home, a reminder of his fun day at the beach. This simple text is less about the "story" and more about the message—capturing the magic of the moment, finding your own completeness.

WHY THIS IS A GOOD BOOK FOR TEACHING THIS OBJECTIVE

Pebble is a good book for this objective because it is not your "garden variety" story with amusing characters and an intriguing adventure. This is a "story" that will be best appreciated if readers recognize that it is not, in fact, about a little pebble and a little boy; it is about you and me. It is an allegory for the need we all have to fit in and hold special moments close to us forever. This is a good book for this objective because children who do not understand the message of this text may *not* be terribly impressed by it. This book will separate the deep thinkers from those who just read the words.

OTHER OBJECTIVES THAT MAY BE ADDRESSED BY RE-READING THIS BOOK

- **A1-b:** What is the theme of this story?
- **C1-b:** Make a personal connection to a feeling.

OTHER BOOKS MATCHED TO THIS OBJECTIVE TO LEAD STUDENTS TOWARD INDEPENDENCE (Remember to chart the evidence when you use a picture book so that students may provide specific details from the text)

These "stories" are all allegories with a deeper meaning:

- ***The Little Boy Star: An Allegory of the Holocaust* by Rachel Hausfater**
  At the beginning of this story a little Jewish boy is given a star to wear, which he initially finds quite festive. Gradually, however, the star begins to overtake him such that people see only the star, not the boy. He becomes increasingly scared and lonely as other star-wearers are led away in the night. This is a good text to introduce children to the horrors of the Holocaust and includes much symbolism.

- ***A Bad Case of Stripes* by David Shannon**
  This is a moral tale about a little girl who succumbs to peer-pressure on a regular basis, changing her stripes—literally (red, white, and blue when she says the Pledge of Allegiance in school, etc.). She finally admits her horrifying secret, risking unpopularity: she, alone *loves* lima beans. Now, true to herself, she returns to normal and lives happily ever after.

- ***Eggbert, the Slightly Cracked Egg* by Tom Ross**
  Eggbert enjoys a delightful life in the refrigerator until he discovers that he I "slightly cracked." At first he attempts to disguise his cracks, but soon discovers that his cracks are what make him interesting. What "interesting cracks" make your students special?

SCORING STUDENTS' RESPONSES

 Did you like the book *Pebble*? Why or why not?

Score = 2

I liked this book. I enjoy stories where there is an important message, and there really was an important message in this book. The author was trying to show how important it is to feel like you are complete and fulfilled. She didn't do this in the ordinary way with regular kids or adults as characters. She used a pebble as a main character. I thought that was very clever and creative which is another reason why I liked this story. I would recommend this book to people who like to think at a deep level, because you have to think to understand this book.

> (This response would receive full score because the student has clear criteria for her opinion and backs it up with evidence from the text. The response also shows good understanding of the author's message.)

Score = 1

I didn't really like this book. It wasn't interesting to me. You could never have a talking pebble, so that didn't make sense. This seemed like a baby book, not a story to read to fourth graders. I would only recommend this book to kindergarten or first grade.

> (This response would receive partial credit. It is fine that the student did not like the story—and the opinion is quite strong—but there is no indication that she actually understood it. In fact, describing this as a "baby book" leads me to believe that the level of comprehension was weak.)

Score = 0

When I go to the beach I pick up rocks. I have a whole collection of rocks at home. Some of them are smooth like the pebble in this story. This book made me think about my rock collection. I think I have about a hundred rocks. They all have different shapes.

> (This student would most likely receive a "0" on this response. There may be an underlying assumption that he liked the story, but that is never stated and most of the response is just about his own rock collection. It doesn't even make a clear connection to the content of the text.)

PLANNER FOR SHARED READING

Objective (strategy focus): <u>C2-c:</u> <u>Did you like this book? Why or why not?</u>

 <u>Explain why you did or did not like the book *Pebble*</u>
How will student learning be measured at the end of the lesson? (What will count as "success?")

Text: *Pebble: A Story About Belonging* by Susan Milord   **Pages:** Whole book

<table>
<tr><td rowspan="3" style="vertical-align:middle">BEFORE READING</td><td>Establish prior knowledge, purpose, and predictions</td><td>Prior knowledge: Before reading this book: bring in an assortment of pebbles and let students choose one that they like. Why do they like this particular pebble? Where might this pebble have come from? What sort of adventure might this pebble have experienced?
Predictions: Based on the title and cover of this book, what do you anticipate that it might be about?
Purpose for reading: Today as we read, try to decide whether or not you like this story. Here's a hint: This book may have a deeper meaning than the story alone suggests. Figuring out that deeper meaning might help you decide what you think of this book.</td></tr>
<tr><td>Introduce/ review vocabulary</td><td>pebble   retreat   boulder   foundation
       flecks   longing   brilliant   pondering</td></tr>
<tr><td>Introduce the objective (How to find and use the evidence)</td><td>Making the <u>reading</u> strategic
When you say that you like a book, what actually makes you like it? Some people like books with:
A topic they like to read about (something they can connect to)
Main characters that are boys
Main characters that are girls
Lots of adventure
Lots of description
Humor
An important message
Great illustrations and graphics
Be sure you can explain the *reason* why you like a particular book. It could be one of the reasons listed above, or it could be another reason.</td></tr>
</table>

		The best evidence:
DURING READING	**Model and practice finding evidence for the objective**	**Model:** **p. 2:** I love the seashore. I can make a lot of "seashore connections," so I will probably like this book. **pp. 3-8:** I'm noticing that the pebble in this book is being treated as if it was a person (bathed by the rain; it was frightened). **p. 9:** the pebble longed for more (this pebble has feelings). **Practice:** **pp. 11-12:** Pebble said he would like to be part of something more: a stone wall or a building's foundation—but he's too small. **pp. 13-14:** Pebble said he would like to be shaped into a sand castle or stained glass window, —but he's too big. **p. 16:** Pebble wanted something more from life, but he didn't know what. **pp. 17-18:** Despite the good things in his world, Pebble still wanted more. **p. 20:** We're meeting a new character here. I wonder if the boy will meet the pebble. **pp. 21-24:** I'm noticing that the boy is a little like the pebble. He can't fid exactly what he is looking for, either. **pp. 25-26:** The boy found just what he was looking for—the pebble **pp. 27-28:** The pebble found what he was looking for, too.
	Model and practice other strategies	**Connecting?** What kind of connections do you think the author wants readers to make as they read this book? **Visualizing/Picturing?** How did the author help you create pictures in your mind in this story? **Wondering?** What did you wonder about as we read this story? What questions did you have? **Predicting/Guessing?** Could you predict how this story would end? At what point could you make that prediction? What clues did the author provide to help you predict? **Noticing?** What did you notice about this story that made it different from other stories? **Figuring out?** Did you figure out the author's message in this story?

Discussion questions	**Question related to the objective** **C2-c:** Explain why you did or did not like the book *Pebble*. **Other questions** **A1-b:** What is the theme of this story? **A2-d:** How did the pebble change from the beginning to the end of the story? **C1-a:** Make a personal connection to the pebble or the boy. (Make sure you are connecting to the "big idea" of the story.
Written response to text	**Making the <u>writing</u> strategic** • See *That's a Great Answer*, p. 137, for a template matched to this objective. • Model the response using the template. • Remove your response and ask students to write the response themselves using the template if necessary—choosing their own reasons.
Other follow-up activities	**Oral language, fluency, vocabulary, comprehension, reading extensions, writing extensions** **Oral language/fluency:** What tone do you think the author had in mind for this story: Sad? Haunting? Hopeful? Another emotion? Practice reading this story, or a part of it until your tone fits the mood of the story. **Vocabulary:** See the *Vocabulary Connections* activity for this book on the CD. **Comprehension:** These follow-up activities may be found in *Constructing Meaning through Kid-Friendly Strategy Instruction*: Active Reader Report, p. 155; Best Quote, p. 175; A Message from the Author, p. 186. **Reading extensions:** These stories all focus on self-fulfillment: • *Ish* by Peter H. Reynolds • *Wings* by Christopher Myers • *Dream: A Tale of Wonder, Wisdom & Wishes* by Susan V. Bosak **Writing extensions:** In this story, the author gives a pebble human characteristics. It thinks, talks, and has feelings. Write a story in which you give human characteristics to an object. (It could be a pencil, item of clothing, or something else.) Write a story that includes this object as a main character.
Reflect on reading and writing strategy	• When you decide whether or not you like a particular book, what do you need to consider? • Why is it important to know what qualities you like in a book?

*(Left vertical label: **AFTER READING**)*

C2-d: What was your first reaction to this text?

BOOK

Four Feet, Two Sandals by Karen Lynn Williams and Khadra Mohammed

INTRODUCTION TO THE BOOK

This book is about two refugee children who each find one sandal when relief workers bring a shipment of clothing to their refugee camp. The two girls decide that it makes more sense to share the sandals (Lina will wear them one day, and Feroza will wear them the next day) rather than each of them wearing one sandal. As the story unfolds, the plight of refugees on the Afghanistan/Pakistan border becomes clear. In the end, Lina and her family are among those selected for resettlement in America. Now what will become of the sandals? The girls' decision to each retain one of the sandals is a tribute to the friendship that has developed between them.

WHY THIS IS A GOOD BOOK FOR TEACHING THIS OBJECTIVE

In order for students to react to text, the story needs to have an emotional impact. This story surely qualifies as it gently, without preaching, gives a voice to the millions of children victimized by war. (At the time this book was written there were more than 20 million refugees worldwide, the majority of which were children.) Students will get to know two families torn apart by war; each of the girls has lost family members to war's violence. The girls live in tents in a refugee camp. They have no shoes. They are not allowed to go to school. They long for resettlement in America where there is hope for a brighter future. Compassion for these circumstances evoke strong feelings and much reaction from students who have not faced the realities of war in their day-to-day lives.

OTHER OBJECTIVES THAT MAY BE ADDRESSED BY RE-READING THIS BOOK

- **A1-b:** What is the theme of this story?
- **A2-e:** What is the setting of this story? Give details from the story to support your answer.
- **B1-a:** What caused _____ to happen in the story?
- **B2-b:** Why did the author write a [picture book] on this topic?
- **D2-c:** Using information in the text, write a paragraph that could have appeared in _____'s journal after _____ occurred.

OTHER BOOKS MATCHED TO THIS OBJECTIVE TO LEAD STUDENTS TOWARD INDEPENDENCE (Remember to chart the evidence when you use a picture book so that students may provide specific details from the text)

These books, all depicting the devastation of war and its unintended victims, will surely generate strong reactions from students.

- *The Librarian of Basra: A True Story from Iraq* by Jeanette Winter
  In this true story, the chief librarian of Basra's Central Library realizes that her library will likely be bombed as the war continues. She is determined to save the library's books and with the help of friends, gets the books out just before her library is burned to the ground. She then moves the books a second time to keep them safe until a new library can be built. Students will react to the courage and determination of this librarian.

- *Sami and the Time of the Troubles* by Florence Parry Heide and Judith Heide Gilliland
  This story set in Beirut, Lebanon conveys that war threatens both one's physical well-being as well as the human spirit. To avoid the bombs, Sami and his family retreat to an underground cave where they "listen to the noises of the night" and stare at a rug that Sami's mother has brought with them to keep alive their memory of more normal times. This is a sensitive, but intense story.

- *The Bracelet* by Yoshiko Uchida
  This story, which takes place following World War II, is about a young Japanese-American child, who with her family, is moved from her home in Berkeley, California to an internment camp. Most children are not aware of this dark period in American history and are horrified by such blatant racial profiling.

SCORING STUDENTS' RESPONSES

 What was your first reaction to *Four Feet, Two Sandals*?

Score = 2

This whole story was shocking to me in a sad and upsetting way. I didn't even know that there was something called Refugee Camps, and to be truthful, I didn't even know what a refugee was. I couldn't believe the bad living conditions, and that children wouldn't have shoes to wear for years and years. On the news you see places in the Middle East getting bombed, and I knew people got killed, but seeing the girls in this story made this more real because it was their parents and family members who died.

> (This response would receive full credit because this student is truly speaking from the heart. The reaction is powerful and is based on specific evidence from the text.)

Score = 1

This story was pretty sad in the beginning, but then it got happier when the girls got to be friends and shared the sandals. I think they will always be friends and that Feroza will get to go to America to be with Lina.

> (This response would receive partial credit because it represents the story fairly accurately (sad at the beginning, happier at the end). It also mentions the sandals. Beyond that, there are no details, and the final thought about being friends in America is off-topic.)

Score = 0

I liked this story. It was about two girls who became friends because they shared sandals. At the end Lina went to America but Feroza couldn't go.

> (Although this student indicated that he liked the story, there is no mention of *why* he liked it. Instead, there is a brief summary—which is not what the question asked.)

PLANNER FOR SHARED READING

Objective (strategy focus): <u>C2-d:</u> <u>What was your first reaction to this text?</u>

 <u>What was your first reaction to *Four Feet, Two Sandals?*</u>
How will student learning be measured at the end of the lesson? (What will count as "success?")

Text: <u>*Four Feet, Two Sandals* by Karen Williams and Khadra Mohammed</u> **Pages:** <u>Whole book</u>

<table>
<tr>
<td rowspan="3" style="writing-mode: vertical-rl;">BEFORE READING</td>
<td>Establish prior knowledge, purpose, and predictions</td>
<td>Prior knowledge: Where is the Middle East? What are some of the countries in the Middle East? What do we know about these countries from what we see and hear on the news? What is a refugee? (You may need to build background knowledge if students are unfamiliar with these concepts.)
Predictions: Based on the cover and title, what do you anticipate this story will be about?
Purpose for reading: As we read this story, decide how you feel about it: What is your reaction? Is this story comforting, disturbing, joyful, hopeful, shocking? Why do you feel this way?</td>
</tr>
<tr>
<td>Introduce/ review vocabulary</td>
<td>***refugee and refugee camp (these words are essential to understanding the story. Other possible vocabulary words from the text are)
      resettled   Ramadan   flee   makeshift</td>
</tr>
<tr>
<td>Introduce the objective (How to find and use the evidence)</td>
<td>Making the <u>reading</u> strategic
Your first reaction to a text is based more on feeling than thinking. As you read this text, notice the details of the events and the things that happen. Pause to react to each of these events. You will get a stronger reaction if you put yourself in the place of the main character: How would you feel if you were experiencing the events in the story yourself? After you have read the whole story, decide on one word that sums up your feelings/reaction to the story in general.</td>
</tr>
</table>

DURING READING	**Model and practice finding evidence for the objective**	**The best evidence:** **Model:** **p. 2:** Children grabbing used clothing from the back of a truck (This doesn't sound like a good situation) **p. 3:** Lina hadn't worn shoes for two years (sounds like she is very poor). **p. 6:** The girl's feet were cracked and swollen; this "camp" doesn't look like the kind of camp kids go to in the summer (more evidence of poverty and poor living conditions). **p. 7:** Washed clothes in the river; had to walk from Afghanistan carrying her brother (people living in a war-torn country endure many hardships for the sake of safety). **p. 10:** The girls would share the sandals: one day for Lina and one day for Feroza) (amazing—so poor that there was only 1 pair of sandals for two children). **Practice:** **p. 12:** Waiting in a long line for a jug of water (the effects of war) **p. 13:** Families were waiting to be resettled in a new home; both girls had lost family members in the war (my heart aches for these girls and all they have had to endure). **p. 16:** School was just for boys; does not look like our schools (so sad that there was little opportunity for education—especially for girls). **p. 18:** Dreamed of a new home (amazing that these girls are still hopeful. **pp. 20-21:** Lina's name is on the list for resettlement. (I can imagine her excitement, but also the disappointment of Feroza.) **p. 23:** Lina has tears in her eyes (will miss her friend; probably scared about what the future will bring). **p. 25:** Feroza gave a sandal to Lina as a sign of their friendship (little things meant so much…). **p. 27:** Lina said they would share again in America (wonder if Feroza felt hopeful or hopeless at this moment).
	Model and practice other strategies	**Connecting?** Connect to sharing something really special with a friend; sacrificing something for a friend **Visualizing/Picturing?** What does the author describe that paints a vivid picture in your mind? What do you have a hard time picturing? Why? **Wondering?** Wonder what it would be like to be Lina or Feroza **Predicting/Guessing?** Do you predict Lina and Feroza will see each other again? Explain **Noticing?** What do you notice in particular that causes you to react to this story? **Figuring out?** How do you feel about this story? What is your reaction? Why?

Discussion questions	**Question related to the objective** **C2-d:** What was your first reaction to this text? **Other questions** **A4-b:** If the author added another paragraph to the end of the story it would <u>most likely</u> tell about _____. **B2-b:** Why did the author create a picture book on this topic? **D2-c:** Using information in the text, write a paragraph that could have appeared in Lina's's journal after she found the sandal.
Written response to text	**Making the <u>writing</u> strategic** • See *That's a Great Answer*, p. 139, or *Teaching Written Response*, pp. 76-77, for a template matched to this objective. • Model the response using the template. • Remove your response and ask students to write the response themselves using the template if necessary—choosing their own reaction and evidence.
Other follow-up activities	**Oral language, fluency, vocabulary, comprehension, reading extensions, writing extensions** **Oral language/fluency:** Practice reading the page where Feroza returns the sandal she found to Lina. Change your voice so you sound like both Lina and Feroza. Another page to practice might be the one where Lina sees her name on the list for America, and Feroza realizes that her name is not on the list. **Vocabulary:** Vocabulary: See *Vocabulary Connections* activity for this book on the CD. **Comprehension:** *Constructing Meaning*: What's in a Picture, p. 165; Reading with All of my Senses, p. 168; The Question is…, p. 172; Stopping Point, p. 180 **Reading extensions:** These books extend students' understanding of the Middle East: • *Sitti's Secrets* by Naomi Shihab Nye • *The Flag of Childhood: Poems From the Middle East* by Naomi Shihab Nye • *The Day of Ahmed's Secrets* by Florence Parry Heide and Judith Heide Gilliland • *The Golden Sandal: A Middle Eastern Cinderella Story* by Rebecca Hickox **Writing extensions:** Imagine that Lina and Feroza meet many years later in America. Write the dialogue that might occur between them. Think about: What has become of the two sandals? What do they discuss of their past? What will their future hold? Will they continue to be friends?
Reflect on reading and writing strategy	• When you react to a story what should you keep in mind? • What are some different reactions you might have to stories you read?

Left margin: **AFTER READING**

Chapter Eleven

STRAND D LESSONS

Examining Content and Structure

D1-a: What words does the author use to help you picture _____?

BOOK

Water Dance by Thomas Locker

INTRODUCTION TO THE BOOK

Is this book fiction or nonfiction, science or poetry? However you define it, *Water Dance* is a captivating explanation of the water cycle, combining Locker's characteristic, dramatic seascapes and landscapes with a free verse "first person" narrative. The book begins, "Some people say that I am one thing./ Others say that I am many./ Ever since the world began/I have been moving in an endless circle./ Sometimes I fall from the sky./ *I am the rain*". Subsequent pages define a mountain stream, a waterfall, and a thunderhead—among others. Words truly do dance across the pages here as Locker's words and images come together to help readers ponder the wonder of water.

WHY THIS IS A GOOD BOOK FOR TEACHING THIS OBJECTIVE

I have used this book for years and it never lets me down. I'm not sure that many students would choose this book independently from a library shelf; it is not a "story" in the usual sense—no characters, no action, no problem to be solved. But once the text is introduced, children are fascinated. It's hard to say which they find more compelling—the words or the paintings. My guess is that in this case, the whole is somehow more than the sum of the parts. To add intrigue I often cover the identity of the term (cloud, storm, mist, etc.) at the bottom of each page, and encourage students to figure out what it is from the words alone. I don't let them look at the picture initially. In this way, students *must* draw on the word clues.

OTHER OBJECTIVES THAT MAY BE ADDRESSED BY RE-READING THIS BOOK

- **A1-c:** What is the main idea of this text?
- **B2-b:** Why did the author combine poetry and art in this way?
- **D1-d:** Find an example of personification in this text.
- **D2-a:** What two questions would you like to ask the author that were not answered in this text?

D TO THIS OBJECTIVE TO LEAD STUDENTS

E (Remember to chart the evidence when you use a ay provide specific details from the text)

g mental images are not "stories" with the usual progression of ometimes a "story" can actually get in the way of appreciating r books that inspire visualization, I seek works by some of my Thomas Locker provides a feast of images. Some possibilities *Tree: Seeing Science through Art; Thirteen Moons on Turtle's Begins.* Other authors and representative picture books are:

eenhouse; Welcome to the Sea of Sand; Birdwatch; Owl Moon Scarecrow; In November; Snow; The Wonderful Happens; Night in the Country; When I was Young in the Mountains
- Robert Burleigh: *Hoops; Stealing Home: Jackie Robinson: Against the Odds; Black Whiteness: Admiral Byrd Alone in the Antarctic*
- Charlotte Zolotow: *The Seashore Book; I Know a Lady; The Moon was the Best*

SCORING STUDENTS' RESPONSES

◎ **D1-d: Choose two words that help you picture [the waterfall] and explain the picture in your mind (may substitute another term explained in the text).**

Score = 2

The words that help me picture the waterfall are <u>leaping</u>, <u>spiraling</u>, and <u>plunging</u>. First I can see the water <u>leaping</u> from someplace high up. Then in my mind I see the water <u>spiraling</u> really fast as it heads downward. At last, the water <u>plunges</u> into the river at the bottom making a loud splashing sound.

> (This response would receive a "2" because it identifies specific words and goes on to explain how each one helps to create a mental image of the waterfall. It also relates the image to both seeing and hearing, a "loud splashing sound").

Score = 1

The words that helped me picture the waterfall were leaping and plunging because I could see the water leaping and plunging.

> (This response would receive a score of "1" because it does identify the words that created the mental image, but the actual image just repeats the words rather than explaining it in greater detail.)

Score = 0

I can picture at the foot of the mountains, I leap from a stone cliff. Spiraling. Plunging.

> (This response would receive a "0" because it just copies the text word-for-word. There is no indication that particular words are noteworthy, or that the student is really picturing anything.)

PLANNER FOR SHARED READING

Objective (strategy focus): <u>D1-a:</u> <u>What words help you picture [   ]?</u>

◎ <u>Choose two words that help you picture [the waterfall] and explain the picture in</u>
<u>your mind.</u>
How will student learning be measured at the end of the lesson? (What will count as "success?")

Text: <u>*Water Dance* by Thomas Locker</u>   **Pages:** <u>Whole book</u>

<table>
<tr>
<td rowspan="3">BEFORE READING</td>
<td>Establish prior knowledge, purpose, and predictions</td>
<td>Prior knowledge: What is the water cycle? What do you know about the water cycle? What are some different bodies of water that you know (such as lake and river)? (author) Have you read other books by Thomas Locker? What do you expect to find in books by this author? (stories about nature, beautiful paintings as illustrations
Predictions: Do you expect this book to be fiction or nonfiction? What do you expect to find out in this book?
Purpose for reading: As we read, look for words that help to create pictures in your mind. What do you see in your mental pictures?</td>
</tr>
<tr>
<td>Introduce/ review vocabulary</td>
<td>tumble   plunging   still   drift   gleaming   drench</td>
</tr>
<tr>
<td>Introduce the objective (How to find and use the evidence)</td>
<td>Making the <u>reading</u> strategic
Although we often think of adjectives and adverbs as describing words, the best images usually come from strong verbs and specific nouns. As you read, notice especially the nouns and verbs that help you make pictures in your mind. Try to go beyond just the words on the page to imagine the picture that the illustrator might draw.</td>
</tr>
</table>

DURING READING	**Model and practice the focus strategy**	**The best evidence:** **Model:** **p. 3:** cascade, tumble, moss-covered rocks, forest shadows: These words help me picture a stream in a deep, dark forest. The water looks white as it is moving and there are little rocks jutting up. **p. 5:** leap, spiraling, plunging: I can see a waterfall in my mind. It's flying off a tall cliff and crashing into the water. **p. 7:** still, deep, shadows of the mountain: I can see the lake, calm and peaceful without any ripples with mountains surrounding it. **Practice:** **p. 9:** What words help you picture this river? What do you see? **p. 11:** What words help you picture the sea? What do you see? **p. 13:** What words help you picture the mist? What do you see? **p. 15:** What words help you picture the clouds? What do you see? **p. 17:** What words help you picture the storm front? What do you see? **p. 19:** What words help you picture the thunderhead? What do you see? **p. 21:** What words help you picture the rainbow? What do you see?
	Model and practice other strategies	**Connecting?** Have you seen a waterfall or anything else described in this text? Where? Explain. **Visualizing/Picturing?** What can you picture the most clearly in this text? **Wondering?** As you read this text, what did you wonder about? **Predicting/Guessing?** What else could this author have included in this text? **Noticing?** What details in this book (either words or pictures) made this book memorable for you? **Figuring out?** What did you figure out through this book about combining poetry, science, and art.

AFTER READING	**Discussion questions**	**Question related to the objective** **D1-a:** Choose two words that help you picture [the waterfall] and explain the picture in your mind. **Other questions** **A1-c:** What is the main idea of this text? **C2-d:** What was your first reaction to this text? **D2-a:** What two questions would you like to ask the author that were not answered in this text?
	Written response to text	**Making the <u>writing</u> strategic** • See *That's a Great Answer*, p. 143, for a template matched to this objective. • Model the response using the template. • Remove your response and ask students to write the response themselves about the waterfall or another image in the book, using the template if they wish.
	Other follow-up activities	**Oral language, fluency, vocabulary, comprehension, reading extensions, writing extensions** **Oral language/fluency:** Students can "perform" this entire text. Assign individuals or pairs of children different pages. Rehearse the words on each page until they are fluent and expressive. Draw some accompanying illustrations (mist, rainbow, etc.) and perform your own classroom version of *Water Dance*. **Vocabulary:** See *Vocabulary Connections* activity for this book on the CD **Comprehension:** These follow-up activities may be found in *Constructing Meaning through Kid-Friendly Comprehension Strategy Instruction*: Picture This, p. 164; Reading with all of my Senses, p. 168. **Reading extensions:** These books are about water: • *A Drop of Water* by Walter Wick • *A Drop Around the World* by Barbara McKinney • *A Drop in the Ocean: The Story of Water* by Jacqui Bailey **Writing extension:** There are other bodies of water that this author did not include in *Water Dance* such as a bay, harbor, inlet, pond, and gulf. Write a free verse poem about one of these in the style of Thomas Locker. Illustrate your poem.
	Reflect on reading and writing strategy	• How do you get a good picture in your mind of something an author describes in a text? • Why is it important to go beyond the words on the page to get a really good mental image?

▶ OBJECTIVE

D1-b: Choose a simile and explain why the author chose this simile.

BOOK

The Seashore Book by Charlotte Zolotow

INTRODUCTION TO THE BOOK

In this descriptive narrative a little boy asks his mother, "What is the seashore like?" She takes him there in his mind by describing a mosaic of mental images—the cool, wet sand, the stones washed smooth by the sea, the tiny brown snail shells, the cold water that makes your skin feel like peppermint—and so much more. If the words aren't enough to mentally transport you to your favorite beach, the beautiful water color illustrations will surely bring you there.

WHY THIS IS A GOOD BOOK FOR TEACHING THIS OBJECTIVE

Among the mesmerizing word images in this book are many similes. Whether children are familiar with the seashore, or they've never felt sand between their toes at the edge of an ocean, the similes in this book will help them connect to this experience through all of their senses. Because there's not much of a "story" here in the traditional sense, students can focus on the language—which is elegant by any standard.

OTHER OBJECTIVES THAT MAY BE ADDRESSED BY RE-READING THIS BOOK

- **C1-d:** Using evidence from the text, explain whether you would ever want to _____.
- **C2-c:** Did you like this [story/article]? Why or why not?
- **D1-a:** Choose [2] words from paragraph ____ that help you picture the _____.

OTHER BOOKS MATCHED TO THIS OBJECTIVE TO LEAD STUDENTS TOWARD INDEPENDENCE (Remember to chart the evidence when you use a picture book so that students may provide specific details from the text)

These books also contain lots of similes:

- ***All the Colors of the Earth* by Sheila Hamanaka**
  This little book celebrates children's differences, especially hair and skin color, with poetic language and paintings: Do you have "hair that flows like water" or "hair like bouncy baby lambs?" The similes in this book inspire pride in one's appearance—whatever that might be.

- ***The Whales' Song* by Dyan Sheldon**
  A very old grandmother captures the imagination of her young granddaughter when she shares a haunting tale about whales that sing in the night. And if you listen carefully, the whales might even call your name: Whales as big as hills, whales as peaceful as the moon. There are plenty of similes here to help students visualize.

- ***My Dog is as Smelly as Dirty Socks* by Hanoch Piven**
  This book is very funny. Bold, found-art images accompany a series of similes about each family member: "My daddy is as jumpy as a SPRING and as playful as a SPINNING TOP. He is as fun as a PARTY FAVOR. But sometimes he's as stubborn as a KNOT in a ROPE." (Visualize if you will, a wooden top, one of those noisy party favors, and a frayed piece of rope.)

SCORING STUDENTS' RESPONSES

D1-b: Choose a simile from *The Seashore Book* and explain why the author chose this simile.

Anchor responses are provided for the following simile:

> *A little white sailboat is so far out it <u>seems</u> a toy*

Score = 2

This simile compares a faraway sailboat to a toy. The author used this simile to show that because the sailboat was far out in the ocean, it looked very, very small. The author wants us to get an idea of how far away the boat was, and what it looked like in the distance.

> (This response would receive full score because it correctly identifies the comparison the author made, and why she used this particular comparison.)

Score = 1

This simile says that the sailboat was so far away that it looked like a toy.

> (This response identifies the comparison, but could explain more about why the author used this particular image.)

Score = 0

Toy sailboats are small. They are smaller than regular boats.

> (This reader probably understands this simile, but does not explain it thoroughly enough to convey that understanding.)

PLANNER FOR SHARED READING

Objective (strategy focus): <u>D1-b: Choose a simile and explain why the author chose that simile.</u>

◎ <u>Choose a simile from *The Seashore Book* and explain how this simile helps you to picture the seashore.</u>

How will student learning be measured at the end of the lesson? (What will count as "success?")

Text: <u>*The Seashore Book* by Charlotte Zolotow</u>   **Pages:** <u>Whole book</u>

<table>
<tr>
<td rowspan="3" style="writing-mode:vertical-rl">BEFORE READING</td>
<td>Establish prior knowledge, purpose, and predictions</td>
<td>Prior knowledge: What is "the seashore?" What are some things that you would find at the seashore? Suppose you were trying to describe the seashore to someone who had never been there before. How would you help that person get a picture in their mind of the seashore? (Encourage describing words.)
Predictions: This story is about a little boy who has never been to the seashore. Look at the cover. What do you think we might find out in this book?
Purpose for reading: As we read this book, look at the way the author describes the seashore. In particular, look at the way she uses similes to help readers picture the seashore in their mind.</td>
</tr>
<tr>
<td>Introduce/ review vocabulary</td>
<td>hazy   crusty   skims   lulls (you to sleep)   wade
crescent (moon)</td>
</tr>
<tr>
<td>Introduce the objective (How to find and use the evidence)</td>
<td>Making the <u>reading</u> strategic
A simile is a way of comparing two things by using the word like or as: I'm as hungry as a bear; I felt like a princess in my new party dress. Authors use similes to help you get a better picture of something in your mind. A simile can help you understand something more thoroughly by using your senses. When you find a simile in a text, notice what is being compared. Which one of your senses helps you to understand this better? Think about why the author used this comparison and make sure you can explain it.</td>
</tr>
</table>

DURING READING	**Model and practice finding evidence for the objective**	**The best evidence:** **Model:** **p. 7:** *The cold water makes your skin feel <u>like</u> peppermint:* I'm noticing that the author is comparing the feeling of cold water on your skin to peppermint. I'm thinking this is kind of like a peppermint candy. The cold water makes you feel all tingly and the peppermint candy makes your mouth feel all tingly. By understanding this comparison, I can get a better idea of what the water is like at the seashore. **p. 9:** *The hot noonday sun feels warm <u>as</u> a big soft cat covering you:* I'm noticing that the author is comparing the feeling of the sun on you to the feeling of being covered by a big cat. Although I didn't ever lie in the sun before, I know what a cat would feel like on top of me. I'd probably be really warm and cozy. So I'm figuring out that the sun will make me feel warm and cozy, too. **p. 11:** *The gray sandpipers make claw prints <u>like</u> pencil lines in the sand*: I never saw a sandpiper claw print, but I know what a pencil line looks like, so I have an idea about the bird claw prints. **Practice:** **p. 15:** *A little white sailboat is so far out it <u>seems</u> a toy* **p. 17:** *The airplane's shadow on the sand is <u>like</u> a gigantic bird* **p. 19:** *The fishing pier is white <u>as</u> a snowfall* **p. 21:** *The setting sun is a huge orange ball* (metaphor—comparison without *like* or *as*)
	Model and practice other strategies	**Connecting?** Connect to a time when you've been to the seashore…. What was similar? What was different? **Visualizing/Picturing?** What scene from this book can you visualize really clearly in your mind? **Wondering?** What do you wonder about the seashore? **Predicting/Guessing?** What helped you to predict what you would learn in this book? **Noticing?** Which details helped you picture the seashore most vividly? **Figuring out?** What made this book special?

AFTER READING	**Discussion questions**	**Question related to the objective** **D1-b:** Choose a simile from *The Seashore Book* and explain how this simile helps you to picture the seashore. (See follow-up sheet with similes with the materials for this lesson on the CD.) **Other questions** **C1-d:** Using evidence from the text, explain whether you would ever want to visit the seashore. **C2-c:** Did you like this story? Why or why not? **D2-a:** What two questions would you like to ask the author that were not answered in this text?
	Written response to text	**Making the <u>writing</u> strategic** • See the follow-up sheet of similes with the lesson materials for this book on the CD. • See *That's a Great Answer*, p. 145, for a template matched to this objective. • Model the response using the template. • Remove your response and ask students to write the response themselves using the template if they need it—choosing a different simile.
	Other follow-up activities	**Oral language, fluency, vocabulary, comprehension, reading extensions, writing extensions** **Oral language/fluency:** This book contains many poetic-sounding passages. Practice reading one or two of them until you really sound like a poet (who loves the seashore!) **Vocabulary:** See *Vocabulary Connections* activity for this book on the CD. **Comprehension:** These follow-up activities may be found in *Constructing Meaning through Kid-Friendly Comprehension Strategy Instruction*: Picture This, p. 164; Reading with all of my Senses, p. 168. **Reading extensions:** These classic picture books, all by Holling C. Holling celebrate our natural world: • *Minn of the Mississippi* • *Pagoo* • *Seabird* • *Tree in the Trail* • *Paddle to the Sea* **Writing extensions:** Using the "hyperbole" format, create an elaborated simile related to the seashore. See template for this lesson on the CD.
	Reflect on reading and writing strategy	• What is a simile? • Why does an author use similes? • How does a simile help you understand a text better?

D1-c: How did the author create humor in this book?

BOOK

The School Nurse from the Black Lagoon by Mike Thaler

INTRODUCTION TO THE BOOK

Selecting a text for this objective was difficult. Oh, I have plenty of books that *I* think are humorous. And I can predict where I'll get a laugh or two from the *teachers* observing the lesson. But it's hard to determine what intermediate grade *kids* will find funny. Young children love made-up words, the kind of word-play reminiscent of so many of the Dr. Seuss books. More sophisticated readers enjoy things like fractured fairytales and double entendre—but both of those require a degree of background knowledge and abstract thinking that many students in the intermediate grades do not possess.

WHY THIS IS A GOOD BOOK FOR TEACHING THIS OBJECTIVE

For reasons that are not always apparent to me, kids love these *Black Lagoon* books—and they are universal in their appeal: Old kids, young kids, boys, girls. They all love these farcical tales that are simultaneously highly exaggerated and completely real. The situations themselves are extreme: a school nurse, for example who gives kids shots with a needle as long as a saber. But what rings true is that lots of children do have "school nurse anxiety" and are reluctant to visit the nurse's office because they're not entirely sure what happens there. So maybe this is the kid version of Moliere: black humor where we sort of laugh at ourselves—and enjoy it. Other kinds of humor also appeal to children. You'll soon discover what the students in your class like when you read a story aloud and they laugh—and beg you to read it again.

OTHER OBJECTIVES THAT MAY BE ADDRESSED BY RE-READING THIS BOOK

- **A1-d:** What would be another good title for this book/story?
- **A2-d:** How did _____ change from the beginning to the end of the story?
- **A3-a:** Briefly summarize this story.
- **C1-a:** Make a personal connection to an experience.

OTHER BOOKS MATCHED TO THIS OBJECTIVE TO LEAD STUDENTS TOWARD INDEPENDENCE (Remember to chart the evidence when you use a picture book so that students may provide specific details from the text)

These books are humorous for various reasons:

- ***Double Trouble in Walla Walla* by Andrew Clements**
  What makes this book funny is the word play. The book begins: *"Mrs. Bell, I feel like a nit-wit. My homework is all higgledy-piggledy. Last night it was in tip-top shape, but now it's a big mish-mash."* Mrs. Bell said, *"Nit-wit? Higgledy-piggledy? Mish-mash? Lulu, stop that flip-flop chitter-chatter or you'll be in double trouble!"* And so the story goes. Jeepers-creepers, kids love this and catch on right away. They can try this technique in their own writing, too.

- ***That's Good! That's Bad!* by Margery Cuyler**
  What makes this book funny is its predictive nature—or more accurately, the reader's inability to anticipate the next unlikely twist: As the story begins, a little boy falls into a muddy river and lands on a hippopotamus who carries him to shore. That's good? No, that's bad! The boy encounters baboons who chase him. That's bad? No, that's good because.... Students love to guess what might come next—but this author generally outsmarts them!

- ***17 Things I'm Not Allowed to Do Anymore* by Jenny Offill**
  It's the kid-connections that make this book funny: *I had an idea to staple my brother's hair to his pillow.... I am not allowed to use the stapler anymore. I had an idea to glue my brother's bunny slippers to the floor.... I am not allowed to use the glue anymore.* You get the idea, and students will, too—many of whom have "been there, done that." Most kids probably have at least 17 things *they're* not allowed to do anymore. And after reading this book, maybe they'll tell you about them in their own writing.

SCORING STUDENTS' RESPONSES

◎ **D1-c: Give an example of something that is funny from *The School Nurse from the Black Lagoon* and explain why it is funny.**

Score = 2

It was funny in this book when the school nurse used a surf board as a tongue depressor to check the kid's sore throat. This was funny because it is exaggerated. A surf board is much too big for this, but it is about the same shape. Of course it could never fit in the kid's mouth, but it is a great image watching the nurse standing there with it and the kid looks terrified!

> (This response would receive full score because it identifies a plausible humorous incident and thoroughly explains *why* it is humorous.)

Score = 1

It was funny when the kid got turned into a rug because he was run over by the VCR cart. He is flat, just like a rug and he is lying on the floor. It looks funny.

> (This response identifies a humorous image and describes it using details. The reader says it "looks funny," but doesn't explain what technique the author/illustrator has used to make this so humorous. He could have mentioned exaggeration or even farce—exaggeration to the point of being nonsensical.)

Score = 0

It was funny when there were eyeballs on the pool table.

> (Eyeballs on the pool table would be pretty funny—but *why*? Since the point of this question is to explain the humor, this should not receive credit.)

PLANNER FOR SHARED READING

Objective (strategy focus): <u>D1-c:</u> <u>How did the author create humor in this book?</u>

🎯 **<u>D1-c:</u>** <u>Give an example of something that is funny from *The School Nurse from the Black Lagoon* and explain why it is funny.</u>
How will student learning be measured at the end of the lesson? (What will count as "success?")

Text: <u>*The School Nurse from the Black Lagoon*</u>   **Pages:** <u>Whole book</u>

<table>
<tr>
<td rowspan="3" style="writing-mode: vertical-rl;">BEFORE READING</td>
<td>Establish prior knowledge, purpose, and predictions</td>
<td>Prior knowledge: There are several "Black Lagoon" books. If you've read any of the others, what are they like? What do you expect to find in books in this series?
Predictions: Based on the cover, do you expect this book to be funny or serious? Why?
Purpose for reading: Let's read to enjoy the humor in this book and to think about what makes this book funny.</td>
</tr>
<tr>
<td>Introduce/ review vocabulary</td>
<td>lagoon   ghoul   affliction   vaccination   normal</td>
</tr>
<tr>
<td>Introduce the objective (How to find and use the evidence)</td>
<td>Making the <u>reading</u> strategic
Think about what makes something funny:
<ul>
<li>Made up words or words with a double meaning</li>
<li>Exaggeration—or something that would be unlikely to happen. "Extreme exaggeration" can be considered farce if it is so silly that it could never, ever happen.</li>
<li>Something slightly scary or painful (but you know that you are safe from harm)</li>
<li>Something gross</li>
<li>Words that create a humorous picture in your mind</li>
<li>Pictures that are humorous</li>
<li>Animals or nonliving things that speak or act like people</li>
<li>Surprise ending that contradicts what you expected</li>
</ul></td>
</tr>
</table>

<table>
<tr>
<td rowspan="2"></td>
<td>Model and practice finding evidence for the objective</td>
<td>

***Important:** Read this book all the way through one time. Then go back and reread it to analyze why different parts were funny.

The best evidence:

<u>Model:</u>

p. 3: Miss <u>Hearse</u>, the nurse (play on words)

p. 5: skeleton of kid who had a stomachache (scary/couldn't happen)

p. 7: cut in half by a paper cutter; taped back together backward with a band-aid (couldn't happen)

p. 8: kid got run over by a VCR cart...now a rug (words that create a humorous picture; could never happen)

p. 9: thermometer the size of a flag pole (exaggeration)

<u>Practice:</u>

p. 10: tongue depressor as big as a surfboard (exaggeration)

p. 11: stretched on a rack to help you "grow" (ouch—could never happen)

p. 13: eyeballs for billiard balls (ouch—could never happen)

p. 15: ears in her jewelry collection (ouch—could never happen)

p. 16: vaccination (words that create a humorous picture; ouch; exaggeration)

p. 17: ice (could never happen)

p. 18: cot (ouch; exaggeration

p. 20: toothache (would never happen)

p. 21: sore throat (would never happen)

p. 27: she' a miracle worker (surprise, contradictory ending)

</td>
</tr>
<tr>
<td>Model and practice other strategies</td>
<td>

Connecting? Did you ever hear any "horror stories" about someone, but then discovered that the stories weren't true?

Visualizing/Picturing? What picture can you see really clearly in your mind?

Wondering? What does an author need to think about in order to write with humor?

Predicting/Guessing? Predict what the nurse will *really* be like.

Noticing? Notice some of the details in the illustrations: How do they add to the humor?

Figuring out? Is there one technique that this author uses more than others to create humor?

</td>
</tr>
</table>

<table>
<tr>
<td rowspan="5"></td>
<td>Discussion questions</td>
<td>Question related to the objective
D1-c: Give an example of something that is funny from The School Nurse from the Black Lagoon and explain why it is funny.
Other questions
B2-a: Why does the author include the picture and words on p. 27: "She's a miracle worker. I'm cured!"
C1-a: Make a personal connection to a time when you anticipated the worst from someone, but then were pleasantly surprised.
D1-a: Choose two words or phrases from page 16 that help you picture the vaccination.</td>
</tr>
<tr>
<td>Written response to text</td>
<td>Making the <u>writing</u> strategic
• See That's a Great Answer, p. 147, for a template matched to this objective.
• Model the response using the template.
• Remove your response and ask students to write the response themselves about another incident in the book that they find humorous using the template if necessary.</td>
</tr>
<tr>
<td>Other follow-up activities</td>
<td>Oral language, fluency, vocabulary, comprehension, reading extensions, writing extensions
Oral language/fluency: Practice reading favorite pages from this book until you sound really SCARY!
Vocabulary: See Vocabulary Connections activity for this book on CD.
Comprehension: These follow-up activities may be found in Constructing Meaning through Kid-Friendly Comprehension Strategy Instruction: Picture This, p. 164; Reading with all of My Senses, p. 168.
Reading extensions: Read other "Black Lagoon" books by Mike Thaler. Which one seems funniest? Why?
Examples:
• The Substitute Teacher from the Black Lagoon
• The Librarian from the Black Lagoon
• The School Bus Driver from the Black Lagoon
Writing extensions: Write your own "Black Lagoon" book. Some possible topics might be: The Babysitter from the Black Lagoon, The Coach from the Black Lagoon, The New Kid in Class from the Black Lagoon.</td>
</tr>
<tr>
<td>Reflect on reading and writing strategy</td>
<td>• What are some author's crafts that make a story humorous?
• How did the author create humor in thi book?</td>
</tr>
</table>

OBJECTIVE

D1-d: Give an example of personification in this text.

BOOK

Dear World by Takayo Noda

INTRODUCTION TO THE BOOK

This book is a collection of unrhymed poems where a little child personifies things and creatures by speaking directly to them: Dear dawn…, Dear apples…, Dear sun…, Dear turtle. Each poem captures the child's nuanced thinking, the significant details about the subject from a kid point of view. The cut-paper collage-style illustrations are equally charming and compliment the text perfectly.

WHY THIS IS A GOOD BOOK FOR TEACHING THIS OBJECTIVE

While many books contain examples of personification here and there, it is not easy to find a book that features personification on every page. This book does that. The entire premise of this book is personification—writing to things and creatures as if they are personal friends. While the extent of personification varies from poem to poem, every poem offers some examples: *Dear Snow, I see you/ spinning and dancing/ just like angels in white. Dear Sun, I know/ when you are angry/ because you hide behind/ the dark cloud and/ shout thunder/ and lightning.* Besides being a great resource for reading, this book can also be a wonderful writing resource. Students can use this format to create their own personification poems, writing to things and creatures special to them in their world.

OTHER OBJECTIVES THAT MAY BE ADDRESSED BY RE-READING THIS BOOK

- **A4-b:** If the author added more lines to the end of the poem, it would <u>most likely</u> tell about _____.
- **D1-a:** Choose [2] words from paragraph ___ that help you picture the _____.
- **D1-b:** Choose a simile and explain why the author chose that simile.

OTHER BOOKS MATCHED TO THIS OBJECTIVE TO LEAD STUDENTS TOWARD INDEPENDENCE (Remember to chart the evidence when you use a picture book so that students may provide specific details from the text)

These books all contain beautiful images created through personification:
- ***Is That You, Winter?* by Stephen Gammell**
  Old Man Winter laments that wintertime is here and he has to go to work again. This book follows him through his day as he "lets loose his icy blast" and puzzles over "Who

do I make it snow for?" He ends the day in a good mood, however, when he sees how happy he's made the kids "playing in the snow that fell this morning."

- **Snow by Cynthia Rylant**
  What is it about snow that goes so well with personification? This book is "typical Rylant," a gentle, lyrical study of the way snow warms our heart: *The best snow/ is the snow that/ comes softly in the night,/ like a shy friend/ afraid to knock,/ so she thinks she'll/ just wait in the yard/ until you see her.* By the time you finish reading this book, you may find yourself wishing for snow—even in July.

- **In November by Cynthia Rylant**
  This book has it all: imagery that involves all of the senses, similes, and abundant personification. This is more personal narrative than "story," but children love it—images of bare tree branches, birds readying for winter, cats piling up in the corners of barns, Thanksgiving pies, and the final benediction: *In November, at winter's gate, the stars are brittle. The sun is a sometime friend. And the world has tucked her children in, with a kiss on their heads, till spring.*

SCORING STUDENTS' RESPONSES

 D1-d: Give an example of personification in this text.

Anchor responses are provided here for *Dear Sun*. Responses would look similar for other poems.

Score = 2

In this poem, the sun is acting like a person which is personification. It is shouting when it is angry like in a thunderstorm and winking over a rainbow when it is happy. This helps me to picture the sun in my mind. But a sun doesn't really have feelings like happy and angry and it doesn't shout or wink.

> (The reader correctly identifies two examples of personification here, explains how the personification helps him visualize the image, and explains *why* this is personification.)

Score = 1

Personification in this poem is that the sun bounces on everything like a person.

> (The reader is correct that this is personification, but there is no elaboration as to why this is an example of personification, or how it contributes to the imagery.)

Score = 0

This is personification because it is about the sun. In the end the sun makes a rainbow.

> (This reader does not appear to understand personification. Personification is not created by the topic of a poem, but by how the imagery is created with that topic— with actions like those of a person.)

PLANNER FOR SHARED READING

Objective (strategy focus): <u>D1-d: Give an example of personification in this text.</u>

 <u>Give an example of personification in one of the poems in *Dear World.*</u>
How will student learning be measured at the end of the lesson? (What will count as "success?")

Text: <u>*Dear World* by Takayo Noda</u>   **Pages:** <u>Whole book</u>

<table>
<tr>
<td rowspan="4" style="writing-mode: vertical;">BEFORE READING</td>
<td>Establish prior knowledge, purpose, and predictions</td>
<td>Prior knowledge: How are poems different from stories? Do all poems rhyme? What do you expect to find in a poem other than rhyming words? (Elicit the idea that poems create images that you can appreciate with all of your senses.)
Predictions: Can you make any predictions about this book by looking at the title—and knowing this is a book of poetry? (Children should note the word *dear* and that this implies a "letter" format. Share a few pages so students can see that this book is a series of poems written to things and creatures in our world.)
Purpose for reading: This book contains lots of *personification*. As we read these poems, we will look for examples of personification.</td>
</tr>
<tr>
<td>Introduce/ review vocabulary</td>
<td>dawn   twilight   chorus   tart   (to feel) blue   shelter   wink</td>
</tr>
<tr>
<td>Introduce the objective (How to find and use the evidence)</td>
<td>Making the <u>reading</u> strategic
Personification means that the author is making something that is a "thing" or a "creature" act the way a person would act. Authors use personification because it helps us picture something more clearly in our mind. For example, the author might way, "The sun was dancing across the water." The *sun* doesn't really *dance*; *people dance*. So that is an example of personification. Here's another example: "The wind moaned for hours during the terrible storm." Again, wind doesn't actually *moan*. One way to find personification is to look for the action words (verbs). Then see who's doing the action. If it's a "thing" or a "creature" doing something that only a person could do, that's personification. Personification can also be created by a simile: *The tree with outstretched branches looked <u>like a ballerina</u>.* Sometimes a thing or creature is personified when it talks and carries on a conversation or when the author shows the thoughts in the thing's or creature's mind. (You may not want to share all of these personification techniques during your first lesson.)</td>
</tr>
</table>

DURING READING	**Model and practice finding evidence for the objective**	**The best evidence:** Examples of personification will be identified for some of the poems in this book. Read the other poems in this book for additional examples. **Model:** Notice for all of these poems, that the author is addressing a "thing" or "creature" as if it is a friend—a person. Right away, you can tell there's going to be personification here. **Dear world:** *you* grow berries; *you* give sweet smells; *you* change the colors of leaves in the fall ("The world" doesn't really do any of these things.) **Dear apples:** *your* leaves *tickle* my face; *your* sweet juice *journeys* into my belly (leaves don't tickle or take journeys) **Practice:** **Dear ocean:** Please leave the doors open (an ocean can't leave a door open—what doors?) **Dear snow:** I see you *spinning* and *dancing* (snow doesn't dance—even *spin* is a stretch) **Dear sun:** *shine* and *bounce*; as if you had *tears in your eyes*; *hide* in the dark clouds and *shout* thunder and lightning; *wink* over the rainbow (Notice here that personification is created by a simile—underlined)
	Model and practice other strategies	**Connecting?** Did you ever have any of these same thoughts—or different thoughts—about some of the creatures or things in this book? **Visualizing/Picturing?** How did the pictures in this book help you to enjoy these poems more than if you had just read the poems? **Wondering?** What things or creatures do *you* wonder about that were not described in this book? **Predicting/Guessing?** Make a prediction about what this author might be like based on the poems that she wrote. **Noticing?** What small details in this book really stood out to you? Which details will you remember? Why? **Figuring out?** If you wanted to write a poem in the style of this author, what would you try in your own writing?

AFTER READING	**Discussion questions**	**Question related to the objective** **D1-d:** Give an example of personification in one of the poems in *Dear World.* **Other questions** **A4-b:** If the author added more lines to [title of poem], it would <u>most likely</u> tell about _____. What might the author add? **B2-b:** Why did the author write a book of poems using the "Dear World" format with so much personification? **C1-b:** Make a personal connection to a feeling in one of these poems. Why could you relate to it? **D1-a:** Choose some words from [title of poem] that help you get a good picture in your mind. What do you picture?
	Written response to text	**Making the <u>writing</u> strategic** • See *That's a Great Answer*, p. 83, for a template matched to this objective. • Model the response using the template for one of the poems. • Remove your response and ask students to write the response themselves based on another poem using the template if needed.
	Other follow-up activities	**Oral language, fluency, vocabulary, comprehension, reading extensions, writing extensions** **Oral language/fluency:** These poems are written in free verse meaning that they do not rhyme, and the author has decided where the line breaks should be based on the phrasing that she intends. Practice reading one of the poems, focusing on phrasing. Or, rewrite the poem with different line breaks. Does the poem sound different now that the phrases are different? **Vocabulary:** See *Vocabulary Connections* activity on the CD. **Comprehension:** These follow-up activities may be found in *Constructing Meaning through Kid-Friendly Comprehension Strategy Instruction*: Reading with All of My Senses, p. 168; "Best Quote," p. 175. **Reading extensions:** These poetry books also demonstrate formats that students could try in their own writing: • *Hailstones and Halibut Bones* by Mary O'Neill • *The Important Book* by Margaret Wise Brown • *Runny Babbit: A Billy Sook* by Shel Silverstein • *Silver Seeds* by Paul Paolilli and Dan Brewer **Writing extensions:** Write a "Dear World" poem of your own: Choose a thing or creature to write about. Write your poem in free verse, deciding where to put your line breaks so the phrasing sounds just right. Create images that involve all of your senses. Be sure to include personification.
	Reflect on reading and writing strategy	• What is personification? • Why does an author use personification? • How do you recognize personification?

OBJECTIVE

D1-e: Do you think the author made this story believable? Why or why not?

BOOK

Pictures from Our Vacation by Lynne Rae Perkins

INTRODUCTION TO THE BOOK

I'm sure I'm not the only one who's noticed that the quintessential "family vacation" is never quite the storybook experience we imagine as we plan the trip and look longingly at the online photos of bright sun shining on pristine blue waters, happy brothers and sisters smiling sweetly at each other, and luxurious resorts with every amenity. The author of this book has captured the real deal (perhaps as a stowaway on one of *my* vacations): endless days of rain, destinations that bear little resemblance to the brochure, and kids bickering over who gets to sit next to the window (not that it really matters because there's nothing interesting to see anyway.) This book features all of these realities—and more. In the end, it's the unanticipated moments that are the most memorable. While these mental images may never make it into the family photo album, they become the inspiration for that question that becomes the standard of any good vacation: *When can we do it again?*

WHY THIS IS A GOOD BOOK FOR TEACHING THIS OBJECTIVE

When I began teaching this objective, I used stories with extensive exaggeration—such as tall tales and fantasies. I reasoned that students would be better able to recognize what is "real" by understanding characters that could never exist and adventures that would never happen. Students easily identified the features that made a story "not believable." But this didn't really give them insight into features that make a story realistic. Hmmm. I decided I needed something more "real" than a basic problem/solution story where everything conveniently works out in the end despite some catastrophic near-miss. "Real life" isn't a neat little package that runs like a TV sit-com; it's a string of events with assorted ups and downs—the small details to which all of us can relate. That's what makes this book so perfect. This book is all about the small details that make life quirky. This is one of those honest books that make you think: "Been there, done that"—the stuff of which real connections are made.

OTHER OBJECTIVES THAT MAY BE ADDRESSED BY RE-READING THIS BOOK

- **A4-b:** If the author added another paragraph to the end of the story, it would <u>most likely</u> tell about _____.
- **B2-a:** Why does the author include the photo of the shoes (on the first page)?
- **C1-a:** Make a personal connection to a time when you went on a family vacation or went somewhere with your family?
- **D3-a:** What is important to this author? How can you tell?

OTHER BOOKS MATCHED TO THIS OBJECTIVE TO LEAD STUDENTS TOWARD INDEPENDENCE (Remember to chart the evidence when you use a picture book so that students may provide specific details from the text)

These books are useful for demonstrating the "believable" factor because they provide an honest look at the way life really is—not some glossy, "only in a fairytale" version of the way we'd like it to be.

- ***The Pain and the Great One* by Judy Blume**
  Any kid who has a brother or sister can relate to this book, and even the children in your class without siblings will appreciate this well-loved classic about life first from big sister's point of view, and then from little brother's perspective. About The Pain: *I would really like to know why the cat sleeps on the Pain's bed instead of mind especially since I am the one who feeds her.* About the Great One: *She thinks she's great just because she can play the piano and you can tell the songs are real ones.*

- ***Halloween* by Jerry Seinfeld**
  The author's name alone tells you this book will be a reality check. Seinfeld has a well-honed talent for finding the tiniest detail and exploding it into a mega event. Take, for example, the rubber band on the back of a Halloween mask: *That was a quality item. Thinnest gray rubber in the world. It was good for about ten seconds before it snapped out of that cheap little staple they put it in there with. You go to the first house, "Trick or ... SNAP!*

- ***The Memory String* by Eve Bunting**
  Unlike the two books described above, this one is definitely *not* funny. In fact, a box of tissues is in order. The story features a little girl who is having a hard time adjusting to her new step-mom. Things get much worse when her memory string of special buttons breaks and she loses the most precious button of all—one that came from her mom's favorite nightgown. Your heart will ache for both the child and the stepmother. But in the end, compassion prevails and the little girl begins to realize that this new woman in her life is not trying to be a substitute mom—but she just might be a nice person with whom to share her life.

SCORING STUDENTS' RESPONSES

 D1-e: Figure out what makes *Pictures from Our Vacation* a believable story.

Score = 2

This story is believable because it shows that even though you want your vacation to be perfect, sometimes it might not be that great. For example, the girl wastes a picture when she takes a picture of her shoes by mistake. I know that could really happen because I've taken a picture by mistake before. One time the family went sightseeing, but the hill just looked like a hill, not anything really cool. This could be real because sometimes when we go sightseeing, I get mostly bored.

> (This reader provides two examples of things that could be real as well as *why* they seem real. She also offers her own connections. This is not required. But when something seems real, it is natural to want to connect to it.)

Score = 1

This story could be real because it always rains on vacations, even when it should be sunny. Also, a lot of times, there is nothing to do.

> (This reader gave two reasonable examples, but there is no specific evidence from the text.)

Score = 0

This story could be real because it is about kids going on vacation with their family. They take pictures.

> (In order for this response to receive credit, it would need to indicate what made the vacation and the pictures "real.")

PLANNER FOR SHARED READING

Objective (strategy focus): <u>D1-e:</u> <u>Is this story believable?</u>

🎯 <u>Figure out what makes *Pictures from Our Vacation* a believable story</u>

    How will student learning be measured at the end of the lesson? (What will count as "success?")

Text: *Pictures from our Vacation* by Lynne Rae Perkins   **Pages:** Whole book

<table>
<tr>
<td rowspan="3">BEFORE READING</td>
<td>Establish prior knowledge, purpose, and predictions</td>
<td>Prior knowledge: Think about a time when you've been really excited to go somewhere—but then it hasn't turned out the way you expected. What kinds of things "get in the way" of your "good time?"
Predictions: Look at the cover (and a few pictures from the book). What do you think the "pictures from our vacation" might show?
Purpose for reading: Let's read to find out why this story is believable.</td>
</tr>
<tr>
<td>Introduce/ review vocabulary</td>
<td>nostalgic   motel   memories   gazebo   memorial (service)
ornery</td>
</tr>
<tr>
<td>Introduce the objective (How to find and use the evidence)</td>
<td>Making the <u>reading</u> strategic
To figure out if something is believable, decide: Could events like this happen in real life? Do the characters act like, look like, talk like, and think like real people? In fact, stories sound believable when they are told with honesty—the way something really is, not the way you wish it would be. You can hear the character's (or author's) voice, and you know the person is telling the truth. Look for the small details. That's where you'll find the evidence that makes you say: "This is believable"—because you may have had these same things happen to YOU.</td>
</tr>
</table>

	Model and practice the focus strategy	**The best evidence:** **Model:** **pp. 1-2** (dedication page): Family is leaving for vacation with expectations of having a wonderful time; everyone has their own dream (believable—always leave for vacation with high expectations). **p. 4:** Taking a picture of your shoes by mistake (believable—take lots of bad pictures by mistake) **pp. 5-6:** The scenery from the car window isn't really "beautiful;" It's really *boring* (believable). **pp. 7-8:** Motel promised a pool—but it had no water (believable—lots of times you don't get what you expect—false advertising). **p. 9:** Dad loved the old farmhouse, though it was old and dusty (believable—someone else's happy memory doesn't always mean you will think it's so great). **Practice:** **p. 11:** Just started to play—and it began to rain (believable—lots of good activities get rained out). **pp. 13-14:** It rained for days (believable—often rains *for DAYS* on vacation). **pp. 15-16:** Secret path to lake now overgrown; "Keep Out" sign prevented getting to the lake (believable—things change! More security; more rules). **pp. 17-18:** The "ancient hills" weren't so impressive; more focused on squirrel eating Chinese take-out (believable—kids are often not impressed by the things that adults think are important). **pp. 21-22:** Wanting to go someplace "cool," like Disney World—but going to a funeral instead (believable—sometimes what you do on vacation seems like the "opposite" of fun). **pp. 23-28:** The relatives came and suddenly everyone was having more fun (believable—sometimes things you don't expect to be fun actually *are* fun). **pp. 29-31:** The pictures didn't really capture the important aspects of the vacation (believable—the best memories after a vacation are the feelings inside you and the pictures in your mind).
	Model and practice other strategies	**Connecting?** Connect to a time when you expected something to be great—or not-so-great—and the experience turned out differently for you. **Visualizing/Picturing?** What do you get a really good picture of in your mind? Why? **Wondering?** Wonder how the author made this story so believable? How could you do this in your own writing? **Predicting/Guessing?** Did you predict that this adventure would end happily? Why or why not? **Noticing?** What details gave this story the most voice? **Figuring out?** Why was this story believable?

After Reading	**Discussion questions**	**Focus question** **D1-e:** Is this story believable? Why or why not? **Other questions** **B1-a:** What caused the children's feelings abut their vacation to change at the end of the story? **C1-a:** Make a personal connection to a time when you went someplace and had a better (or worse) time than you expected to have. **C2-c:** Did you like this story? Why or why not?
	Written response to text	**Making the <u>writing</u> strategic** • See *That's a Great Answer*, p. 153, for a template matched to this objective. • Model the response using the template. • Remove your response and ask students to write the response themselves, choosing other examples of "reality." They may use the template if necessary.

	Other follow-up activities	**Extensions: Oral language, fluency, vocabulary, comprehension, reading extensions, writing extensions**
		Oral language/Fluency: Write a dialogue between two sisters (or two brothers) in the back seat of a car on a long car ride. They are getting bored and ornery. Make your conversation believable. Act out this scene for your classmates.
		Vocabulary: See *Vocabulary Connections* activity for this book on the CD.
		Comprehension: *Constructing Meaning*: Active Reader Report, p. 155; Picture This, p. 164; Reading with all of my Senses, p. 168
		Reading extensions: These stories all involve family relationships:
		• *Faraway Home* by Jane Kurtz
		• *Uncle Jed's Barbershop by Margaree King Mitchell*
		• *Down the Road* by Alice Schertle
		Writing extensions: Writing on topics you know a lot about allows you to include the kinds of small details that make your writing believable. Choose something about which you are an "expert" and use lots of small details to make your story believable. Some possible topics might be:
		    • How to annoy your mother when she's on the phone
		    • How to get to stay up past your bed time
		    • How to avoid eating a vegetable you really don't like

	Reflect on reading and writing strategy	• What makes a story believable? • What kind of evidence should you look for to determine whether a story is believable? • How can knowing how to make a character believable help you in your *writing* as well as in your *reading*?

OBJECTIVE

D2-a: What two questions would you like to ask the author that were not answered in this text?

BOOK

Will We Miss Them? Endangered Species by Alexandra Wright

INTRODUCTION TO THE BOOK

This book presents information about thirteen endangered animals in short passages that would be both easy to understand and interesting for intermediate grade students. The accompanying illustrations are simple and clear, contributing to the impact of the information. The final two pages of the book include a map showing where each animal lives, and information about protecting wildlife.

WHY THIS IS A GOOD BOOK FOR TEACHING THIS OBJECTIVE

One of the neat things about this book is that it was written by an eleven year old. It would be wonderful to share with students that a child of their age can be a published author! Another great feature of this book is that it contains descriptions of thirteen specific endangered animals. Having different sections devoted to different animals makes it easy to apply the gradual release model in initial teaching: model, prompt, release. Sections of this book could also be used in a small group with students able to read the text with teacher guidance.

OTHER OBJECTIVES THAT MAY BE ADDRESSED BY RE-READING THIS BOOK

- **A1-c:** What is the main idea of this [portion of the text]?
- **B1-d:** Can this part of the [text] be described as: a description, an explanation, a conversation, an opinion, an argument, or a comparison? How do you know?
- **B2-a:** Why does the author include paragraph ___?
- **B3-b:** Which facts (details) show that _____?
- **C2-b:** Which part of this [text] was most interesting or surprising to you? Why?

OTHER BOOKS MATCHED TO THIS OBJECTIVE TO LEAD STUDENTS TOWARD INDEPENDENCE (Remember to chart the evidence when you use a picture book so that students may provide specific details from the text)

- *She's Wearing a Dead Bird on Her Head* **by Kathryn Lasky**
  When wearing dead birds atop their hats became a fashion statement for fancy ladies at the turn of the century, a few Boston women started the Massachusetts Audubon Society to put an end to this practice. This book raises numerous ethical and environmental issues that will inspire students' thoughtful questions. It also models "girl power," the capacity of ordinary folk to bring about political action, and the importance of caring about the environment.

- *Letting Swift River Go* **by Jane Yolen**
  This book illustrates the impact of modernization on civilization and will lead students to important questions about what really counts as "progress." This book, too is a New England tale, set in Massachusetts. But it speaks to all of us. Sally Jane's community is swallowed up by the forming of the Quabbin Reservoir which will provide water to the people of Boston. One way of life disappears so another can continue. Which is more important? How should similar environmental issues be handled in the future? Reflective students will ask these questions—and more.

- *Planting the Trees of Kenya: The Story of Wangari Maathai* **by Claire A. Nivola**
  Wangari Maathai won the 2004 Nobel Peace Prize and founded the Green Belt Movement. She grew up in Kenya, and was dismayed upon her return there after college to find that much of the land had been cleared and that the country's beautiful trees were nearly gone. How could she bring back the trees and the wellbeing of the people of Kenya? This story will encourage students to think along with Wangari as she attempts to answer that question, and to ask other questions of their own about the role of the environment in determining the fate of civilization: What kind of future do we want?

SCORING STUDENTS' RESPONSES

⊚ **D2-a: Think of two questions you would like to ask about one of the endangered animals in this book that the author did *not* answer?**

Score = 2

In this book the author tells about baby elephants weighing more than grown-up people do. I would like to know exactly how much baby elephants weigh because there is a lot of difference in the size of adults. Does a baby elephant weigh one hundred pounds, two hundred pounds, or more?

> (This response would receive full score because the question came directly from something specific in the text; the question is both relevant and reasonable, and the student even clarifies his thinking by noting the differences in the size of human adults.)

Score = 1

In this book it tells about African elephants. I wonder if these elephants could get a job in a circus. It is funny when they squirt water from their trunks.

> (While this text does reference elephants squirting water from their trunk to their mouth, it is quite a stretch from there to the circus question. This question is only loosely related to the text. This response seems to be more of a personal connection than a question to gain further knowledge about elephants.)

Score = 0

In this book the author tells about elephants. Elephants are endangered because people kill them. It is bad to kill elephants.

> (This question would receive a score of 0 because it doesn't ask a question, but rather, identifies information that the author has provided (elephants are endangered) and gives an opinion (it is bad to kill elephants).)

PLANNER FOR SHARED READING

Objective (strategy focus): <u>D2-a</u>: <u>What two questions would you like to ask the author that were not answered in this text?</u>

◎ <u>Think of two questions you would like to ask about one of the endangered animals in this book that the author did *not* answer</u>

How will student learning be measured at the end of the lesson? (What will count as "success?")

Text: <u>*Will We Miss Them? Endangered Species* by Alexandra Wright</u>   **Pages:** <u>Whole book</u>

<table>
<tr>
<td rowspan="3">BEFORE READING</td>
<td>Establish prior knowledge, purpose, and predictions</td>
<td>Prior knowledge: What do we mean by endangered animal? Do you any animals that are endangered? What makes an animal endangered?
Predictions: Look at the cover and title of this book. What do you predict we will learn in this book?
Purpose for reading: In any nonfiction book, the author gives you information. But sometimes that information raises other questions in your mind. As we read this book, think about what else you would like to know based on the information the author has given you.</td>
</tr>
<tr>
<td>Introduce/ review vocabulary</td>
<td>endangered   species   thriving   conservation   harmony   habitat</td>
</tr>
<tr>
<td>Introduce the objective (How to find and use the evidence)</td>
<td>Making the <u>reading</u> strategic
When you think of questions based on something you read, your questions should come directly from the text. That means that you should be able to point to something specific that the author has told you that created a question in your mind. As you read, underline the sentence or phrase in the text that caused you to think of a question. Think about why you want to know this, and why you think this is an important question.</td>
</tr>
</table>

DURING READING	**Model and practice finding evidence for the objective**	**The best evidence:** **Model:** Bald eagle: (build their nests in big trees): What kinds of trees do eagles build their nest in? (eats small animals): What kinds of small animals do eagles eat? **Practice: (These are just suggested prompts; other information may also generate questions)** African elephant: Stop and prompt students to think of a question based on the following information: (Largest creatures on land), (refuse to buy anything made of ivory) Blue whale: Stop and let students work with a partner to come up with a question based on information about the blue whale ***Continue reading about different animals and having students determine questions based on the reading. Eventually, students should be able to formulate two questions independently for one of these endangered animals.
	Model and practice other strategies	**Connecting?** Have you read about any of these animals anywhere else? What else do you know about them? **Visualizing/Picturing?** What can you really picture in your mind? What words has the author used to help you create this picture in your mind? **Wondering?** Which question that you created seems the most important? Why? **Predicting/Guessing?** What do you predict will happen to these animals in the future? Why? **Noticing?** Did you notice any similarities about why these animals are endangered? **Figuring out?** Can you figure out any solutions to the problem of endangered animals?

Discussion questions	**Question related to the objective** **D2-a:** Think of two questions you would like to ask about one of the endangered animals in this book that the author did *not* answer **Other questions** **A1-c:** Choose one animal that you read about in this book. What is the main idea? Identify two details that support this main idea. **B2-b:** The author of this book was an eleven year old girl. Why do you think she wrote a nonfiction book on this topic? **C2-b:** Which part of this book was the most surprising to you? Explain.
Written response to text	**Making the <u>writing</u> strategic** • See *That's a Great Answer*, p. 156, or *Teaching Written Response*, pp. 158-159, for a template matched to this objective. • Model the response for one animal using the template. • Remove your response and ask students to write the response themselves for another animal (one that you read about together). They may use the template if necessary.
Other follow-up activities	**Oral language, fluency, vocabulary, comprehension, reading extensions, writing extensions** **Oral language/fluency:** Pretend you are a news reporter. Practice reading about one of the endangered animals in this book and read the section aloud sounding like a news reporter. **Vocabulary:** See *Vocabulary Connections* activity for this book on CD **Comprehension:** *Constructing Meaning*: Good Questions to Ask, p. 195; I Predict I'll Remember p. 183; True or False, p. 171 **Reading extensions:** Other books about endangered animals: • *Can We Save Them? Endangered Species of North America* by David Dobson • *The Best Book of Endangered and Extinct Animals* by Christiane Gunzi • *Endangered Animals* by Rhonda Lucas Donald **Writing extensions:** Research another endangered animal. Write about it in the style of Alexandra Wright. Think about how she presented her information and write about your animal in this same style.
Reflect on reading and writing strategy	• What is important to keep in mind when asking questions of an author about information in a text? • Why is it important to ask questions about what you are reading?

D2-b: Imagine you are going to give a talk to your class about _____. What two points would you be sure to include in your speech?

BOOK

So You Want to Be President? by Judith St. George

INTRODUCTION TO THE BOOK

Kids are not accustomed to reading expository text that is quite this much fun! Instead of stodgy, dry facts about presidents (in the tradition of many history books), this book is full of interesting, often humorous anecdotes—accompanied by equally humorous cartoon-style illustrations. Did you know, for example, that your chances of being president might be improved if your name is James? (We've had six "James" presidents—more presidents with this name than any other.) Did you know that Taft's bathtub was four times the size of an average tub—to accommodate his larger-than-average size? This book teaches children that our presidents were, in many ways, just "regular folks" like the rest of us. One minor issue here: This book was published in 2000, so Presidents George W. Bush and Barack Obama are not included.

WHY THIS IS A GOOD BOOK FOR TEACHING THIS OBJECTIVE

When I teach students about information to include in a speech, I want them to know that a good speech is made up of more than a series of main ideas and basic details. What makes a speech interesting? It's the odd details that hold your interest, the improbable facts and figures, the mention of problems that still need solving. This book offers an abundance of these "fun facts," and thus is perfect for teaching this objective.

OTHER OBJECTIVES THAT MAY BE ADDRESSED BY RE-READING THIS BOOK

- **A1-c:** What is the main idea of this text (or part of this text)?
- **B2-b:** Why did the author write a [poem/story/nonfiction book, etc.] about this?
- **B3-b:** Which facts (details) show that _____?
- **C1-d:** Using evidence from the text, explain whether you would ever want to _____.

OTHER BOOKS MATCHED TO THIS OBJECTIVE TO LEAD STUDENTS TOWARD INDEPENDENCE (Remember to chart the evidence when you use a picture book so that students may provide specific details from the text)

These books also contain intriguing facts that would provide interesting material for a speech:

- *The Icky Bug Alphabet Book* by Jerry Pallotta

  Children are often fascinated by bugs they consider "gross." This book offers short segments about various bugs that may be "gross" and "icky" to kids, but useful in the natural world for various reasons.

- *Grossology* by Sylvia Branzei

  In case you've ever wanted more information about barfing, burping, body odor, ear wax, or other subjects that are typically not discussed by polite company, this is the book for you—or your students, many of whom just love these taboo topics. Students will have no difficulty finding facts to entertain their classmates in speeches related to the content of this book.

- *Children's Miscellany: Useless Information that's Essential to Know* by Matthew Morgan and Samantha Barnes

  What are the symptoms of a venomous spider bite? How do you win a fight with an alligator? Which insects are edible? Speeches on topics such as these would surely keep classmates' attention.

SCORING STUDENTS' RESPONSES

D2-b: Imagine you were going to give a talk to your class about our Presidents, what two points would you be sure to include in your speech?

Score = 2

If I gave a speech to my class about the Presidents I would to say that your size doesn't matter. President Taft had a bat tub big enough for four people because he was so big. I would tell that because it's kind of funny. I would also tell that if you want to be President, it is good to be named James because we've had six Presidents with this name. I never thought about that before.

> (This is a good answer. The reader sites two interesting facts and explains why each would be included.)

Score = 1

If I gave a speech about the Presidents I would say that you don't have to eat vegetables you don't like and you have a bowling alley in your house.

> (The details identified are sufficient, but there is no explanation provided: *Why* would these be good pieces of information to include in a speech?)

Score = 0

If I gave a speech I would say Abraham Lincoln was a good man because he stopped slavery and he was tall. He also got shot.

> (This reader is relying on background knowledge and has not paid enough attention to information in the text. There is nothing in this response specifically from the text.)

PLANNER FOR SHARED READING

Objective (strategy focus): <u>D2-b:</u> <u>Imagine you are going to give a talk to your class about</u>
<u>[   ]. What two points would you be sure to include in your speech?</u>

◎ <u>Imagine you were going to give a talk to your class about our presidents, what two</u>
<u>points would you be sure to include in your speech?</u>

> How will student learning be measured at the end of the lesson? (What will count as "success?")

Text: <u>*So You Want to Be President*</u> by Judith St. George   **Pages:** <u>9-17*</u>

Special Instructions: *This book will require more than a day to read. However, even a few
pages will provide plenty of material to address this objective.

<table>
<tr>
<td rowspan="3" style="writing-mode: vertical-rl;">BEFORE READING</td>
<td>Establish prior knowledge, purpose, and predictions</td>
<td>Prior knowledge: Who were some of our past presidents? What do you know about them?
Predictions: What do you expect to learn from this book? Does this book look like it's going to be a "typical" history book? Explain.
Purpose for reading: As we read this book, let's think about points that we might want to include if we were giving a speech about presidents.</td>
</tr>
<tr>
<td>Introduce/ review vocabulary</td>
<td>adversary   mansion   opponents   penny pincher
thrifty   clobbered</td>
</tr>
<tr>
<td>Introduce the objective (How to find and use the evidence)</td>
<td>Making the <u>reading</u> strategic
Think about the kinds of things that people would be interested to hear in a speech. You should talk about important information and a main idea, but you also need to keep people's attention. Mention a fact that they probably never heard before, something surprising, a problem that needs to get solved, a statistic, etc. As you read, try to find interesting facts and ideas to share with your audience.</td>
</tr>
</table>

DURING READING	**Model and practice finding evidence for the objective**	**The best evidence:** **Model:** **p. 9:** Good things about being President: house has a swimming pool, bowling alley, and movie theater; never has to take out the garbage; doesn't have to eat yucky vegetables—like George Bush wouldn't eat broccoli. **p. 10:** Bad things: always have to be dressed up; must always be polite; have lots of homework **Practice:** **p. 11:** People get mad at the President—someone once through a cabbage at President Taft. **p. 12:** Names matter: Six presidents have been named James; 4 Johns, 4 Williams…. **p. 15:** People love "log cabin" presidents—8 lived in a log cabin **p. 16:** Size doesn't matter: Taft was the biggest—had a tub big enough for four people.
	Model and practice other strategies	**Connecting?** Do you have anything in common with any of the presidents? **Visualizing/Picturing?** Which illustration in this book did you especially like? Why? **Wondering?** What else do you wonder about our presidents that would be interesting to know? **Predicting/Guessing?** This book was published before George W. Bush or Barack Obama became presidents. What do you predict this book would say about them? **Noticing?** What details did you find the most interesting? Why? **Figuring out?** Why do you think the author wrote this book?

AFTER READING	**Discussion questions**	**Question related to the objective** **D2-b:** Imagine you were going to give a talk to your class about our presidents, what two points would you be sure to include in your speech? **Other questions** **A4-b:** If the author added another paragraph to the end of this book about President Geoge W. Bush or Barack Obama, it would <u>most likely</u> tell about _____. Why? **B3-b:** Which details show that there are good things (or bad things) about being president? **C2-b:** Which part of this book was most interesting or surprising to you? Why?
	Written response to text	**Making the <u>writing</u> strategic** • See *That's a Great Answer*, p. 159, or *Teaching Written Response*, pp. 192-193, for a template matched to this objective. • Model the response using the template. • Remove your response and ask students to write the response themselves using two other points. They may use the template if necessary.
	Other follow-up activities	**Oral language, fluency, vocabulary, comprehension, reading extensions, writing extensions** **Oral language/fluency:** Give a speech about presidents on one of these topics: Good things about being President; Bad things about being President; Presidents' names; Presidents' size—or any other topic from this book that interests you. **Vocabulary:** See *Vocabulary Connections* activity on the CD. **Comprehension:** These follow-up activities may be found in *Constructing Meaning through Kid-Friendly Comprehension Strategy Instruction*: I Predict I'll Remember, p. 183; Important Words, p. 190; Good Questions to Ask, p. 195 **Reading extensions:** • *The Everything Kids' Presidents Book: Puzzles, Games and Trivia - for Hours of Presidential Fun* by Brian Thornton • *Time for Kids: Presidents of the United States* by The Editors of Time for Kids • *Smart About the Presidents* by Jon Buller **Writing extensions:** Write a page about either George W. Bush or Barack Obama that could be added to this book. Remember, you want to find "fun facts" like the author has included about the rest of our presidents.
	Reflect on reading and writing strategy	• How do decide what information to include in a speech? • Why is it important to include both big ideas *and* small details?

D2-c: Using information in the text, write a paragraph that could have appeared in _____'s journal after _____ occurred.

BOOK

Going Home by Eve Bunting

INTRODUCTION TO THE BOOK

Carlos and his family travel home to Mexico for the Christmas holiday to see their relatives. Mexico is "home" for their parents, but Carlos and his two sisters are being raised in the United States. At first, they have a hard time understanding Mama's and Papa's desire to return to their former village which is a long journey away over bumpy roads in their very old car. Then they arrive at the home of their grandfather and begin to recognize all that their parents have sacrificed for their children's "opportunities." This story not only reminds us once again that "home" truly is where the heart is, but that love also means looking toward the future.

WHY THIS IS A GOOD BOOK FOR TEACHING THIS OBJECTIVE

Eve Bunting has a talent for taking complex subjects and bringing them to life in thoughtful ways that encourage children to reach a deeper level of understanding. Such is the case with *Going Home*. The story, combined with the vibrant south-of-the-border illustrations, invites readers to reflect: Where is "home?" Why do parents make sacrifices for their children? What do you need to consider when you think ahead to your future? These are the kinds of reflections that make wonderful musings for journal entries! This objective is well suited to this book because there is a specific event (the trip to Mexico) that leads students to respond to these matters of the heart. Can they put their "heart on paper" in a journal entry? I think they can!

OTHER OBJECTIVES THAT MAY BE ADDRESSED BY RE-READING THIS BOOK

- **A2-d:** How did _____ change from the beginning to the end of the story?
- **A4-b:** If the author added another paragraph to the end of the story, it would <u>most likely</u> tell about _____. Use information from the story to support your answer.
- **C1-b:** Make a personal connection. Show how something that happened in the story is like something that happened in your own life (connect to a feeling).
- **D3-b:** How are your customs different from the customs described in this story/article?

OTHER BOOKS MATCHED TO THIS OBJECTIVE TO LEAD STUDENTS TOWARD INDEPENDENCE (Remember to chart the evidence when you use a picture book so that students may provide specific details from the text)

The following books all contain an emotionally charged situation that would be a good launching point for writing a journal entry.

- *Far Away Home* **by Jane Kurtz**
  This book not only matches the objective, but also the theme. It is about a father who returns to his native Ethiopia because his mother is ill. His daughter, Desta, doesn't want him to go, telling him that "Ethiopia is so far away." But the father replies, "For me, Ethiopia is never far away." What might Desta have written in her journal the night before her father left to go home to his ailing mother?

- *For the Love of Autumn* **by Patricia Polacco**
  Danielle Parks was a teacher. She loved her students, but she also loved her little cat, Autumn. Unfortunately, Autumn disappears one afternoon and is gone for a very long time. The ending to this story is an especially happy one, but Danielle couldn't predict that before Autumn returned. What might she have written in her journal after her precious kitty had been missing for a few days?

- *One Green Apple* **by Eve Bunting**
  This is Farah's second day in her new school in her new country, and her class is going on a field trip to an apple orchard. Unable to speak the language, Farah feels lonely and lost, and different from everyone else. The dupatta covering her head is one more reminder that she doesn't fit in, and to make matters worse, she endures cruel stares from students who do not seem to like her mid-eastern country. The situation changes a little as she joins her classmates as they try to make cider and she feels like part of the team. The bus ride home is more pleasant. What might Farah write in her journal about this day, and about her new school and classmates?

SCORING STUDENTS' RESPONSES

◎ **D2-c: Using information in the text, write a paragraph that could have appeared in Carlos's journal after his family's first night at their relatives' home in Mexico.**

Score = 2

When I was on my way to our relatives' house I couldn't understand why my parents were so excited to be going to Mexico because America is our home now. Then I saw how happy Mama and Papa were and that made me both happy and sad. I was happy that our parents got to feel the love of their Mexican family, and a little sad that they had given up so much so my sisters and I could have a better future. I wonder if Mama and Papa will come back to Mexico someday. I will visit them, but I feel like America will always be my home.

> (This response would receive full credit because the student shows that he understands the events of the story, and that from these events, he can infer the feelings of the characters and can use those inferences to predict something about what might happen next.)

Score = 1

I didn't really want to go to Mexico for Christmas. Mama and Papa did, and they were happy there. They even danced without any music. They might move back to Mexico sometime in the future.

> (This response would receive partial credit. It accurately describes the events of the story, but the reader has not demonstrated any inferential thinking based on her understanding of the text. Remember: the point of the "D2" objective is to synthesize information and extend one's thinking.)

Score = 0

I think Carlos will be happy to go back to his home in America even though he has to work hard there. He has to sleep in the car. His parents think that is ok, but it might not be safe.

> (This response would receive no credit. The intent of a journal entry is to write in the first person, as if you *are* the character; this student did not do that. Additionally, he has focused on one specific detail that shows no real understanding of the big idea of the story, and there is no inferential thinking that addresses the author's message.)

PLANNER FOR SHARED READING

Objective (strategy focus): <u>D2-c:</u> <u>Using information in the text, write a paragraph that could</u> <u>have appeared in [</u>   <u>'s] journal after [</u>   <u>] occurred.</u>

 <u>Using information in the text, write a paragraph that could have appeared in Carlos's</u> <u>journal after his family's first night at their relatives' home in Mexico.</u>

How will student learning be measured at the end of the lesson? (What will count as "success?")

Text: <u>*Going Home* by Eve Bunting</u>   **Pages:** <u>Whole book</u>

<table>
<tr>
<td rowspan="3">BEFORE READING</td>
<td>Establish prior knowledge, purpose, and predictions</td>
<td>Prior knowledge: What is a migrant worker? (Discuss the meaning of this with students—some families follow the crops to earn a living working for different farmers.) Where is Mexico? (Locate this on the map and show students how many Mexicans have migrated from Mexico to California and other states in order to find work.)
Predictions: Based on the title, the cover, and the author, what do you expect from this book? What kind of stories does Eve Bunting often write (realistic fiction that shows many feelings)?
Purpose for reading: Let's read to understand the story and the feelings of the characters so we can write an entry that the narrator, Carlos, might have written in his journal after his family arrived in Mexico.</td>
</tr>
<tr>
<td>Introduce/ review vocabulary</td>
<td>sparkles   battered   legal   opportunities   stammer
poked</td>
</tr>
<tr>
<td>Introduce the objective (How to find and use the evidence)</td>
<td>Making the <u>reading</u> strategic
When you want to write an entry that could have appeared in a character's journal, think about these things as you read:
• What happened in the story
• What are your feelings about these events?
• What might happen next, or sometime in the future because of these events and feelings?
Also, remember that when you write your journal entry, you need to pretend to actually BE the person. Use the word "I" as you write in your journal.</td>
</tr>
</table>

		The best evidence:
DURING READING	**Model and practice finding evidence for the objective**	**Model:** **p. 2:** the family is going "home" to Mexico, though the children consider America their home. **p. 3:** The parents are excited about the trip, but the children aren't so sure… **p. 5:** It's a long ride; the children are concerned about being allowed back into the U.S.; Mama is very happy about being in Mexico. **pp. 7-8:** Working in America is hard; Mama and Papa went to America for "opportunities." **Practice:** **pp. 9-14:** Life in Mexico seems very different from life in America. **p. 18:** The family arrives at the grandparents' home and they meet their relatives; everyone is happy. **p. 19:** Carlos can tell that Mama is sad about moving away from her family and realizes she did it for him and his sisters—for "opportunities." **p. 22:** Carlos and his sister talk about why their parents like LaPerla so much. **p. 27:** Carlos and his sister discuss how and why their parents view of Mexico is different from their own, and what may happen in the future
	Model and practice other strategies	**Connecting?** Connect to what is special about why your home is special to you **Visualizing/Picturing?** What words that the author uses help you picture Mexico? What picture do you have in your mind? **Wondering?** Would you be willing to leave your home for better opportunities somewhere else? What kinds of opportunities would make it worthwhile to you to move far away from your relatives and friends? **Predicting/Guessing?** What do you predict about this family's future? Will the parents return to Mexico eventually? What about the children? What do you predict about their future in America? **Noticing?** What details did you notice about the parents' true feelings about Mexico and why they left LaPerla to live in America. **Figuring out?** What was important to Carlos's parents? How can you tell?

AFTER READING	**Discussion questions**	**Question related to the objective** **D2-c:** Using information in the text, what do you think Carlos might have written in his journal after his family's first night at their relatives' home in Mexico. **Other questions** **A1-a:** What lesson does Carlos learn in this story? **B1-c:** Compare Carlos and his mom. How are they the same? How are they different? **C2-a:** Which part of this story do you think was *most* important? Use information from the story to explain why you chose that part.
	Written response to text	**Making the <u>writing</u> strategic** • See *That's a Great Answer*, p. 163, or *Teaching Written Response*, pp. 153-154, for a template matched to this objective. • Model the response using the template. • Remove your response and ask students to write the response themselves based on their own idea using the template if necessary.
	Other follow-up activities	**Oral language, fluency, vocabulary, comprehension, reading extensions, writing extensions** **Oral language/fluency:** Choose a page in this book where the characters are talking to each other. Practice reading the page until you can read it fluently with lots of expression. Try to make your voice sound like the different characters. **Vocabulary:** See *Vocabulary Connections* activity on the CD. **Comprehension:** These follow-up activities may be found in *Constructing Meaning through Kid-Friendly Comprehension Strategy Instruction*: Active Reader Report, p. 155; One Word; p. 160; What's in a Picture, p. 165; Best Quote, p. 175. **Reading extensions:** These books all focus on the concept of home: • *Faraway Home* by Jane Kurtz • *Little Cliff and the Porch People* by Clifton Taulbert • *Momma, Where Are You From* by Marie Bradby • *In My Momma's Kitchen* by Jerdine Nolen • *Appalachia* by Cynthia Rylant • *Let's Go Home* by Cynthia Rylant • *All the Places to Love* by Patricia MacLachlan • *Coming on Home Soon* by Jacqueline Woodson **Writing extensions:** Write about an opportunity for which you are grateful. This does not need to be something that costs money. It could be an opportunity for a good education, an opportunity to have a family who loves you, or anything else that you consider an opportunity. You could write about your opportunity in a paragraph, as a poem, or in some other form.
	Reflect on reading and writing strategy	• When you want to write a journal entry that a character might have written, what do you need to think about? • Why is it sometimes difficult to write this kind of journal entry? (Need to write from the character's point of view)

D3-a: What is important to the author/ character? How does the author/character show this?

BOOK

Weslandia by Paul Fleischman

INTRODUCTION TO THE BOOK

In this story Wesley, an avowed nonconformist needs to find a way to keep himself busy during summer vacation. He thinks professional football is stupid, refused to follow the trend at his school of shaving half of his head, and is perpetually tormented by his peers for his inability to fit in. So, for lack of a better plan, he invents a civilization! By the end of the summer he has developed a new language, a sustainable staple crop, clothing suited to his new environment, a means of telling time, appropriate shelter, and sports that require logic and collaboration instead of brute strength and competition. By the time he returns to school in the fall, his former tormenters have become allies in his quest for creativity.

WHY THIS IS A GOOD BOOK FOR TEACHING THIS OBJECTIVE

This book is well-matched to this objective because what is important to the author is very clear: While Wesley initially must endure much taunting for his nonconformist ways, in the end, his independent thinking pays big dividends; he makes the world a better place, and in the process, wins the respect of his peers. This is a great message for intermediate grade students to consider as many kids of this age have little tolerance for those who march to the beat of a different drummer. Furthermore, the author gets his point across here in a manner that is really quite humorous if you are tuned in to subtle comments such as, "Passing his neighborhood's two styles of housing—garage on the left and garage on the right—Wesley alone dreamed of more exciting forms of shelter." Even sophisticated students who are initially skeptical about the likelihood of actually learning something from a picture book, are quickly captivated by this clever story of a very clever boy.

OTHER OBJECTIVES THAT MAY BE ADDRESSED BY RE-READING THIS BOOK

- **A2-c:** How did _____ solve his/her problem? Give details from the story to support your answer.
- **A4-b:** If the author added another paragraph to the end of the story, it would most likely tell about _____. Use information from the story to support your answer.
- **B1-d:** Can this part of the story be described as: a description, an explanation, a conversation, an opinion, an argument, or a comparison?
- **C2-c:** Did you like this story? Why or why not?

OTHER BOOKS MATCHED TO THIS OBJECTIVE TO LEAD STUDENTS TOWARD INDEPENDENCE (Remember to chart the evidence when you use a picture book so that students may provide specific details from the text)

These books also show the importance of particular character traits:

- ***Wings* by Christopher Myers**
  Icarus Jackson's unique ability to fly is the source of derision, not delight as he is chastised by his peers, and even his teacher and a policeman. One, lone student, also something of an outcast, sees Icarus differently, and ultimately finds the courage to stand up to his tormenters. The illustrations in this book also contribute to the author's message about the importance of celebrating your personal gifts.

- ***Odd Boy Out: Young Albert Einstein* by Don Brown**
  As a child, Albert Einstein's quirky brilliance often left him misunderstood by his parents, peers, and teachers (one of whom tells him "he will never get anywhere in life.") This story demonstrates that one's personal gifts are not always readily apparent; we all bloom in our own good time.

- ***The Goat Lady* by Jane Bregoli**
  The goat lady is not well-received by her neighbors who think she is just plain strange for the odd clothes she wears, her barnyard full of goats, and her ramshackle house. But opinions begin to change when they see her kindness and the many selfless deeds that have improved the lives of so many people. This book helps students look beyond the surface level of a person or character into her soul.

SCORING STUDENTS' RESPONSES

 D3-a: What is important to the author of *Weslandia*? How does the author show this?

Score = 2

I think that <u>being a problem-solver</u> was important to the author of this story. Some examples that show this are that Wesley invented kinds of clothing like a hat and a robe that were better suited to warm weather than heavy jeans, which can be very hot. He also invented suntan lotion and mosquito repellent and then figured out a way to sell them to make money for himself. In the end, the biggest thing Wesley probably did was solve his problem of having no friends. Now other kids respected him for his creativity.

> (This response would receive full score because it identifies an appropriate value [problem-solving ability] and then provides solid pieces of evidence to support that claim. The final piece of evidence, solving the problem of no friends, is particularly insightful—but would not be required for maximum score.)

Score = 1

I think that <u>being creative</u> was important to the author. In the story Wesley is creative with his summer project of inventing a civilization, like his clothes, and his garden, and his words.

> (This student obviously understood the story and chose an appropriate value [creativity], but the references to the text are too general: Tell something about the civilization that was creative. Explain a bit about the clothing or the garden. This response would receive only partial credit for although it is accurate, it lacks specifics.)

Score = 0

I think this author likes people who are weird. Wesley is very weird. He does strange things. Maybe the author likes Harry Potter, too because Wesley looks like Harry.

> (This response would most likely receive a score of "0" because the student missed the whole point of the story and does not defend her response with any actual information from the text. The comment about Harry Potter is random and in this case, irrelevant.)

PLANNER FOR SHARED READING

Objective (strategy focus): <u>How does the author show that [   ] is important to him?</u>

◎ <u>What is important to the author of *Weslandia*? How does he show this?</u>
How will student learning be measured at the end of the lesson? (What will count as "success?")

Text: <u>*Weslandia* by Paul Fleischman</u>   **Pages:** <u>Whole book</u>

<table>
<tr>
<td rowspan="3" style="writing-mode: vertical-rl">BEFORE READING</td>
<td>Establish prior knowledge, purpose, and predictions</td>
<td>Prior knowledge: What is a civilization? Give some examples of things that are part of a civilization? (You may need to help students build this concept)
Predictions: Based on the title and the cover, what do you think this story will be about?
Purpose for reading: As we read this story, let's try to figure out what is important to this author. What are some of the things that this author values?</td>
</tr>
<tr>
<td>Introduce/ review vocabulary</td>
<td>outcast   civilization   tormentor   fleeing   entrancing
scornful   innovations   traditional   spectators   morale</td>
</tr>
<tr>
<td>Introduce the objective (How to find and use the evidence)</td>
<td>Making the <u>reading</u> strategic
Authors often write stories to reveal something that is important to them by speaking through the voice of their main character. Read the text through one time to get a general impression of what was important to this author. What is important to the author is often reinforced at the end of the text, so notice in particular how the story ends. Now go back and find the details that provide *evidence* to support your answer.</td>
</tr>
</table>

DURING READING	**Model and practice finding evidence for the objective**	**The best evidence:** **Model:** **p. 2:** Disliked pizza and soda; found professional football stupid; refused to shave half his head **p. 3:** Two styles of houses: garage on the left, garage on the right **p. 6:** Wesley could *use* what he'd learned to found his own civilization. **p. 9:** Wesley opened his land to chance, to the new and unknown. **p. 13:** Developed a new kind of fruit that blended flavors **p. 14:** Dried a rind to make a cup and built his own squeezing device; created other recipes **Practice:** **p. 15:** Wesley wove himself a sunhat and a robe to wear (comfortable in warm weather). **p. 17:** Friends were scornful, then curious; invented suntan lotion and mosquito repellent; sold this to former tormentors. **p. 19:** Invented new system for telling time and counting **p. 21:** Invented games that required strategy and complex scoring **p. 24:** Made himself a flute and renamed constellations **p. 27:** Invented a language to label the things he'd invented **p. 29:** Invented own alphabet and writing system **p.31:** Wesley had many friends when he returned to school.
	Model and practice other strategies	**Connecting?** Connect to creativity that paid off for you **Visualizing/Picturing?** How does this author make Wesley's civilization easy to picture? **Wondering?** Wonder what makes this story so entrancing? **Predicting/Guessing?** Predict Wesley's relationship with his peers in the future **Noticing?** Notice the humor in this story **Figuring out?** Figure out the author's values based on the events of the story—and it's outcome

AFTER READING	**Discussion questions**	**Question related to the objective** **D3-a:** What is important to the author of *Weslandia*? How does he show this? **Other questions** **A2-d:** How did Wesley change from the beginning to the end of the story? Why did he change? **C2-d:** What was your first reaction to this story? Explain. **D1-e:** What are some things about this story that are believable? What is *not* believable?
	Written response to text	**Making the <u>writing</u> strategic** • See *That's a Great Answer*, p.165, or *Teaching Written Response*, pp. 143-144, for a template matched to this objective. • Model the response using the template. • Remove your response and ask students to write their own response based on the incident you chose, or another incident in the story. They may use the template if necessary.
	Other follow-up activities	**Oral language, fluency, vocabulary, comprehension, reading extensions, writing extensions** **Oral language/fluency:** Invent your own words for some common classroom objects (pencil, eraser, book, computer, etc.) and practice saying sentences aloud that use these words. Can your classmates figure out the word's meaning? **Vocabulary:** Complete the *Vocabulary Connections* activity for this book found on the (CD). **Comprehension:** These follow-up strategy activities may be found in *Constructing Meaning through Kid-Friendly Comprehension Strategy Instruction*: Active Reader Report, p. 155; Summary Frame for Story Text, p. 188; Character Study, p. 195. **Reading extensions:** These books from the *Childhood of World Figures* series bring to life the character traits that contributed to the renown of each person: • *Marie Curie: Young Scientist* by Beatrice Gormley • *Gandhi: Young Nation Builder* by Kathleen Kudlinski • *Christopher Columbus: Young Explorer* by Kathleen Kudlinski • *Leonardo da Vinci: Young Artist, Writer, and Inventor* by George Stanley **Writing extensions:** Pretend you are Wesley on the first day of school. Your teacher has asked you to write about "What I Did on my Summer Vacation." Write the essay that Wesley might have written on this topic.
	Reflect on reading and writing strategy	• How do you go about figuring out what is important to an author? • Why is it important to consider what is important to the author?

D3-b: How are your customs and values different from the customs/values described in this story/article?

BOOK

The Lotus Seed by Sherry Garland

INTRODUCTION TO THE BOOK

The narrator of this text is the granddaughter of a Vietnamese woman who sees her emperor cry on the day he hands over the leadership of his country to Ho Chi Minh. To remember him, the grandmother (then a young girl) plucks a seed from a lotus pod in the Imperial garden and carries it with her through life's most difficult moments, including her escape in an over-crowded boat from war-torn Vietnam. Decades later in America, the narrator's little brother finds the lotus seed, and unaware of its significance, plants it in a pool of mud. The grandmother is overcome with grief until one day the lotus blooms in all of its magnificence. When the blossom fades, the old woman gives one of its seeds to each of her grandchildren and keeps one for herself.

WHY THIS IS A GOOD BOOK FOR TEACHING THIS OBJECTIVE

Although I've known about this book for a long while, I began using it for instruction just recently. So often I would take it from my book shelf and contemplate its potential effectiveness: Would intermediate grade students "get it?" Would they understand the symbolism of the lotus seed? One day I tossed *The Lotus Seed* into my book bag, not for the shared reading lesson I would teach in this fourth grade, but for some independent follow-up reading for whatever objective I was teaching that day. Still, I was skeptical. I wasn't even sure anyone would choose this book, but one student did. When I called on him during the reflection at the end of the reading block he shared that he thought it was amazing that something as small as a seed could have a double meaning: "It was not just a seed; it stood for everything important to this grandmother about her culture." Okay, I thought to myself. I guess I should get serious about using this book. Since then, I've used it often. Students always "get it" and they love the oil-paintings that accompany the sparse text. Another advantage of this book is its brevity. It can easily be read in its entirety and discussed in a thirty-minute lesson.

OTHER OBJECTIVES THAT MAY BE ADDRESSED BY RE-READING THIS BOOK

- **A1-b:** What is the theme of this story?
- **A3-a:** Briefly summarize this story.
- **C1-b:** Make a personal connection to a feeling in this story.
- **C2-d:** What was your first reaction to this text? Explain.

OTHER BOOKS MATCHED TO THIS OBJECTIVE TO LEAD STUDENTS TOWARD INDEPENDENCE (Remember to chart the evidence when you use a picture book so that students may provide specific details from the text)

These books celebrate traditions and rituals of different cultures and portray positive features of different cultures:

- ***Young Cornrows Callin out the Moon* by Ruth Forman**
  This book immerses you in the energy and spirit of city life and will make you want to move there to experience it yourself if you don't already live in an urban area: *we got double dutch n freeze tag n kickball so many place to hide n seek n ... we got the ice cream man ... we got the corner store....*" This story is told in rap with illustrations as happy and up-beat as the text.

- ***Long Night Moon* by Cynthia Rylant**
  Native American "moons" (the months of the year) are celebrated in this book of lyrical prose: *Each month had a moon, and each moon had its name....* Each moonlit night reveals its magic and mystery through both the illustration and the text: *In January/ the Stormy Moon shines/ in mist,/ in ice,/ on a wild wolf's back./ Find it/ and find your way home.* Readers will find their way to a heightened respect for nature, reminiscent of Native Americans' love for the natural world.

- ***Sitti's Secrets* by Naomi Shihab Nye**
  This is the story of a little girl who visits her Grandma in a Palestinian village. Although they don't speak each other's language, they learn to communicate in their own way, and in the process, come to appreciate the nuances of the different cultures from which each comes. They discover that they have more similarities than differences and though the visit ends, they remain "neighbors" in spirit.

- ***14 Cows for America* by Carmen Agra Deedy**
  It is nine months after September 11, 2001. Far away in Kenya, a Maasai tribe learns of the horrific events of this day from young Kimeli, who has traveled back to his homeland after attending medical school in New York City. The people of his tribe, moved by this tale of great suffering, ask, "What can we do for these poor people?" To the Maasai, the cow is life. And so, in a ceremony of sacred ritual, fourteen cows are presented to an American diplomat because "There is no nation so powerful it cannot be wounded, nor a people so small they cannot offer mighty comfort."

SCORING STUDENTS' RESPONSES

◎ **D3-b: Tell why the lotus seed was so important to the grandmother. In America, is there anything we treasure like the grandmother treasured the lotus seed?**

Score = 2

The lotus seed was important to the grandmother because it reminded her of the emperor in her homeland and it was a good luck charm for her. She even brought it with her to her new country, America. She said the lotus was the flower of life and hope. In America we have symbols that we treasure, too, such as the bald eagle. This bird is a symbol of strength and can soar high, just like Americans.

> (This response thoroughly explains the significance of the lotus seed and identifies the meaning of a comparable American symbol.)

Score = 1

The lotus seed meant so much to the grandmother that she brought it to America with her. If I moved to a different country I would bring baseball cards since they symbolize an American sport.

> (This response indicates that the lotus seed was very important to the grandmother, but doesn't say why. The baseball cards may not be a commonly recognized symbol, but the reader does make an adequate case for their symbolism.)

Score = 0

The grandmother brought the lotus seed to America and she cried when her grandson planted it. Then she was happy when the seed grew into a beautiful flower. My favorite flowers are lilacs because they smell so beautiful.

> (This reader doesn't seem to understand the meaning of symbolism. He simply explains what became of the lotus seed, and then makes a connection to his favorite flower.)

PLANNER FOR SHARED READING

Objective (strategy focus): <u>D3-b:</u> <u>How are your customs or values different from the customs/values described in this story/article?</u>

◎ <u>Tell why the lotus seed was so important to the grandmother. In America, is there anything we treasure like the grandmother treasured the lotus seed?</u>

<small>How will student learning be measured at the end of the lesson? (What will count as "success?")</small>

Text: <u>*The Lotus Seed*</u> by Sherry Garland   **Pages:** <u>Whole book</u>

<table>
<tr>
<td rowspan="3" style="writing-mode: vertical-lr">BEFORE READING</td>
<td>Establish prior knowledge, purpose, and predictions</td>
<td>Prior knowledge: Where is Vietnam? What do you know about the war that took place in Vietnam? (The author's note at the end of this book can help you build your students' background knowledge about this country.)

Predictions: Look at the title of this book and the picture on the cover. What do you think this book may be about?

Purpose for reading: This book describes a cultural tradition important to someone from Vietnam. As we read this book, think about this tradition, and how it is similar to or different from traditions in our country. (Also discuss meaning of culture and tradition)</td>
</tr>
<tr>
<td>Introduce/ review vocabulary</td>
<td>plucked   clamored   scrambled   unfurling</td>
</tr>
<tr>
<td>Introduce the objective (How to find and use the evidence)</td>
<td>Making the <u>reading</u> strategic
"Customs" are the things people of a particular region do and the way they live day-to-day, like the way they celebrate special holidays, what they do in their free time, etc. As you read, look for customs, examples of things in the characters' or people's lives that are different from your own life. For example, do people live in different kinds of houses? Are their schools different? What about the games they play? Do they celebrate holidays that you don't celebrate? Try to find at least two or three customs that are different from your customs.

People's customs show the things that they value (what is important to them). Sometimes you can figure out what is important to the characters in a story based on the customs of their country.</td>
</tr>
</table>

DURING READING	**Model and practice the focus strategy**	**The best evidence: (elements of Vietnamese culture)** **Model:** **p. 2:** emperor, golden dragon throne **p. 3:** lotus pod, Imperial garden **p. 5:** family altar **Practice:** **p. 7:** married young man chosen by her parents **p. 9:** mother-of-pearl hair combs **p. 21:** the flower of life and hope; the flower of my country **p. 25:** wrapped the seed in silk
	Model and practice other strategies	**Connecting?** Connect to a special family tradition, or connect to a special treasure that you would never want to lose. **Visualizing/Picturing?** Which words help you picture the lotus in bloom? Which words help you picture Vietnam? **Wondering?** What questions do you have about Vietnam that this author didn't answer? **Predicting/Guessing?** Predict what will become of these new lotus seeds. Will the children lose them? **Noticing?** Notice clues that show the importance of family to the Vietnamese culture. **Figuring out?** Figure out what was important to this author. Why did the author write this book?

AFTER READING	**Discussion questions**	**Follow-up to the objective:** **D3-b:** Tell why the lotus seed was so important to the grandmother. In America, is there anything we treasure like the grandmother treasured the lotus seed? **D3-b:** There are many examples of Vietnamese culture in this book. Find some examples of things that are part of Vietnamese culture that are not a part of our American culture. **Other questions:** **B3-a:** In this story, it is clear that Vietnamese families really "stick together." Find evidence that supports this. **A1-d:** What would be another good title for this story?
	Written response to text	**Making the <u>writing</u> strategic** • See *That's a Great Answer*, p. 168, for a template matched to this objective. • Model the response using the template. • Remove your response and ask students to write the response themselves using a different example of Vietnamese culture. They may use the template if necessary.
	Other follow-up activities	**Oral language, fluency, vocabulary, comprehension, reading extensions, writing extensions** **Oral language/fluency:** Find a page in this book that shows lots of feeling. Practice reading it until your voice shows the kind of feeling that you think the author intended. **Vocabulary:** See *Vocabulary Connections* activity for this book on the CD. **Comprehension:** These follow-up activities may be found in *Constructing Meaning through Kid-Friendly Comprehension Strategy Instruction*: Active Reader Report, p. 155; I'm Connected, p. 159; What's in a Picture, p. 165; Character Study, p. 185. **Reading extensions:** These books would extend students' understanding of Vietnam and Vietnamese culture: • *Vietnam Abc's: A Book about the People and Places of Vietnam* by Theresa Alberti • *Toad is the Uncle of Heaven: a Vietnamese Folktale* by Jeanne M. Lee • *Going Home, Coming Home/ Ve Nha, Tham Que Huong* by Truong Tran **Writing extensions:** Choose a flower that you just love. What could it symbolize for you? Write a description of your special flower and what it symbolizes for you.
	Reflect on reading and writing strategy	• What do we mean by "cultural traditions?" • How do we identify cultural traditions as we read? • What other cultures could we read about to find out about cultural traditions?